Online Auctions at EBay®

3rd Edition

The Expert's Guide to Buying and Selling

Online Auctions at EBay®

3rd Edition

The Expert's Guide to Buying and Selling

Dennis L. Prince

Premier
Press

SVP, Retail Strategic Market Group: Andy Shafran

Publisher/Acquisitions Editor: Stacy L. Hiquet

Senior Marketing Manager: Sarah O'Donnell

Marketing Manager: Heather Hurley

Manager of Editorial Services: Heather Talbot

Associate Marketing Manager: Kristin Eisenzopf

Project/Copy Editor: Karen A. Gill

Technical Reviewer: Andy Harris

Retail Market Coordinator: Sarah Dubois

Interior Layout: Marian Hartsough

Cover Designer: Mike Tanamachi

Indexer: Kevin Broccoli

Proofreader: Kezia Endsley

ISBN: 1-59200-193-9

Library of Congress Catalog Card Number: 2003114352

Printed in the United States of America

04 05 06 07 BH 10 9 8 7 6 5 4 3

Premier Press, a division of Course Technology
25 Thomson Place
Boston, MA 02210

For my dear grandmother,
Eleanor Thompson,
in thanks for her perpetual smile
and fun-loving style.

Acknowledgments

It's always a terrific opportunity to pen a new book but, when working with the folks at Premier Press, the opportunity is more pleasurable than ever. My sincere thanks to my Publisher and Acquisitions Editor, Stacy Hiquet, for recognizing the need to revise this edition and for the unwavering support she has provided on this project as with every other project in the past in which we've worked together. Special thanks to SVP Andy Shafran for giving this project the green light and offering me the opportunity to work with his fine team.

Of course, this author is only as effective and fluent as his direct editor enables and, therefore, my deepest thanks and warm appreciation for Project and Copy Editor Karen Gill. Thanks for sticking close by as we tackled this revision together and thanks, too, for your lighthearted attitude and penchant for having a good time every step of the way. Then, I heartily applaud the insight and input from Technical Editor Andy Harris, who has demonstrated his knack for transforming what might be a dry text into an enjoyable jaunt that's as pleasant as it is precise. I truly hope the three of us will have the opportunity to work as a team again—soon.

Thanks also to the fine work of Proofreader Kezia Endsley and Indexer Kevin Broccoli, who added the final touches to ensure accuracy and accessibility to the information contained herein. And to the rest of the Premier team: Marian Hartsough for the excellent layout, Mike Tanamachi for the stellar cover, and the Marketing team of Sarah O'Donnell, Heather Hurley, and Heather Dubois for helping to get this book into the hands of the readers who are eager and ready to absorb everything within these pages.

Last, but certainly not least, I must acknowledge the community of members at eBay. It's been my privilege to have met thousands of you over the years of trading. And to those of you who have read my previous books, thank you for taking the time to write to me to share your thoughts, experiences, and excitement for online auctioning. I hope to have the sustained opportunity to interact with and serve you for years to come.

About the Author

DENNIS L. PRINCE is a business professional with a background in technical (computer) applications and corporate procurement principles. As a longtime online auction enthusiast, analyst, and advocate, he has studied the growth and potential of Internet auctioning as well as other forms of e-commerce since 1995. Dennis has authored many successful books, including *How to Sell Anything at EBay . . . and Make a Fortune!* (McGraw-Hill, 2003) and *Starting Your Online Auction Business* (Premier Press, 2000). He has been recognized by Vendio (formerly AuctionWatch) as one of the "Top 10 Online Auction Movers and Shakers."

Acclaimed for his commitment to promoting better understanding and execution in online selling, Dennis has regularly contributed to a variety of noted Internet and auction service sites, such as Vendio, Auctiva, Krause, Collector Online, and ZDNet. He has been featured in the nationally distributed *Access Magazine* (2000) and *Entrepreneur Magazine* (2003), and he has been a guest of highly rated television and radio programs such as TechTV and C/Net Radio with Alex Bennett.

Contents at a Glance

Contents

Preface

The vigilante reviewer pulled no punches:

> "Words, words, words. This book takes nearly 500 pages to say what I think needs less than 100 pages. Padding is a serious problem with many books."

Ouch. That's gonna leave a mark.

On June 28, 2003, John Wilson, an Amazon.com customer and self-appointed literary critic, stopped by to publicly proclaim his opinion of my book, *Online Auctions @ eBay: 2nd Edition.* Oh c'mon, John, tell me how you *really* feel.

Now, I could immediately leap into a defensive argument that illuminates the difficulty of writing a book, of satisfying an editor, and of ensuring adequate explanation and so on and so forth, but I won't.

Why not? Because John's right.

When I wrote the first edition of this book in April 1999, I was excited— everyone was excited—about the new online trading oasis, eBay. I became a self-made eBay expert, driven by my desire to harness all its potential to serve my personal needs and aspirations. In no time, friends, family, and co-workers got wind of my exploits and demanded step-by-step instruction to achieve the same. When my publisher, likewise, became interested in the information, it was clear that every detail, every nuance, of online auctioning—from how to log on to the site to how to package and ship an item and every aspect of the human interaction in between—would need to be shared in painstaking precision. "Don't ever assume the reader knows what you know" became the mantra I was instructed to work by.

Upon publication, those same friends and family members, those who literally begged me to impart all the secrets of my eBay success responded, "Well, I don't want to read that much; I just want to know how to do it."

What's the vernacular about being damned if you do and damned if you don't?

That was then. Now, as eBay has been around some eight years and computer literacy is on the rise, I can dispose of the virtual training wheels and get this new edition off to a running start. Thank goodness, really, because in this microwave mentality we live by ("Damn! Must I wait an entire 30 seconds to heat this miserable slice of meatloaf?"), people demand fast answers, quick results, and immediate gratification. Fair enough. As it is with leftovers, so shall it be with a book that imparts the ways and wiles of effective auctioning at eBay—now quicker and tastier than ever.

So, thanks John. Your blunt statement has left a mark . . . available here in this new and improved edition.

Introduction

Suppose you had a yard sale . . . and 50 million people showed up.

Suppose you went to work tomorrow . . . in your bathrobe and slippers.

Suppose you opened a new business . . . in a single weekend.

Sounds crazy; it's not. Millions of people around the world are doing these things and more, their way, on their terms, and in their own homes. Thanks to eBay, the premiere online auction and cyber-store marketplace, people from all backgrounds, all levels of experience, and all economic sectors are finding a refreshing new way to buy, sell, work, and play. It's no dream; it's a reality, and it's time for you to join in.

Now, You're in Command

I'd venture to guess that you're curious about new ways to add improvement and enjoyment into your life, and I gather you might be looking to eBay to become a part of the answer, a first step toward taking control of that aspect of your life.

Consumption is a mainstay of our lives, yet *how* we consume—how we buy and maybe sell goods—has never been more exciting and has never offered such opportunity for you and me to exercise our will in this consumer culture. It's *that* opportunity—the ability to exercise our will and influence how we will consume goods and services to suit our individual needs—that provides the options, the alternatives, and the freedom to redefine how we live and work from this day forward.

Why Does EBay Matter?

We're in the midst of an entrepreneurial explosion, everyday people establishing themselves as bona fide businesspersons, running their virtual stores with ease and efficiency. Thanks to eBay, the landmark auction site, the one that has become a firm fixture in our popular culture yet which started out as a quirky hobby for some, has had a major impact on millions of lives (including mine) and continues to reshape and redefine how you and I and the rest of the world will trade goods and services. The core of eBay's potential, though, is that it provides options, alternatives, and individual freedom because it enables us to take matters into our own hands, to seize new opportunities of supplementing an income, and to finally have the ability to go into business for ourselves without having to mortgage the house or risk retirement to open up a storefront. All of this is at your fingertips today, and the best news is that you can get it on the cheap. No kidding.

Why Another EBay Book?

Even though there have been dozens of books written on eBay, thousands of articles published on the ins and outs, ups and downs of online auctioning, there's still plenty to be discovered and much to be learned. Why? EBay is commerce; eBay is economics; eBay is evolving. Why else would I be presenting this much-needed update if there wasn't much to talk about? The fact is, eBay, the site, has undergone considerable changes and will continue to change up to the moment and likely soon after this book goes to print. More importantly, though, the tactics, methods, and prospects of utilizing eBay change faster still. That is, mining the full potential of auctioning, direct selling, and online marketing changes as often as you and I change our minds about our goals and how we'll achieve them.

The difference between this book and all the other technical books that pander to you as if you're a "dummy" or an "idiot" (I ruefully regard them as *tech-dreck*) is the reason for my excitement here: The teach-yourself instructional marketplace is woefully in need of an overhaul. The fact is, with computers becoming as commonplace as toasters and the Internet now about as mysterious as the newspaper on your doorstep, people of the world are smarter, more aware, and more capable to take bigger strides at a faster pace when it comes to learning about the cyber-world. Look at you. You're no moron who needs to be schooled about the "right clicker" and "left clicker" on your computer's mouse; that's insulting, yet that's what too many of the instructional texts still persist in doing today. Well, I won't have it. Your money is not to be wasted, and your time is more precious than ever.

But, have I not been such an offender myself? Good point. Looking back to my previous edition of this book, I see that I, too, have blathered on and on about rudimentary tasks and pedestrian concepts related to computers and online auctions. Guilty as charged but, if I can speak in my own defense, at that time (1999), the population of those who were *not* yet online was quite sizable (only about 25% of the population was actively surfing), yet many newcomers were turning out in droves to hop on board and jump into eBay—it being one of the key reasons many decided to finally get into computers and the Internet. That being the audience, the book, as it was written then, spoke to the newcomer and guided him along, step-by-step. Although the previous edition was heavily detailed in all the minutiae of navigating the Web and eBay, it was well received by the readership. That was then; this is now. We've all grown, and I'm ready to make amends.

This book, therefore, is ready to speed ahead, recognizing your marked advancement in computer literacy and online familiarity. For me, it's good news since I can now spend more time speaking to the intrinsics of auctioning, the details of how to get the most from your effort. I want to get you from here to there much quicker but, out of respect to those who might still want to review some of the terminology, concepts, and e-commerce developments that I might take for granted as "common knowledge," I've sprinkled links and references throughout this new edition, leading you to Web sites, publications, and other pools of knowledge and instruction that can clear up any questions you might have. If ever you feel I've gone too quickly, please stop and take the time to explore the resources I'll point out along the way.

What's This Book All About?

So, in presenting this new eBay book based on today's evolved computer and Internet sensibilities, here's what you'll find within these pages.

Part 1: Tracing the Auction Phenomenon

The journey begins with a brief look back, a compressed retrospective of eBay's humble beginnings and unprecedented growth in the decade of the dot-com. Next comes the opportunity to learn more about auctioning and the reasons why dynamic pricing (and fixed pricing) can be of such benefit to you in helping you reach your goals. What are your aspirations? That will be discussed, too, as you zero in on what it is you want to achieve and what sorts of things you *can* achieve, many of which you might never have previously considered. Although this information might seem inconsequential, it serves as the bedrock of your ultimate eBay experience that—trust me—will serve you well.

Part 2: The EBay Way—Policies, Practices, and Preliminary Steps

Here's where I'll roll out the ways and means of getting into the auction game. First, I'll explain how to cut through all the busyness the site pours forth, helping you efficiently navigate to the areas that matter most. Then I'll show you how to become an auction miner *par excellence* by teaching you the best ways to sift through and analyze the tens of millions of items up for auction every day. Bidding comes next, and I'll show you how easy it is to stake a claim on an item while recognizing what critical things to do first to ensure your bidding experience is beneficial. Finally, I'll break down the personality of the eBay community, introducing you to the different sorts of people you'll meet and how to avoid some of the bad folks who might try to rain on your parade.

Part 3: Becoming a Savvy Bidder

Here's where I'll roll out the specific tactics for becoming an expert buyer. I've been working eBay for eight years now, and I've seen and done it all. It's not difficult to become a savvy bidder, a discerning buyer, despite the assertions of "magic and mystery" others might proclaim to possess. Upon completing this section, you'll stand proud among your peers, full of confidence that you know how to find a good deal and how to seize the best items at the best prices.

Part 4: Selling at EBay: For Fun and Profit

Yes, eBay is fun and, yes, it is profitable—*very* profitable. This section will show you how simple it can be to become a seller and how to best present items you want to sell to the millions of active bidders who crowd the virtual marketplace every day. Here, I *will* sweat the details and point out some of the seemingly insignificant points that can actually make or break your selling success. You'll learn everything from timing your auctions, understanding product positioning, and taking better photos to tried-and-true techniques for collecting payment, cutting costs, and shipping the goods with ease. Everything you need to know (including some things you might never have considered) is laid out and properly explained to gain you immediate success.

Part 5: Beyond EBay

So why settle on just eBay when there are other venues to be explored and exploited as you continue your quest for income and acquisition? Here I'll show you how to run parallel activities and how to explore becoming a full-fledged business for yourself.

Gear Up Before You Get Going

Okay. Rather than take pages and pages to describe the details of securing a useful computer, hooking up to the Internet via an Internet Service Provider (ISP), and expounding on the various vanilla software applications you'll need before you begin searching, bidding, and selling, I'll just state it simply: Be sure you have all this before moving ahead. With so many options and alternatives available today, I'd exasperate us both if I tried to give useful instruction on the matter here. I'll assume, then, that you're properly geared up and appropriately hooked up, ready to roll into the auction nation. Still, my conscience is nagging at me, insisting that, at the very least, I offer a list of those tools and tasks you'll need to check off your "get ready" list. Here goes:

- **A computer.** I'm assuming that you have a suitable computer (PC or Mac) and know how to use it and that it's properly equipped with a mouse, keyboard, and storage device (disc drives—internal or external).

- **An Internet connection.** Whether you pay a monthly fee or have free access, use a dial-up (phone), cable modem, or DSL connection, you're connected to the Internet.

- **An e-mail account.** How stupid can I be? Of course you have an e-mail account, which is good because you'll need it the moment you begin your eBay adventure.

Now, if you're lacking in this commonplace online attire, don't fret and don't be embarrassed; plenty of folks still haven't made the leap into the Internet and are now compelled to do so to make use of eBay and other popular Web destinations. Visit any local electronics superstore, and you'll find that buying a computer and even getting hooked up to the Internet can be done in less than an hour. You'll be right up to speed with your peer group in the blink of an eye.

Help Along the Way

How many times have you had a conversation with someone, perhaps seeking instruction in some sort of task or situation, and wound up off the beaten path, so to speak, the dialogue having diverted away from the immediate topic at hand? If you're like me, this happens too often, and you and I, when in these wayward exchanges, struggle and strain to bring the original subject of discussion back into focus. Well, when it comes to the Internet, e-commerce, and eBay, there are so many side roads to be explored, so many corner case scenarios that spin off of the current point of discussion (many that will emanate from your *own* questions), that it sometimes becomes difficult to keep to the task at hand. But, with the goal always in sight, I've identified these areas for sidebar discussion, if you will, with markers like this:

NOTE If there's other information you might benefit from, other resources, or a relevant thought that I think could offer clarity or another perspective, I'll capture it in spaces like this.

ALERT If there's information that could be more critical—perhaps dire—that you understand, recognize, or respond to quickly, I'll flag it in this manner.

DID YOU KNOW? If I have additional thoughts or information to share that, although not necessarily crucial to your success but perhaps interesting and maybe just fun to consider, you'll find that in spaces like this.

My Promise to You

I don't work for eBay, and I never have; I work for *you*. In my years of using, analyzing, and reporting about eBay and the online auction industry, I've maintained that I am the user's advocate, not the site's PR man. To that end, I'll be quite candid in letting you know what's good about eBay and what's not so good. Face it: EBay is in the business of making money, but so are you. To that end, it makes sense that I explain how *you* can best prosper from your efforts and endeavors, even if it means declining some spiffy service eBay would like you to sign up for (read: pay for). I'm not any sort of *eBay-Buster*, some sort of vigilante would-be superhero who's come to bring an evil empire to its knees; I'm just here to point out what's worthwhile, what's reasonable, and what's most effective in utilizing eBay (as well as other venues) in helping you reach your goals and exercise your options in your pursuit of fun and perhaps fortune.

EBay will undergo changes, though, and the industry will shift. New services will spring up while others might dry up. The Internet undergoes perpetual change, and there will be times when what you read here might not exactly match what you see on the screen, have read in the news, or have heard through the grapevine. Any time you have questions that I haven't answered or come across situations where my instruction might seem contradictory to recent changes at eBay or elsewhere, please drop me a line at dlprince@bigfoot.com.

I'll try to answer all mail to the best of my ability because, like I said, I'm in this for you. That's my promise to you.

But, I also promised to help you become an eBay expert in record time, so let's get this show on the road.

part 1

Tracing the Auction Phenomenon

chapter 1

EBay and E-Commerce: How We Got Here and Where We're Going

For starters, let me take you on a brief journey into the history of the Internet, the ways of e-commerce, and the roots of eBay itself. Although it's not critical to your day-to-day success at online selling, I've found a greater sense of perspective, understanding, and personal enlightenment by having been a part of this modern-day Industrial Revolution known as the Computer Age. This will be a quick trip, I promise, because I know you're eager to jump into the eBay experience. Humor me, though, because I think you'll find this abbreviated journey into the recent past fascinating as well as instrumental to establish your foundation and enable you to harness the power and potential of the cyber-market.

It's a Dog's Life

Technology in general and the Internet in particular seem to subscribe to the "dog year" theory of time: So much occurs in such a short span of time that the ratio must be 7-to-1 — arguably seven years' worth of advance in a single year's time. Yes, our current state of technology has enabled us to reach further, achieve greater feats, and acquire more and more of whatever it is we pine for with greater ease and greater speed. The future we dreamed of (and that which Alvin Toffler predicted) a few decades ago is here, now, and has changed forever the way we work, play, learn, and grow. *Future Shock* is now.

Dogs, though, are probably oblivious to all this.

Interestingly enough, our ability to have most everything we want in a fast-paced, electronically charged society has not seemed to bring a sense of greater satisfaction; rather, we now seem to be more intensely afflicted with the need for immediate gratification while having unwittingly adopted an "everything's disposable" mindset along the way. Think about it: Doesn't it seem that anything more than 3 months old is contentiously relegated as, well, dog crap?

Look at all this crap! This crap is outdated and useless! This computer is crap. This television is crap. What will I do with all this CRAP?

Okay, perhaps that's a bit of an exaggeration, but think about how technology that advances like dog years effectively retires itself, making last month's new computer a dinosaur before the new smell has fully worn off. As we have advanced in our manufacturing methods, excelled in our ubiquitous consumerism and collected mountains of goods that would give rise to a whole new industry—self storage—we've effectively situated ourselves into a cluttered existence. In this life, our old crap (a mere 3 month's old, that is) overwhelms us regularly, yet the allure of new crap appears as today's temptation that we simply cannot resist, even though we'll be disinterested in it soon enough.

The trick to dealing with this conundrum is to take a dog's-eye view of the situation and turn this trash into treasure. Hey, there's arguably never been a better time for crap.

A New Place for Old Junk

Pierre Omidyar could scarcely believe what just transpired: He sold his broken laser pointer for $14. It didn't work and was worth essentially nothing to the 28-year-old computer programmer and entrepreneurial dreamer, yet someone he had never met before now wanted it. That $14 transaction was the beginning of a multi-billion dollar venture, the harbinger of an incredible fortune that would be amassed in less than five years' time. (That's 35 dog years if you're still making the conversion.)

EBay was initially christened as *AuctionWeb* (see Figure 1-1), an amateurish Web page launched on Labor Day, 1995. Omidyar's broken laser pointer was the first item ever to be auctioned at the fledgling site, and it happened from the code jockey's cramped Silicon Valley townhouse. He had originally purchased the now malfunctioning tech-toy with visions of grandeur in his head: He'd use it in some big presentation to a board of executives who would be both awed and inspired by the young man's command of the computer industry, his uncanny intellect paving the way to a revolution in the way the world would communicate, commerce, and coexist. The laser pointer broke within two weeks, its most important engagement being that with his cat who fancifully chased the emitted red dot around on the carpet. It was a bust, or was it?

Omidyar's goal in AuctionWeb was to enable buyers and sellers to meet and trade goods in a neutral venue. By utilizing the auction format, of which he admits he was not an expert, he delivered what he considered a "perfect market" where supply would meet demand and precise market value could be achieved every time. It was a theory, anyway, and buoyed by a strictly hobbyist mentality, it seemed like great fun, an interesting experiment, and a lark.

Initially, the site was to play host to trading of computer goods, the sort of "crap" that Omidyar acquired and quickly outgrew. Popular lore also reveals that Omidyar's fiancée was looking for a place to meet and trade with collectors of PEZ novelties; she was an avid hobbyist in her own right, smitten by the hydrocephalic candy dispensers. For both opportunists, utilizing the electronic airwaves seemed like a reasonable approach that might yield modest returns.

Modest, they said.

The Usenet, that network of electronic *newsgroups* that catered to discussions of anything from the latest programmatic bug fixes to the unadulterated conspiracy to viciously dispatch a certain purple dinosaur, played host

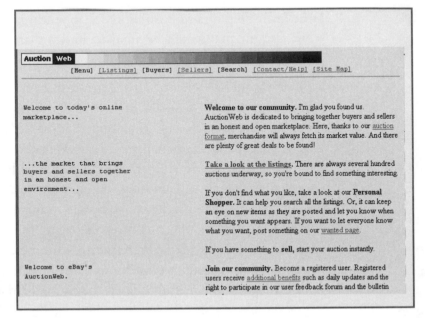

figure 1-1

Screen grabs of the original
AuctionWeb site are almost as
rare as hen's teeth and horse toes.

to thousands of individuals who were eager buy and sell items. These electronic classified ads that touted just about anything for direct sale (with an emphasis, of course, on geek gear) were soon infiltrated by a new sort of listing: items *up for bid* at the URL of http://www.ebay.com/auctionweb (the original URL; it doesn't work today). With that, fueled by rampant and highly positive word of mouth, AuctionWeb became host to thousands of goods to be sold person-to-person. Let the games begin!

A Money-Making Venture

Originally, AuctionWeb was made available free of charge. Omidyar, forever the altruist, was content to provide his public service trading post to all who chose to use it, his personal gain being the coding and Web design experience he'd garner from the effort. Soon, his online service provider, Best, complained that his site was hogging valuable computing cycles and practically crippling response time to other sites hosted on the main server;

Omidyar would need to relocate AuctionWeb to the ISP's business server, jacking up his monthly fees from the $30 range to $250. Suddenly, the hobby was costing the entrepreneur, forcing Omidyar to (almost ashamedly) collect a fee from sellers, which was a small commission based on an item's final selling price. Upon this news, the sellers unanimously . . . *agreed* without retort. Omidyar was soon collecting thousands of dollars in paid fees within a few short months (you figure the dog-year equivalent) and delighted in the site's growth, even when he was forced to install his own server at Best's site. (AuctionWeb had efficiently overtaken all other tenants on the shared business server.) The auction site was a huge and unexpected success.

EBay, This Is Your Life

In 1996, the AuctionWeb name was changed to eBay.com, Omidyar reluctantly dropping a couple of other pet project home pages that were hosted alongside the original auction venue. Working with a new partner, a believer in startups and unmitigated workaholic, Jeff Skoll, the two worked diligently to grow awareness of eBay beyond the modest community of Netizens who had already landed in the opportunistic oasis. The community of users was growing, largely by word of mouth, but it wasn't growing fast enough for Skoll, who set about to establish it as a full-fledged corporation.

By 1998, the Internet was in full commercial bloom. While venture capitalists were becoming the Supermen and women of the day, the growing executive staff at eBay saw an opportunity to significantly expand the site. All that was required was money—lots of it. Because Initial Public Offerings (IPOs) were also the rage of the exploding stock market, eBay's chiefs decided it was time to go public. To gain trust, both of potential shareholders as well as Wall Street, eBay would need a new CEO, one that would be readily recognized with a proven track record in the tough business world.

Meg Whitman, fresh off a stint with Hasbro, Inc., was named the new CEO in March 1998. For better or worse, she brought corporate structure and stability to eBay. Able to thwart off advances by both Amazon.com and Yahoo in bids to acquire eBay, Whitman and Omidyar marched ahead to lay the groundwork for the company's IPO.

DID YOU KNOW? After talks fell through with Yahoo to acquire eBay, Yahoo!Auctions was unveiled just days before eBay's IPO, hoping to steal some of the thunder and dilute the IPO price. The ploy failed.

On September 23, 1998, eBay began trading on Wall Street under the symbol *EBAY*. As the dot-com boom continued, eBay's stock price soared. Despite some controversial moves on eBay's part, such as permanently banning all forms of firearms from the site, the venue continued to prosper, attracting thousands of new users every month.

Even though many of the outspoken long-time *eBaysians* (as they liked to call themselves) decried the chilly corporate feel eBay was adopting, the secret to the site's success lay in its original model: eBay was fully stocked with millions of goods but never had to bother itself with warehousing. The users brought the goods, stored the goods, and managed the sales overhead. Although they sometimes felt underappreciated by Meg Whitman and Co., the buyers and sellers continued to flock to the site.

DID YOU KNOW? On June 10, 1999, eBay suffered the worst outage in its history—it was completely unavailable for 22 hours. Whitman and Omidyar's greatest fear—that all data would be forever lost and the site would have to rebuild from the ground up—was narrowly averted. From that point on, eBay never doubted the need for a redundant (backup) server system. More sobering was the loss of $6 billion in market value attributed directly to the crash. Ouch!

When the dot-com bubble burst in 2000, it had nothing to do with Y2K fears and everything to do with an overstimulated stock market where fortunes that once existed on paper quickly vaporized into the ether. The Internet certainly can't be explained away as a fad, but the fevered attraction was definitely on the decline. Somehow, eBay navigated the choppy waters, buoyed by millions of sellers, many who simply needed to garner income and found a reasonably steady business in the auction venue. Other would-be competitors closed their doors while eBay trudged forward, committed to its business model and determined to continue investing in site enhancements.

Today, eBay is fueled by the buying and selling energy of more than 45 million registered users. Even in the down-turned economy of 2003, the site remains busy as sellers gain income selling virtually anything and everything while buyers find good deals, great treasures, and all manner of other indulgences along the way.

Caught in the Net

Certainly, eBay is the biggest success story of the New Economy and one of the most prolific survivors of the dot-com crash of 2000. If ever you wondered, though, how the rest of the Internet economy is faring, consider these quick statistics as published by the U.S. Department of Commerce:

- In 2002, total online sales were reported in excess of $45 billion.
- E-commerce made up 1.4 percent of total retail expenditures that year.
- During the fourth quarter of 2002 alone, online sales rose 28 percent to $14.3 billion.

Online commerce is expected to maintain and even surpass these levels when 2003 statistics are fully analyzed. But beyond commerce, the Internet itself continues to grow at a staggering rate:

- There are approximately 170 million Internet users worldwide, a figure that's expected to increase to one billion by 2005 (Source: IDC Research).
- About 61 percent of American adults go online every day and, by percentage, spend their time as follows:
  - 93 percent send e-mail.
  - 85 percent use a search engine to find information.

- 83 percent research a product or service before buying it.

- 79 percent search for a map or driving directions.

- 74 percent get news.

- 67 percent surf the Web for fun.

- 61 percent buy a product.

(Source: Pew Internet Research)

The Internet has become a firm fixture in our lives, and the personal computer has become as commonplace as a toaster. Despite economic downturns and various other growing pains the online realm is experiencing, it's clear that online activity is hardly on the verge of fading away, and online auctions will probably never cease to exist so long as people like you and me have goods to offer.

There Was a Time When I Hated Auctions

Initially, I disliked auctions. Having been involved in many face-to-face and many conducted via call-in phone bids, the process of competitive bidding—my money versus yours—held little appeal. Invariably, some big spender would jump in and trounce my pithy offerings, sending me on my way, empty handed and economically dispirited. I changed my tune upon finding eBay.

Being offered $46 outright for a whimsical California Raisins premium (shown in Figure 1-2) seemed like highway robbery when the woman responded to my Usenet ad. I hesitated, though, when I saw another recently sell for more than $50 at AuctionWeb. After politely declining the would-be buyer's offer, I listed the item and let the bidding begin. Though a watched pot might not boil, a heavily monitored auction will still pay off—to the tune of $79. Those singing raisins of mine had coaxed more than 20 bids and gave me my first taste of auction manna.

figure 1-2

These singin', swingin' California Raisins drummed up my first auction profits. I earned it through the grapevine.

And with that, my personal eBay experience began and has never seen interruption. Although I might take a break from active selling from time to time (perhaps when writing a new book), I continue to visit the site at least once a week—usually daily, truth be told—in search of market information, shifts in commodity popularity, or just to snag a peculiar trinket for my own enjoyment. Thanks to the auction, folks like me are compelled and rewarded for entering into the new land of online trading, a land and bartering method which, as you'll learn in the next chapter, isn't new at all.

chapter 2

The Benefits of Auctioning for Buyers and Sellers

Time and again, the question is posed to me:

"Why auction? Why not just sell an item for a certain price and be done with it?"

It's a good question, and the sentiment behind it has merit. Why not simply forego the activity of accepting bids for an item, a process that, on eBay, can span anywhere from 3 to 10 days, and just sell the thing, whatever it is, for a set price? At what price will you sell, though? What if you set too high a price and nobody bites? Worse yet, what if you set too low a price, allowing some lucky buyer to make off with a steal at your expense? And, with those opposing dilemmas facing you, how will you confidently arrive at a proper price?

The auction exists to solve these problems, to gain you fair market value for whatever you might sell and, likewise, ensure that, when buying, you'll be paying the same. Nobody wants to get ripped off (in fact, many fear they will) whether operating as buyer or seller, and the auction model—the principle of dynamic pricing—strikes the balance and returns the proper price every time.

Birth of a Free and Open Market

Really, this is the heart of what makes eBay work: Buyers and sellers meet to establish, real time, the accepted value of an item. The practice of auctioning isn't new, however; its roots have been traced as far back as 500 B.C. (It's true!)

DID YOU KNOW? I'll spare you the historic details of auctions in the dusty days of the Roman Empire and through their glorious days of eminence in 1700s England in this edition. If, however, you are curious to learn more of auctions' origin and evolution, I suggest you grab a copy of my Second Edition of this book and read pages 5–7 to gain a quick background. What's that you say? You can't find a copy of the Second Edition? Look to eBay, silly.

Auctions—that is, using a method of establishing an accepted price for anything from land to rare artifacts and everything in between—employ the methods of *dynamic pricing* to arrive at fair market value; a price is determined by weighing supply to demand, enabling buyers to offer a price they're willing to pay (some will offer more than others) while ensuring a seller can collect a price that truly reflects the present-day value of the goods for sale. For example, every day when fishermen unload their holds, fish buyers gather to bid for a portion of the day's catch. Depending on the demand from other buyers in attendance, the price to the assembly of buyers can and will fluctuate from day to day depending on their need for a portion of the catch. This fluctuation is then passed on to you and me when we visit our favorite seafood restaurant. Naturally, if the catch is limited, yet the attending buyers must meet their steady demand (the patrons who will be visiting the restaurant, for example), each will need to bid higher to gain a portion of the limited catch yet will be constricted to bidding only as much as can be absorbed in menu prices. If the price escalates, restaurant patrons will react to the increase in per-plate cost (as sort of *latent* bidders) by deciding whether they're willing to pay more for the seafood meal. In all of this, the supply side and the demand side both complement and oppose one another, fisherman meeting the public's culinary desires balanced by that same public's tolerance for price fluctuation. In the end, a fair market value is typically reached.

Pierre Omidyar confessed he was not an auction expert when he created AuctionWeb yet understood, in layman's terms, the concepts behind supply-versus-demand valuation. It made sense to him that sellers should have the opportunity to offer items to potential buyers, with those buyers deserving an opportunity to offer up a price they would be willing to pay. In the end, dynamic pricing has worked and continues to work well. EBay was the grand (albeit unwitting) experiment that proved this age-old method of bartering is just as applicable in the Computer Age as it has been throughout world history. Auctions and auctioning have become a staple of our 21st Century economy.

Finding a Fair and Balanced Market

It's one thing to consider the fish buyer whose duty it is to ensure seafood for the restaurant by which he is employed, but what about when these dynamics of dynamic pricing are to be managed by you and me, one of us a buyer, the other a seller? How will either of us, in a one-on-one negotiation, feel confident that the price we settle upon is a true market value? I don't want to get screwed and neither do you, yet somehow we must agree on a price.

So let's have a bit of fun here with a slightly odd yet perfectly plausible scenario, one I originally proposed back in 1999 and which I find still, uh, *sticks*, today. For grins, let's assume you have an original undergarment worn by Darth Vader during the destruction of the Death Star (*Star Wars,* "Episode IV," right?). No doubt, as odd as it might be, you possess a truly rare item: the Lord of the Sith's skivvies. Star Wars *completists* (that is, those folks who are obsessed with owning everything and anything related to topic, idea, or franchise) would probably claw one another to own and proudly display the Evil Emperor's briefs. As unique and uncommon as these must be, these fearful Fruit of the Looms could likely command almost any price—a price that would be offered up, if nothing else, for the sheer bragging rights of ownership. (And, yeah, I'm sure the owner would brag about these.)

What's a fellow to accept, he who no longer wishes to posses (or possibly be possessed by) the evil underpants? The auction, then, comes into play to help this seller unload (ugh!) the prize upon an audience of anticipative bidders.

NOTE Sometimes, auction prices are realized based on the true rarity of an item, with the ultimate value being placed not so much on the usefulness of the item but upon the coveted *opportunity to own* the item. Bargain hunts be damned, these are some rare Jedi Jockeys, and the seller who offers them up to an eager—and likely unsuspecting—group of motivated bidders will probably fare well.

So, working from this aspect of item scarcity, the present owner (perhaps a prop man who scurried off with the Dark Lord's tighty-whities) might not know what price he could get for them. A spokesperson for the Collectors of Celebrity Undergarments Society might try to dupe the owner with a mere pittance for the shorts, thinking the prop man has no clue how precious the "pocket protectors" really are. The seller wisely dismisses the offensive offer and places the desirable drawers up for bid at—you guessed it—eBay, and the response is overwhelming with all manner of fans, fanatics, and film enthusiasts clamoring for this previously unknown *Soily Grail* of a find. All fun aside now, the auction can work to help a seller establish and sell at current market value, the value of a rare find like this being determined by how available the item is, how *many* are available, and, bottom line (sorry), how much someone is willing to pay for the right of ownership. Let's just hope that, after all of this, Darth hasn't decided he enjoys going *commando*.

Run Luke, run . . .

The Buyers Strike Back

Sellers aren't the only ones to prosper from auctioning, and although one may, one day, proclaim to have the only known pair of Darth Vader underoos in existence, buyers are rescued from out and out exploitation by being able to shop the wares of other, competing sellers. Suddenly, one seller's word isn't cosmic law, a price that dare not be challenged; auctions bring *many* buyers from geographies far, far away, and the buyers now have choices.

Not only have auctions served to regulate prices in an open marketplace, disallowing the opportunistic seller from playing the high-pressure sales schtick, but they've also kept sellers from the temptation of "gilding the lily," that is, talking up the quality and appeal of an item in a way that, prior to open and global competition, left a buyer without much opportunity to confirm, compare, and verify the seller's assertions. Buyers are now able to bring their virtual bidding paddles (their online purchasing power) and select from among several—or maybe several hundred—sellers all peddling the same or similar wares. There are no secrets, there are no cuffed aces, and buyers are able to quickly and easily decide, in real time, how *they* value goods up for auction.

Defining Your Purpose

And here's the good news that is eBay: The online auction market is available and adaptable to suit your personal wants, needs, desires. EBay, you'll find, can serve you on a variety of levels:

- If you're a collector, you'll find plenty of items to add to your collection, usually discovering those once hard-to-find pieces are no longer as obscure as they once might have been.

- If you're looking to buy practical and new items, there are plenty of big and small businesses offering new-in-box goods such as electronics, computer goods, housewares, and more.

- If you're looking to clean out your closet, attic, garage, or other makeshift repositories of life's artifacts, eBay is the place to sell your unwanted goods. ***Don't throw it away; throw it on eBay!***

- If you've ever wanted to experiment with starting your own business, eBay is the perfect place to test your plan, allowing you the freedom to work when and how you like, managing as much volume as you care to tackle.

- If you're already a business owner and are looking for an easy way to extend your business's reach, eBay gets your goods in front of millions of eyes throughout the world.

- Before jumping headlong into the world of eBay, take a bit of time to consider what you want out of the experience and what you're willing to invest into it. Don't be surprised if your plans change along the way; many folks adjust their expectations as they gain experience, and that's the beauty of eBay: *It's your business, just the way you like it.*

Whoa! Wasn't that sort of a quick jump from, "How much do you think these underwear are worth?" to "Let's start a business . . . tonight!" Yes, the segue was less than subtle, yet the ability for you to harness eBay and other online venues—as buyer or seller—can be affected in much the same way: quick and calculated. Why? Well, although I've used a broad brush stroke here to paint the background for eBay and online auctions, the next chapter will explain a bit more about *dynamic pricing* and why you'll want to understand its philosophy as you ready yourself for the ultimate eBay experience.

chapter 3

Entrepreneur Alert!
Understanding and
Applying the Auction
Model to Your Business

It's been the best news to greet you and me since the advent of sliced bread and indoor plumbing: Dynamic pricing is back, and it's restoring power to the average citizen in a consumer market that was previously dominated— arguably exclusively—by a relatively few number of large sellers. In other words, good ol' Joe Meat-and-Potatoes has a prominent economic voice in that he (or she) is actively influencing consumer pricing and can affordably enter and compete in the reselling arena. The change is largely thanks to eBay, and it's definitely about time.

NOTE You might ask, "It's back? When did it ever leave?" Recall the mention in the previous chapter of the history of the auction in ancient times on up to modern day, yet ask yourself how often, in the past decade or so, you have been able to shop for goods, by and large, in a haggling manner. Largely, the negotiation of goods trailed off during the past century (the early 20th Century, that is) due mainly to an increase in trading via mail order catalogs as well as trading over a great distance. As the one-on-one meeting of seller and buyer became geographically impractical, sellers took to setting *fixed prices* to maintain consistency in pricing for their catalog and other long-distance sales. Over time, the practice took hold and set the standard for what we consider "retail prices." Yet, today, who wants to pay retail prices? Not me.

So, to sharpen the discussion of auctioning and why a site like eBay has done so well, consider how dynamic pricing has resurfaced in the New Economy, what it means to you, and how you can harness and adapt it to meet your needs, to support your goals, and to allow you to operate a business, no matter how big or small. Although you might contend it doesn't really matter, that just getting *stuff* listed for sale at eBay is all there is to kicking off an auction venture, you'll soon learn that there's quite a bit to know about dynamic pricing and its present-day offshoots and that there are many intrinsic details that will help you become an expert online seller (and buyer) when you recognize how and why dynamic pricing works and how it can be fine-tuned to yield a result that fits your needs and expectations.

Why Does Dynamic Pricing Work?

If you believe the reason eBay has been a phenomenal success is simply because "people like to bid on stuff," you're partly right. Although bidding on goods can be an attraction by its own right, the answer to online auction success goes deeper than that.

For starters, let's agree on the term *dynamic pricing*. From the economist's view, the definition goes something like this:

> Dynamic pricing can be formally defined as the buying and selling of goods and services in markets where prices are free to move in response to supply and demand conditions.

(Source: The CRM Project, 1999)

Nicely enough, this "academic" definition is quite clear in its intent: The dynamic pricing model supports and delivers *true market value* of a given commodity, allowing price to fluctuate up or down as demand rises or falls, affected by the elements of overall availability, temporary or seasonal appeal, perception of rarity or obscurity, and general usefulness. My, aren't we the educated bunch?

Now, as eBay has found its footing and has continued to soar largely fueled by the enticing collectibles market (yes, the collectibles category is still tops in terms of remaining the most popular category of goods bought and sold), buyers and sellers of collectible items—including antiques, glassware, pottery, toys and games, and so on—quickly saw their market shift. That is, item availability and market accessibility for both buyers and sellers changed such that more goods were made available to more buyers as offered by more sellers, thereby affecting the previously accepted prices for such items. In some cases, prices dropped because eBay was able to extend buyer and seller access beyond the previously limited market of local trade shows or distribution of catalogs to a subscriber base; eBay offered a greater selection and, in cases where supply naturally increased, buyers had more choices regarding from whom to buy and at what price. On the other hand, some item prices rose sharply as more buyers entered the market and put additional demand on items that were, perhaps, more finite in supply; prices for those items increased.

Fine, but what if collectibles aren't your bag? That really doesn't matter because, as you might expect, the dynamic pricing model applies to any commodity (goods or service) where one seller can cater to the wants and needs of many buyers. Regardless of whether the commodity is computer goods, books, movies, clothing, jewelry, or whatever else you might imagine, the bottom line is that whenever more than one person wants an item, there is the opportunity to apply dynamic pricing principles.

The Dynamics of Dynamic Pricing

But simply offering an item up for bid isn't all that's required to stir and retain the potential of a dynamic market. Certain other conditions must also exist to ensure that the market is truly dynamic and can yield maximum benefits to participants. In rapid fashion, here are the characteristics that help ensure a dynamic market is free to be all it can be:

- The bigger the market the better. Dynamic pricing is best suited to large markets that have a large supply of goods to be traded. Achieving and maintaining a "critical mass" is essential to driving a dynamic market.

- The greater number of small players, the greater the gain. A market made up of a large population of smaller agents (buyers and sellers, individuals, or small businesses) helps ensure proper competition and drives dynamic pricing. A market dominated by only a few large buyers or sellers can stifle dynamic activity and thereby offer the least potential to gain.

- The greater the volatility, the better. The dynamic market must be driven by ever-changing conditions of supply and demand, a fluid market perception of value (therefore price), and a relatively stable cost of business.

- Participation cost (to buyers and sellers) must remain low for the dynamic market to attain and maintain critical mass and peak activity.

- The customer must be empowered. The success of e-commerce rests firmly upon buyers' ability to compare products and prices easily and accurately, resulting in highly sophisticated consumers with heightened value expectations.

- The consumer experience plays an important role. Participating in a dynamic pricing "event" (if it goes well) can be intoxicating and can lead to repeat participation, especially if the event culminates in a positive transaction.

Without question, many dynamics are required to power and propel a dynamic market. Perhaps you hadn't considered these aspects before but, if you consider eBay itself, you'll likely recognize that it embodies these attributes just described. That's been key to eBay's unbounded success.

A Fair and Balanced Model?

With the dynamic market in place, consider further how this economic model benefits the buyer and the seller. The good news here is that *both* benefit, neither maintaining unfair advantage.

First, consider these benefits to the buyer:

- Increased customer power allows buyers to shop and compare items and prices in real-time fashion.

- Access to a larger and more diverse set of suppliers (sellers) sustains choice and comparison.

- The ability to participate in multiple auctions concurrently further increases the buyers' ability to compare and contrast market demand and price sensitivity.

- An increased ability to *pull* items through the market, where buyers are able to become more selective and precise in purchase decisions, means buyers aren't forced to settle for limited goods or selection in a market dominated by fewer sellers who would merely *push* goods (of the seller's choice) through the market.

With that, it might seem that this is a buyer's market and the seller is the mere pawn who must jump through hoops if sales goals are ever to be realized. Not so. Here's how sellers likewise benefit from the dynamic pricing model:

- Access to a significantly larger market of buyers and easy access to new customers mean increased sales opportunity.

- The ability to effectively specialize while still catering to a substantial audience of consumers allows sellers additional options of product focus.

- Similar access to real-time market trends and conditions (as the buyers enjoy) enable fast and effective alteration of product offerings, pricing strategies, and response to competitive pressures.

- Lowered cost of sales, marketing and advertising, and transaction completion reduce overhead costs and improve profits.

- It provides a safe opportunity to experiment with new pricing methods and marketing approaches.

Clearly, there's opportunity for both camps to prosper, that being the keystone success factor of the dynamic pricing model. It explains why online auctioning succeeds for reasons beyond the fact that bidding can be fun or sellers can peddle their wares from the privacy of their own homes, garbed only in a bathrobe and slippers.

The Secret Ingredient of Auctioning: Private Data

When you think of online privacy, you're likely to conjure up thoughts (or apprehensions) regarding identity theft, computer viruses, and other unwelcome personal data affronts. I'll discuss *those* issues at length in the next chapter, but for now, let's wrap up this immediate discussion of the dynamic pricing model and of auctioning specifically by recognizing the infrequently discussed element that makes the whole thing work.

In dynamic bartering, "private information" is of ultimate importance to upholding the model's effectiveness. When entering into a bid or barter, the buyer maintains privacy—that is, he consciously does not reveal information regarding how much he or she will pay for a particular item. This *buyer valuation* is founded on the buyer's belief of the item's value both in terms of market price as well as personal desire for ownership. Much like the proverbial game of poker, the buyer must keep a straight face when deciding to go after an item; if the buyer "tips the hand," the seller can exploit that information against the buyer as well as against other buyers who might also be in contention for ownership.

Likewise, the seller has to play the cards close to the chest. Here, the seller is careful not to divulge the actual cost or investment in the item being offered, does not let on what sort of price is expected, and never (or rarely) announces the lowest acceptable selling cost during the course of the auction. If this information is revealed, the buyers in assembly might begrudge a significant profit the seller might collect or, conversely, might choose not to participate in bidding if they consider the seller's initial valuation as excessive. To this end, both buyer and seller *must* maintain secrecy of this vital information if the true market value, derived by supply and demand alone, is ever to be reached.

Dynamic Domination: Why Has EBay Become and Remained the Biggest Player in Online Auctions?

If you've followed the evolution of online auctions over the past five or so years, you'll know that there have been plenty of other contenders envious and determined to bring eBay—the virtual 300-pound gorilla—down from its reigning perch; many have tried, many have failed, most have folded, and few remain to offer much of an alternative venue. So is eBay just so damned superior and so incredibly wise that advances by competitors are destined to fail by some cosmic predetermination, or is it, in fact, that others have tried end-runs that, while in theory might have seemed certain to succeed, in all practically were undermined by lack of forward thinking? It's probably a bit of both.

To begin with, eBay benefited from uncanny timing, point blank. Pierre Omidyar's lucky experiment came at a time when the Internet was poised to boom. Then the dot-com boom fueled it, where almost anything online garnered a frenzy by right of its very existence. (New surfers were simply mesmerized by being able to rapidly surf from here to there.) But beyond timing, eBay also benefited from *brand recognition*, possessing an easy-to-remember moniker and having the enviable word-of-mouth confidence of a growing community that was further blossoming as each day passed. *EBay* was the word on the tip of many Internet enthusiasts' tongues.

Or maybe it was just the beanie baby. Face it. At the time eBay came into being, so did a nationwide—no, *worldwide*—feeding frenzy fueled by these simple bean bag critters. As folks clamored for the cleverly *retired* characters that were in finite supply, they turned to eBay to find that which they so desperately sought. The "haves" who possessed these coveted creations learned of the online demand for beanies and gleefully complied by listing beanie babies for auction and then sat back and watched the frenzy unfold (and the dollars roll in). Now, with some hindsight, I have to wonder if one could have ever existed without the other: In a true "chicken and the egg" juxtaposition, if beanie babies didn't exist, could eBay have gained such critical mass, or if eBay didn't exist, could beanie babies ever have become so wildly popular? That's one to stew on for a time. No matter the answer, eBay became first on the block and quickly soared into success, heralding the shape of things to come in the New Economy.

As eBay continued to grow, so did its need to collect nominal fees from sellers to ensure the site could keep pace with the increased demand of its features and services. Although some balked at the need for these fees (and I'll reference the listing fee specifically), it might have been these levies that kept independent sellers soundly in business. You need only look at Yahoo!Auctions to see that it was the sellers, perhaps, who summarily crippled that venue.

Yahoo sought to unseat eBay from its lofty throne by creating an alternative bid-and-sell venue with the added attraction of *no listing fees*. That's right—where eBay charged an *insertion fee* based on the minimum bid amount (and later by the optional *reserve price* amount), Yahoo invited all sellers to list whatever they had at whichever opening bid they chose without paying to do so. The result—Yahoo auctions sputtered and largely failed, the majority of auctions closing without a sale. Although some sellers argued eBay had too much of a stranglehold on the auction market and that Yahoo's venue simply wasn't enticing enough, it all came back to the core principle of dynamic pricing: Sellers were freely establishing minimum bid values in excess of what the market (the buyers, that is) would bear. Because there was no fee (you could call it a *penalty* perhaps) for listing items at premium prices, sellers effectively short-circuited the dynamic pricing model and actually discouraged bidders from participating in the auction experience. Sellers grumbled, "There aren't any buyers at Yahoo. What a waste of time," while potential buyers asserted, "The prices at Yahoo!Auctions are way too high. I can find better deals at eBay!" That's a point well taken (if unknowingly) because eBay *did* charge fees based on opening bid and reserve prices, encouraging sellers to set more reasonable prices and allowing bidders to participate at lower opening prices. Go figure; you could say eBay lucked out again.

And how about Amazon Auctions? Well, theirs is arguably a case where perhaps brand recognition hurt their effort to challenge eBay's grip on the auction market. Although I don't have empirical data to this point, I and many I've talked to have agreed that when we think Amazon, we think books (and sadly few ever think of the actual winding river that runs through South America). At the time Jeff Bezos, Amazon.com CEO, was eager to take on eBay's Meg Whitman in a virtual *Celebrity Deathmatch*, the book site was likewise branching (or splintering) into just about every other conceivable commodity, hoping to become *the* end-all, be-all Internet destination. It didn't work. Amazon Auctions, like Yahoo!Auctions, is still live at this writing, but their share of the auction industry is practically negligible when compared to eBay. EBay, again, lucked out because it focused solely on auctions and the auctioning experience.

Fixed Versus Dynamic: A New Price War?

Lastly, consider the newest dynamic of the auction market, which isn't dynamic at all—fixed pricing. Interestingly enough, eBay began to become increasingly pressured by buyers and sellers who wanted the option to avoid the usual auction game, to shorten the sales process, and to close a deal quickly and noncompetitively. To achieve this, the market required a *fixed price* to sell by. This circumvented the back-and-forth bidding process and established a "take it" price (at eBay, it's called the *Buy-It-Now* price) that sellers could establish and which buyers could elect to accept. But isn't this blasphemy in the auction space, a "retail" pricing methodology that would send the dynamic market and dynamic pricing back to the recesses of the Old Economy? More critical, couldn't the fixed-pricing methodology effectively short-circuit the dynamic market?

Actually, no. The good news is both pricing methods have proven they can peacefully and successfully coexist and, if exercised to their fullest, could further propel the dynamic market. Of course, the key for both buyers and sellers is knowing when to utilize the bidding process and when to defer to the alternate fixed-price format.

From a seller's perspective, your best bet when offering goods for sale is to give the buyers what they really want: options. Whether they choose to battle other bidders for goods or elect to buy items outright, customers appreciate the opportunity to decide for themselves. As you'll learn later in this book, there are strategies to use—for both buyers and sellers—to gain the greatest advantage in the market when you know how and when to use the different pricing and sales approaches in the dynamic market.

Now, before jumping into the auction action, ready to apply all you've learned about dynamic markets, I urge you to familiarize yourself with some of the darker elements of the online realm. The fact is, there are some traps out there that you'll need to anticipate and avoid. The next chapter will guide you through the dark spaces of the Internet but bring you back alive and ready to eBay.

chapter 4

Security and Privacy in the Cyber-Market

When it comes to online privacy and security, the first step in broaching the subject is to admit the following: You are at risk. Read it; repeat it; believe it. Whether someone's trying to lift your credit card number or attempting to infiltrate the sensitive data on your computer, hacking, spamming, and data mining have become the white-collar crimes of our era. While you needn't allow that to frighten you away from rightful online pursuits, it is important that you become familiar with the array of cyber-crimes being committed every day and then guard yourself, your PC, and even your auction exploits from assault.

NOTE Although it wouldn't be practical to fully articulate *every* aspect of the security and privacy issues online or attempt to instruct you in each precise step to take in avoiding and preventing online troubles, this chapter does provide specific tasks and checkpoints to bolster your online safety. Where appropriate, I've also included links and references to additional resources that will help you further the fight against cyber-crime.

A Rogues Gallery of Online Ruses

To begin, take a look at this rundown of online shenanigans that occur every day with the potential to impact each of us who choose to make use of the Internet, eBay, and everything else on the World Wide Web.

Identity Theft

Identity theft skyrocketed 81 percent in 2002. It was reported that 700,000 people were victims of identity theft in the United States that year, based on data released by the Federal Trade Commission. Shockingly, that statistic gains frightening new relevance when compared to the 418,000 robberies committed in the United States in 2002 (as reported by the FBI's Uniform Crime Reporting Program).

"The bulk of identity crimes are committed through decidedly old-fashioned means," confirmed Gartner Group analyst Avivah Litan in a previous interview. "Information stolen in pre-existing relationships, pickpockets taking wallets and purses, mail interception where the thief opens financial mail, copies the information, and reseals the envelope all play a large part [in identity theft]."

The Internet adds a potentially easier method to abscond an individual's personal information: online pickpocketing. As you'll learn later in this chapter, there are numerous ways for crooks to obtain your vital information and ways for you to prevent it.

Computer Viruses

Even those who might never have surfed the Internet are probably well aware of the widespread and negative impact computer viruses have had on computer users. Most viruses arrive in the form of a *Trojan horse*, a file that secretly accompanies some unsolicited e-mail message or which could be attached to a seemingly harmless file stored on a floppy disk or CD-ROM. Another class of malicious software is called *worms*. These programs exploit weaknesses in existing computer systems and propagate without requiring any action on the user's part. (How thoughtful of the pranksters.) Fortunately, most worm programs, like other viruses, can be controlled by keeping your virus scanning software up to date. Whichever the case, after the intruding program is unleashed on your computer, the agent of harm can immediately begin its dirty deeds of corrupting your other files, erasing your vital data, and generally disabling your computer's operating system.

Spam, Adware, and Spyware

At one time they were merely annoyances. I'm talking about the occasional virtual junk mail and pop-up ads that find their way into your e-mail and onto your computer screen. Today, though, junk mail and junk advertising have spread to epidemic proportions, responsible for clogging server relays, harboring virus-infected files, and capable of surreptitiously installing clandestine programs onto your computer to strip personal information for use in identifying and forwarding even more garbage to your account. Some have called these tools methods in which to personalize and enhance online experiences; the rest of us call them invasive, intrusive, and unwanted.

Credit Card Fraud

As you might have guessed, identity theft and spam are both after this vital information: your credit card data. All that is required to purchase items with stolen credit cards is a number and expiration date. Worse yet, armed with an ill-obtained credit card number and social security number, crooks can quickly and easily set up new accounts to buy and sell goods under the guise of *your* identity. Thieves will aggressively pursue high volumes of credit card data and then either use that data themselves or barter it off to others for unauthorized activity. Again, this is critical data to safeguard. When you're online, this potential for fraud requires you to lock down your computer and be certain where and when you'll offer up the data yourself.

Auction Fraud

EBay, too, has been fertile soil for online crime. Not only will you need to be able to spot a fraud in action (auction scams are covered fully in Chapter 8, "E-Motions and Auction Affronts"), but you'll again need to remain vigilant in protecting your eBay-specific information to ensure some scoundrel can't make off with your data and run a rampage of illicit activity. For starters, visit GetNetWise (see Figure 4-1) for a sound introduction to online security and the safety issues that face us all.

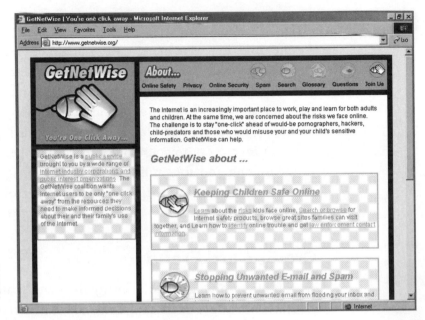

figure 4-1

If you want to know more about online security and safety risks, please visit http://www.getnetwise.com.

Securing Your Computer

Your task, prior to venturing into an eBay goods-grabbing, fortune-finding journey, is to ensure that your computer is safe and your data is safe. Here are the steps to consider to ensure that your online adventure begins in a safe vehicle.

Step 1: Secure the Line

With the allure of blazing-fast Internet surfing made available by broadband Internet connections (DSL or cable modems, for example), PC users need to recognize the risk and responsibility when enjoying the convenience of an "always on" Internet connection. Essentially, your PC remains open to the Internet 24 × 7 while it's dutifully humming awaiting your next command or request. In the meantime, others could be stopping by, unannounced, usually to cause harm, mayhem, or data theft. Don't yank the connection from the wall just yet, though. Instead, look to a Firewall application that can effectively screen unauthorized access to your PC from that open broad-band line. ZoneAlarm and BlackICE PC Protection are but a couple of the firewall applications available to protect your PC. Search the Internet for "firewall" and compare and contrast the features and costs.

 TIP Be sure your firewall goes both ways—that is, it should scan and alert you of network traffic *bi-directionally*, monitoring both inbound as well as outbound (from your computer) activity.

DID YOU KNOW? If you're completely new to firewalls, visit http://www.securityfocus.com for an extremely well con-structed beginner's guide to firewalls; you'll be glad you did.

Step 2: Batten Down Your Browser

With the direct line into your computer appropriately guarded, now secure your browser to help ensure *you* don't unwitting allow trouble into your trading space while innocently surfing the Internet. The security settings, options, and preferences in your browser will help you add the next level of protection.

If you're using Internet Explorer, choose Tools, Internet Options, click the Security tab, and select the Internet icon. Then confirm that the Security level slider is set at least to Medium, effectively blocking most activities that could introduce illicit scripts and programs to execute while you browse.

 NOTE If you're sharing your computer, especially with youngsters, you might also want to specify restricted sites by clicking on the appropriate icon. Chances are you've been warned by friends or family of specific sites that aren't kid friendly; specify those sites to ensure little hands can't accidentally stray off the beaten path.

If you're using an alternative browser such as Mozilla or Netscape, you can enable the same security features by choosing Edit, Preferences. Then double-click the Privacy & Security category title as it appears in the Preferences pop-up window.

DID YOU KNOW? Finally, when you've finished tweaking your browser's security settings, visit one of the many browser security-check Web sites. Scanit (http://www.scanit.be) and Qualys (http://www.qualsys.com/security) will point out any chinks in your browser's armor and suggest a fix.

Step 3: Clear Your Cookies; Erase Your History

Although they're typically not destructive in nature, those cute little cookie files that Web sites use to personalize your online experience do often tell tales that you might want to keep to yourself. Cookies offer up information about which sites you like to surf, what sort of preferences you have in shopping, and other details about how you've customized your online exploits at various Web sites. If you're an IE user and are curious just how much information cookies can reveal, choose Tools, Internet Options; then on the General tab, click the Settings button in the Temporary Internet files area. In the Settings dialog box, click the View Files button to see all the cookies sitting in your virtual cookie jar. Mozilla and Netscape users should choose Tools, Cookie Manager, Manage Stored Cookies. The real risk in having cookie files hanging around is that the information could be retrieved by a virus, a hacker, or a spybot (more on those later) to collect information about your Internet habits, using that information to bombard you with even more e-mails, advertisements, and other such annoying come-ons.

Besides cookies, all browsers maintain a history of the URL destinations you've visited (which is handy in allowing the browser to complete a Web page address from the drop-down address window but could also be . . . well . . . incriminating if your spouse, kids, grandma, boss, or whomever else might peek in to see—Oh my!—where you've been surfing; no problem if you have a clean conscience).

To view history records in any of the browsers previously mentioned, simply press Ctrl+H on your keyboard to open the History frame that will appear on the left side of your browser window. Here you can see sites that have been visited in the past day, week, or beyond. To clear this trail of events (perhaps you've been Christmas shopping and don't want that special someone to find out; yeah, yeah, that's it), simply right-click on any entry or header for a group of entries and choose Delete.

To quickly erase all history entries in IE, choose Tools, Internet Options and click the Clear History button. In Netscape or Mozilla, click Edit, Preferences, select History under the Navigator category, and click the Clear History button. A quicker method is to right-click in the Taskbar area, select Properties, click the Start Menu Programs tab, and then click Clear. These methods achieve the same result.

Establish a Virtual Vigilance

After you've taken steps to secure your computer against assault and any prying eyes, you'll need to continually monitor and safeguard it from weaknesses and holes in the protective barriers. Just as brick-and-mortar shop owners need to protect their establishments against the disruption of physical theft and vandalism, as a virtual shop owner, you'll likewise need to be equally vigilant against cyber-vandals. Following are the additional safeguards, guidelines, and countermeasures that will help ensure that your ultimate online venture can withstand new and unannounced affronts.

Virus Vigilance

Despite ongoing warnings, many computer users simply aren't using anti-virus software or have not kept their virus definitions current. These users are at high risk of contracting and redistributing viruses to their friends, family, and—most important in this context—their *customers*. Because new viruses are being unleashed all the time, it's up to you to keep your PC properly protected to avoid disruption to your business and ensure that you don't unwittingly infect others' systems.

The good news is that you can often spot a virus on sight if you know what to look for. Because most viruses are spread via e-mail attachments, be suspicious of messages from unrecognized sources that harbor files with these file extensions: VBS, WSH, SHS, WSC, JS, PIF, CMD, BAT, SCR, LNK, COM, EXE, and REG. Also, recognize that many more viruses infect files that use applications containing *macro languages* such as Microsoft Word and Excel. When an infected document or spreadsheet file is opened, the concealed virus is enabled as if it were a macro definition. This means you can contract such a virus by sharing infected files via floppy disk and CD-ROM as well as via e-mail distribution.

To avoid viruses and their fallout, remember these key safeguards to best ensure protection:

- Scan your PC files on a regular basis; scan boot files on each power-up and conduct full system scans on a weekly basis.

- Update your virus definitions weekly. (Symantec updates their Norton AntiVirus definitions every Wednesday.)

- Keep the automatic virus shield enabled at all times.

- Ensure that the virus checking function is set to scan downloadable (Internet) and e-mail files upon receipt.

- Ensure that removable media scanning (floppies and CD-ROMs) functions are enabled.

- If you use Microsoft Outlook, install the security updates to prevent infected files from automatically executing. (Outlook 2002 offers this as a standard security feature.)

- Keep up to date on new virus threats by visiting http://www.sarc.com.

Update, Update, Update

Another way to help safeguard your computer from viruses and their ilk is to ensure that your operating system is kept up to date by regularly checking for and installing updates (sometimes called software patches). Microsoft's Windows Update site (http://windowsupdate.microsoft.com), for example, provides patches that can close up security holes in the suite of Microsoft products as exposed by viruses. Whatever your platform, whatever your operating system, visit the appropriate Web site to ensure that you keep your computer's core functions and protections current.

And, if you haven't already been prompted, most other programs and utilities that you've added to your computer could stand a regular freshening up, too. Whether it's a browser tool, a security tool, a graphics package, or whatever, be sure to keep current on those program updates as well; just seek out the manufacturer's Web site and follow their update recommendations.

Backup and Disaster Recovery

Dutifully secured, virus free, and up to snuff, the best gift you can give to your computer (and online business) is a healthy backup. Because the onslaught of computer nasties will undoubtedly persist, regular operating system and file backups are essential as the last line of defense should a cyber-cretin find a way in and summarily corrupt your data. For about $1 a disc, backing up to CD-ROM (read or read/write) discs is the lowest-cost protection you can buy and will prove invaluable to your business ventures if ever you need to restore important personal and business data. Also, be sure you have all necessary program and driver files for add-on hardware (such as modems, accessory cards, and printers) safely stored away on removable media as well as on the recovery disc that likely accompanied your system. (This would be used in extreme cases in which a full disc reformatting would be required.)

 NOTE You might also consider establishing a backup internal hard drive if your business swells such that continually storing off to a CD-ROM media becomes overly time consuming and generally inefficient. A second backup drive can be configured to become the recipient of automatic system backups. (They can run at night while you sleep.) Be sure to run a regular virus scan on that backup drive, though.

Keeping Spam in the Can

Spam, that ceaseless onslaught of messages promising overnight weight loss, work-at-home fortunes, and any sort of physical enhancement you might dare to imagine, has become more than an annoyance; it's a federal issue these days. (No kidding.) It used to be that spammers harvested e-mail addresses from sites like Amazon.com, eBay, AOL, and others and then used those addresses to begin their junk-mail junket. Nowadays, in response to heightened security features, spammers have devised ways to gain access to individual systems by taking advantage of open relays or open proxies—that is, *pass throughs*, which are basically security vulnerabilities in your mail server or in the software that allow several computers to share an Internet link. When access has been gained, a spammer's message is then rerouted just about anywhere but now utilizes random sources (perhaps a proxy site or even an e-mail address like yours), making it difficult to trace the true origin of the bothersome message.

So what can you do to eliminate spam? Sadly, the spam-slingers get more and more clever with their approaches so, really, the best thing you can do is simply delete the spam, *without responding*. Chances are, after you've responded to any sort of spam, no matter how irate your retort might be, the senders will know that they've made a "hit" and will target your e-mail address for even more spam.

Try utilizing spam filters that are available on most e-mail programs (Eudora, Outlook, Yahoo!Mail, and so on). Then be ready to sign up for the *Antispam Registry*. (This registry is a new effort similar to the national Do Not Call list of 2003 intended to reduce the number of junk phone solicitations you've likely been receiving. To learn more, check out http://www.pcworld.com/news/article/0,aid,110398,00.asp.) Beyond that, be patient, use your Delete key generously, and keep your other computer and Internet connections up to ward off the truly troublesome door-to-door denizens.

Beware the New (Criminal) Kids on the Block

As business and personal technology progresses, so does criminal technology. Whether left to fend for themselves in the daytime, bored with their game decks, or simply fueled by the challenge of inventing new methods of cyber-assault, computer-savvy freaks and geeks are constantly at work to disrupt your online exploits. Just when you think you have a good handle on your exposure online, some new twisted trick comes along to further punish your processing power. Beyond the well-known spam, viruses, and other such annoyances, be on the lookout for these newer computing traps.

Adware, Spyware, and Dialers

Adware is a newer sort of software that, upon successful installation on your PC, proceeds to pop up browser windows that contain unwanted advertisements or redirect the window to another Web site (some not suitable for all ages). In essence, adware is a new breed of spam that doesn't wait for you to respond to an unsolicited invitation; it takes you there, ready or not. Some adware programs also track your Web browsing activity, using the information gathered to initiate targeted advertising based on the sites you've been browsing. Your Internet privacy, once again, is under attack.

Spyware is a dark cousin to adware, its purpose being that of scanning your computer's drives to acquire personal data or to identify your e-mail address for use by other spam proliferators. If this isn't concerning enough, be especially cautious of the insipid *dialers*, which are programs that freely make use of your Internet connection and quietly route you through toll numbers that can cost several dollars per minute. Dialers, like spyware, are often contained within online program downloads (watch out for shareware) or can be automatically invoked upon opening a complex spam e-mail. (Watch out for the porn spam; it's the worst.)

Numerous applications can help you wrangle and remove these computer pests. Check out the free software noted in Table 4-1.

DID YOU KNOW? Most adware and spyware utilities come bundled with desirable free programs, most often in the popular peer-to-peer file-sharing programs like Kazaa, IMesh, and BearShare. Installing one of these can dump dozens of additional programs on your PC.

Table 4-1 Free Applications to Battle Adware and Spyware

Application Name	Use	Operating System(s) or Browser(s) Supported	Web Site
Ad-aware v6.181	Effectively removes adware and spyware	Windows Me, Windows 2000, Windows XP, Windows NT, Windows 98	http://www.lavasoftusa.com
Spybot Search and Destroy v1.2	Cleverly removes spybots, replacing them with empty dummy files	Windows 9.x, Windows Me, Windows 2000, Windows XP, Windows NT	http://spybot.eon.net.au/
PrcView (Process Viewer) v3.7.25	Allows verification and debugging of processes that are actively running in a Windows session	Windows 9.x, Windows Me, Windows 2000, Windows XP, Windows NT	http://www.prcview.com
Spychecker v1.1	Detects spyware that's hiding on your PC	Windows 9.x, Windows Me, Windows 2000, Windows XP	http://www.spychecker.com
WinPatrol v5.2	Detects and destroys unwanted background programs	Windows 9.x, Windows Me, Windows 2000, Windows XP, Windows NT	http://www.winpatrol.com

Spoof! You've Just Been Robbed

Finally, the most recent "hack," if you will, that targets online auction-goers and other such shoppers directly is a fraud known as *spoofing*, or *phishing*. Here, recipients are presented authentic-looking e-mail messages (entreaties, warnings, alerts, and so on) that contain links to allow the updating of sensitive information—credit cards, passwords, SSNs—to ensure the recipient's account remains "in good standing." Spoof! The site where you just entered your vital information was a fake and someone just gathered your data so that he could run amuck disguised as you. (See Figures 4-2 and 4-3 for examples of spoofs that came my way.)

Can You Spot a Spoof?

Actually, most spoofs are easy to detect regardless of the pains the spoofers go to in trying to dupe you and me with their clever graphics and a few legitimate links sprinkled in.

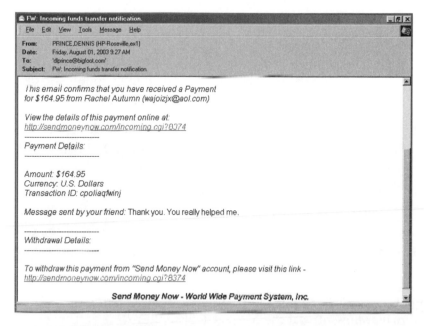

figure 4-2

Although not fancy in design, this spoof promised me cash I never earned if I simply visited the bogus link and entered my info.

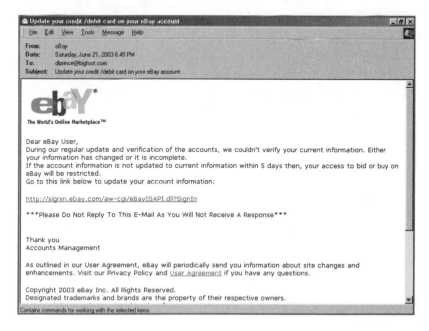

figure 4-3

This convincing-looking spoof indicated my eBay account was about to expire unless I visited the embedded link and ponied up my personal data.

First, always read the message thoroughly and look for grammatical errors and typos; most spoofs have 'em and are an immediate tip off.

Next, when you roll your mouse over the embedded links that would be used to navigate through to enter the illicitly requested data, check the Web URL. I've seen bogus examples like www.ebayupdate.net and www.change-ebay.com, both of them garbage. Likewise, I've seen similar spoofs for sites like PayPal (always a favorite target of fraudsters) and Buy.com.

If you really want to get into the meat of the spoof, right-click on the suspected spoof-email header and click Properties from the pull-down menu; then choose the Details tab. Scan the display to determine the Received From source; usually this will specify an IP address such as 207.44.196.35. With that IP address, visit http://www.arin.net, the American Registry for Internet Numbers, and plug the IP address into the Whois field of the displayed search form; you'll be amazed where some of these messages have hailed from—it's not eBay or Buy.com headquarters.

Bottom line for your safety here: *Never* respond to an e-mail request from any site, no matter how official the message looks, to provide your personal user data or private information. Sites like eBay insist they will never ask for such information in an e-mail message (although they often do send legitimate e-mail messages loaded with active links—sillies). When in doubt, travel to the Web site directly via a Web browser (don't utilize the spoof links) and check your data there. In several cases, my purportedly jeopardized account was in perfect order. Fools. EBay also requests that you forward any such spoof messages directly to them at spoof@ebay.com.

Is It Safe Yet?

Well, much has changed regarding online safety, security, and privacy since the Second Edition of this book was published. Although this chapter has been somewhat lengthy on steps to ensure your safe trading online, understand it's of prime importance that you become aware of some of the snares awaiting you out there. Follow the guidelines presented here, check into the sites of additional information noted, and keep an eye on the headlines to ensure that you're aware when online mischief takes an upswing.

Now it's time to get to work and get your eBay adventure rolling. Next stop—fun and fortune.

part 2

The EBay Way — Policies, Practices, and Preliminary Steps

chapter 5

Seeing the Site,
Learning the Rules,
and Getting Started

Welcome to eBay, the mother of all online trading venues. If you've read the company's latest Annual Report (dated 12/31/02), you would know the site boasts a whopping 62 million registered users, 28 million of those being truly "active," spanning 37 countries worldwide. To serve this vast community of busy buyers and sellers, eBay has grown its item categories to 22,000 unique distinctions, allowing users to narrow their focus for the items they'll buy or sell. Every day, tens of millions of items are readily available for bid or fixed-price purchase. As a result, eBay's system volume is mammoth, managing up to 580 million page views every day, 60 million item searches every day, and 4.5 gigabits per second of data traffic.

Are you impressed?

This hasn't been a commercial for the site nor was it a sly attempt to encourage you to call your stockbroker and buy up shares; rather, it's just a quick overview to let you know what's really going on inside of eBay and with whom you'll be rubbing elbows. The site is big. The site is popular. Although it might seem overwhelming at times, the site can be tamed for your individual use. To that end, this chapter provides the bare-bones tour of eBay in which you'll learn the key points of interest, the areas of "fluff"— glitz and glamour that makes eBay look pretty but might not be of ultimate benefit to you—of which you should be aware, the rules of the site, and, of course, the way to get registered so that you can get to work (or play, whichever you prefer).

EBay Attributes: The Best of the Least

Having been an active eBay user since December 1995, I've seen the site change dramatically. I'm lucky, I suppose, that I learned the ways and means of auctioning when the site was relatively simple, allowing me to become proficient with the core site processes without the distraction of the numerous extra tools, banners, and you-name-its that now plague the portal. Really, new users confide that eBay has become intimidating in all its superfluous design and unrelenting visual noise. No problem: Here's where you find out what's necessary to getting into the action without having to make a grab for the Excedrin just to get past the home page.

The EBay Home Page

Okay. Power up your favorite Web browser and head off to http://www.ebay.com (see Figure 5-1).

Wow! There's a lot going on at eBay by the looks of the active home page that greets visitors. EBay has gone to great pains to make their home page as full-bodied as possible but, I must confess, it's fallen to the same mindset that's delivered cellphones that display text messages, take and send pictures, provide Web access, and play games; all I wanted to do was make a quick phone call. Not to knock on eBay because it is a highly useful and lucrative site for me (and it will be for you, too), but it's getting quite bogged down with *feature bloat*. Rather than look at the main page, roll your eyes, and sigh in exasperation because you're not sure where you really need to begin, here are the key features of the home page, the elements that you'll use every time you visit:

- **The main toolbar.** Expect to become fast friends with this grouping of fast links. Then forget that some of the labels are larger and

figure 5-1

It's a site to see. EBay's home page is a busy place, hinting at the bustling business going on inside.

enclosed in boxes; that makes them no more important than the smaller text-only links that rest above. Although eBay enjoys mixing these links around every other year, it generally holds fast that the Browse, Sell, Services, Search, Help, Site Map, and other links are most useful to you and has graciously positioned this toolbar configuration on practically every other eBay page you'll visit within the site. This is the #1 most useful feature of the site's home page.

■ **The Search box.** Labeled What Are You Looking For, this useful search box allows you to immediately begin hunting for specific goods the moment you arrive at the site. If I'm not here to sell something, this is the point of immediate use to me when I visit eBay.

■ **Categories.** The left side pane links to all the different categories of goods, each with numerous subcategories and each containing thousands of items. If you're less specific about what you might want to search for or are looking to become better acquainted with the categories under which you might list an item for sale, take the time to click the main Categories link at the top of the pane for a view of the entire category landscape.

And that's about it, folks. Beyond those key points of interest, the rest of what you see on the home page is design and marketing oriented. Much like a virtual billboard, the home page theme will change upon every visit (this example promoting the eBay Motors branch). The other links you'll see either take you to featured item listing pages, allow you to navigate to specially themed groupings of listings, visit sponsor and partner sites, and so on. Although sometimes serviceable and nice to look at, this balance of "fluffy" links is not of much immediate use for the buyer who came looking for a particular item or the seller who is ready to list an item. In the next chapters, you'll learn more about each of the key functions mentioned here but, first, let's review the pertinent laws of the land.

Basic Site Rules

Before reviewing the registration process that allows you to become an active buyer or seller, consider the site rules by which the vast eBay community is to abide. There's no real peril inherent to these rules, but you should be aware of a few conditions and technicalities that you'll be signing up to.

A Deeper Look at the User Agreement

When you register at eBay, you'll be required to acknowledge your understanding and acceptance to the site's *user agreement*. Largely, it's an agreement that establishes how users are to conduct themselves in the site-sponsored online transactions, how they are to expected to fulfill obligations to one another, and how they are to refrain from dealing in certain goods. Briefly, here are the key points of the user agreement.

Must Be 18 to Play

By law, online auctioning and other similar intentions to buy or sell goods are restricted to individuals who can "form legally binding agreements." EBay use, therefore, is restricted to members who are 18 years old or older. An adult must accompany youngsters. (Really, it's in the agreement.)

The Fee to Which You Agree

EBay is a fee-based service for sellers and, by accepting the agreement, sellers understand that fees will be assessed in accordance with the site's published fee structure. (More details on that are available in Chapter 13, "Immediate Success with Your First Listing.")

A Contract to Transact

Simply put, if you bid and win, you're expected to pay up. If you list an item for sale, you're expected to be legally able to sell the item (no bridges or swampland, please). This provision is really to ensure that flighty bidders don't renege on their obligation to pay and sellers don't skip town after money has been received.

Don't Monkey with the Mechanism

Here, eBay explicitly prohibits auction interference or other forms of manipulation that might artificially impact a sale. This is all about auction fraud, a problem that stayed high on the Consumer League's top list of online offenses. You'll learn more about the various frauds in Chapter 8, "E-Motions and Auction Affronts."

Privacy Policy

Online privacy remains a topic of heated discussion, and eBay has taken heat for some ambiguous language in previous renditions of its site privacy policy. I urge everyone to read the policy and understand it. While not 100-percent fail-safe, the policy does maintain that your personal information (name, address, and so on) will not be shared with third-parties—law enforcement being the exception, and only if you've been involved in a matter of potential litigation. The policy is generally safe and, unless you agree to it, you'll not be allowed to use the site.

Restricted Items

Yes, there are some things you are prohibited from selling at eBay (not just bridges and swampland, but also tactical nuclear devices and such). Most notably, eBay disallows sale of firearms, animals, alcohol, drugs and paraphernalia, and human remains or body parts. (Anyone remember the auctioned kidney back in 1999?) For the full rundown on prohibited items, click the Help selection from the home page toolbar and then enter a search for "prohibited items" in the pop-up help window; you'll be given the necessary links to review the entire list and accompanying explanations (see Figure 5-2).

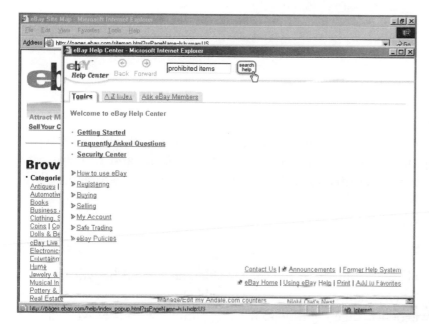

figure 5-2

From the Help link on the toolbar, enter a search term in the pop-up help window.

It's Only a Venue

Lastly, understand that, by accepting the user agreement, you recognize eBay as "only a venue" in your online trading activities. EBay maintains it is not to be held liable for actual transaction results in regards to the content or quality of items bought and sold, is not required to intervene in user disputes, and is generally held free of any and all liability in the course of a transaction. The site will offer some assistance, which you'll learn about a bit later but, truly, you enter this activity at your own risk. Don't worry, though; millions of folks have been doing this successfully for years.

Other Points of Interest Before Proceeding

Before turning you loose in the realm of eBay, here are a few more things that might be of help, use, or general interest to you. EBay is a large site filled with numerous resources that you'll likely want to investigate as time and need dictate. Most important to your immediate efforts are the following.

Where to Find Help

EBay has gone to great lengths to provide online help, links, tutorials, and message boards to answer almost any question you might have. To leverage off the significant instructional content within the site and to help speed along the content of this book, I encourage you to visit the following help areas within eBay.

Site Map

Click on this link from the main page toolbar, and you'll be whisked to a new page containing nearly every other possible link you could ever need in your eBay exploits. Take the time to become familiar with the layout of this page. In the future, if ever you're unable to find eBay-provided information by other means, the site map will get you what you need, guaranteed.

EBay Help Center

Click the Help link on the main page toolbar, and you'll gain access to the pop-up eBay Help Center (as shown in Figure 5-2). Here you can further mine for help and instruction about eBay's features and functions. I'll refer you to this tool frequently throughout the rest of this book.

EBay University Learning Center

And yet another eBay learning tool, this one piggy-backing off the eBay University traveling seminars. The information found here tends to follow the eBay protocol too much (that is, it caters to eBay's proliferation and not always to *your* ultimate gain), but there is some information to be gleaned. I promised to take you into eBay quickly and efficiently, but if ever you want to read eBay's own words about auction formats, rules, bidding practices, and so on, eBay Education is where you'll find the site's explanations.

(Finish this book first, though, because I'll give you the unbiased information you'll want for success.) To access eBay University, click the eBay Education link from the Site Map; then find and click the eBay University link.

Getting Registered

When you're ready to register, return to the eBay home page. Notice, just below the main search box, the grouping of three buttons in a shaded area labeled Welcome New Users. The last button you'll see is labeled Register Now. Click it to begin the registration process (see Figure 5-3).

DID YOU KNOW? The registration link, as well as links to all other eBay pages, can be conveniently located within the Site Map page. Access the site map by clicking on the link on the home page toolbar.

Creating a User's Account

From this point, registering at eBay is a relatively straightforward process in which you'll provide personal information that allows the site to verify your identity and ensures you can be successfully contacted (by other users or by the site itself) as you conduct your business. Getting registered can be accomplished quickly and easily.

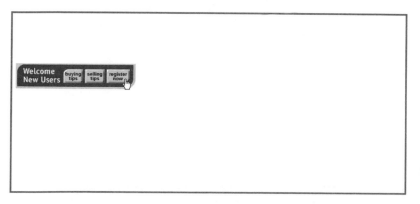

figure 5-3

The quickest way to getting registered is to click on the aptly named button on the eBay home page.

After having clicked the Register Now button, the first registration screen prompts you to enter your personal contact information (see Figure 5-4).

On that first screen, scroll down to enter your e-mail address; choose your user ID, password, and secret question; and fill in your birth date. Click Continue (see Figure 5-5).

DID YOU KNOW? When you register to use eBay, you'll automatically be registered to use the fixed-price selling site, Half.com. You can buy and sell at both sites using the same user ID and password. You'll learn more about using Half.com in Chapter 22, "Venturing Outside of eBay."

In the next screen, read and agree to the eBay user agreement and privacy policy (see Figure 5-6).

Far be it from me to goad you into an irresponsible act, so take the time to read the agreement and privacy policy text within both of the inset scrollable windows. Click on the check boxes at the bottom indicating you're at least 18 years old and you understand you can change your eBay notification

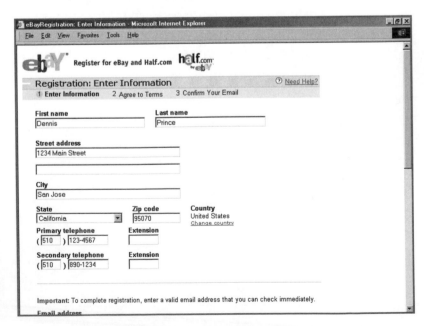

figure 5-4

Enter your name, address, and telephone information in the first portion of the initial registration screen.

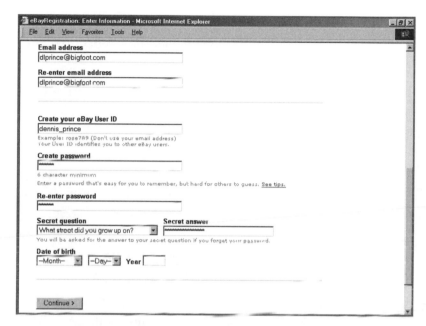

figure 5-5

Complete your identification information and then choose your user ID and password.

figure 5-6

There's no need to call your lawyer; just review and determine if you'll agree to the site's user agreement and privacy policy.

preferences whenever you like (thereby altering the amount of site-generated e-mail you might want or not want to receive). Click the I Agree to These Terms button.

Upon agreeing to the terms, you'll be instructed to check your e-mail account for a special registration message that allows you to complete the registration process and activate your new user ID.

DID YOU KNOW? If you provided an unsecured e-mail account such as Hotmail, Yahoo!, or others, eBay will require you to provide a valid debit or credit card number as a point of further verification.

Lastly, respond to registration e-mail and activate your user ID (see Figure 5-7).

In the e-mail account you specified, you'll receive a message from eBay that contains an active link to confirm your address and activate your user ID. Click on the link within the message to return to eBay and complete the creation of your user account (see Figure 5-8). You can choose to respond to or ignore the inquisitive pop-up window that appears when your registration is complete.

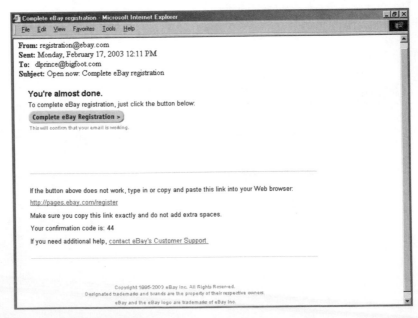

figure 5-7

Click the link on the registration e-mail to complete your account setup.

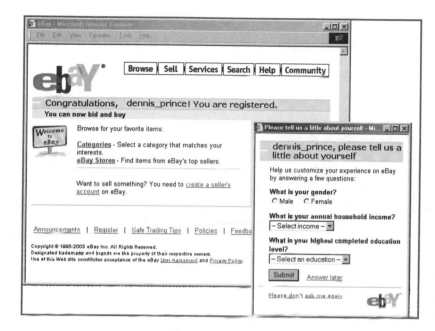

figure 5-8

Voilà! You have activated your eBay account.

Creating a Seller's Account

Even if you believe you'll only be using eBay to browse and buy, odds are you'll be enticed to sell something of your own sooner rather than later. Therefore, now's a good time to create your seller's account so that you'll be able to list goods for auction the moment the urge strikes. Creating your seller's account is as simple as was the initial registration, although the information required of you is somewhat more sensitive.

When creating your seller's account, you'll be asked to provide credit card and bank account information. This is enough to raise the eyebrows (and sometimes hackles) on some folks, so you'll need to be certain you feel comfortable doing so.

DID YOU KNOW? Although eBay has been largely successful in protecting users' sensitive information, it's also a good idea to check with your credit card issuer and financial institution to determine what safeguards they offer in the form of protecting you from invalid or unauthorized use of your account.

ALERT Be sure you understand the difference between credit cards and the seem-ingly cloned debit cards. Debit cards often do not offer the same protections as a bona-fide credit card because funds supplied by a debit card are drawn directly from your checking account. Just be sure you check with your financial institution to determine which is the best choice for you. (Hint: I defer to the credit card, myself.)

To create your seller's account, you can click on the Sell button on the main toolbar and follow the appropriate link, or you can immediately create your account by clicking on the appropriately labeled text link available when your user ID was activated (refer to Figure 5-8).

After you're in the Account Setup screen, enter your credit card information (see Figure 5-9).

On that same screen, scroll down and enter your bank (checking) account information (see Figure 5-10).

Scroll down further to indicate how you want to pay your eBay seller's fees: by credit card or by automated bank account withdrawal (see Figure 5-11).

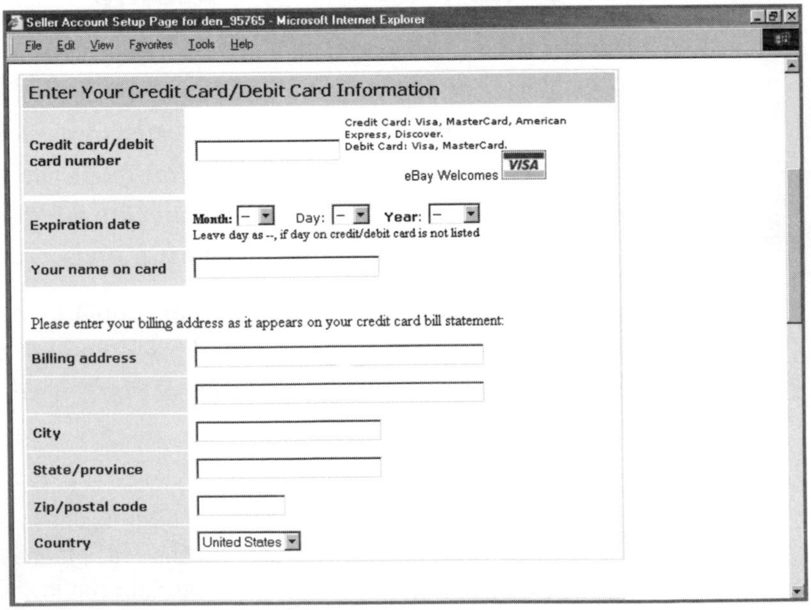

figure 5-9

Begin creating your seller's account by entering your credit card information.

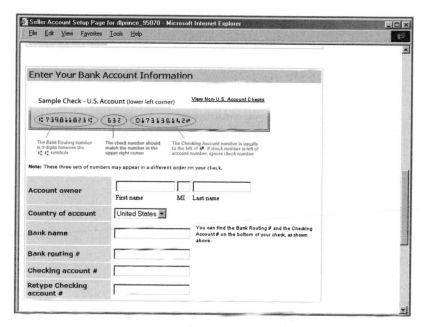

figure 5-10

Enter your bank account (checking) information next.

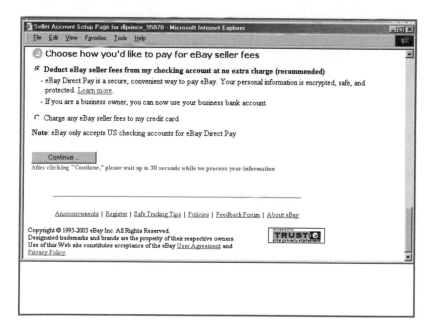

figure 5-11

Select how you want to pay your fees to complete the account setup process.

After you click the Continue button, the account information you provided will be verified through VeriSign and utilizing SSL (encrypted) data transfer. When complete, eBay will display a new screen indicating your seller's account is active and ready for use (see Figure 5-12).

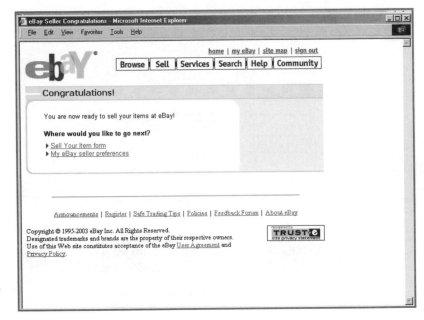

figure 5-12

More congratulations! You're now ready to become an eBay seller.

With that, you're ready to begin blazing through the auction space to stake your claim and make your presence known. Next up: the keys to effectively mining the millions of offerings.

chapter 6

In Search Of . . . Anything and Everything

To begin mastery of eBay, you'll need to become skilled in mining the site. Let's face it: With tens of millions of items available daily, you'll benefit if you can cut through offerings with purpose and precision. In this chapter, you'll learn how to scan the available items via numerous methods, each which can be useful in achieving different results. And although searching the goods on eBay might suggest a shopping spree (which it can easily become), you'll see how searching the site will prove invaluable for anyone who's eager to sell and wants to take command in the competitive marketplace.

Browsing the Categories

Because it's host to tens of millions of items every day, eBay has offered up categories and subcategories (22,000 of them to date) to better organize everything in a logical and intuitive manner. You've already seen how eBay utilizes main categories and subcategories to collate the myriad goods being offered by the legions of sellers. But if you worry that finding a specific item on the site is analogous to finding the proverbial needle in a haystack, rest assured that the task can be as simple as finding a telephone number in the Yellow Pages (even simpler).

Searching through the categories is the least effective method of mining the site but is by no means a useless endeavor. Strolling the categories, truthfully, rarely goes unrewarded. At any time, you're likely to stumble across items you never knew existed, those which you presently own and never knew were of any value to anyone, or cherished items you had outright forgotten and will be stunned to find awaiting your bid.

NOTE I try to make time to browse the categories on a weekly basis for two reasons: I, too, stumble across items I had forgotten about and am glad to find but, more importantly, as a collector of baby boomer goods, I often find items that serve as valuable information to my areas of expertise.

Although it does take time, simple category browsing is also a useful way to find those misplaced gems. Recognizing that sellers are able to choose the category under which their items will be listed, it's not uncommon to find stuff that might seem out of place—miscategorized, if you will. From a buyer's perspective, this is one way to uncover hidden treasure and possibly sneak away with a bargain. From the seller's perspective, category browsing provides opportunity to see how others are listing their goods and whether their categorical choices seem profitable. Of course, browsing the entire site would be an overwhelming task, but it's a useful exercise for those who want to specialize in certain types of goods, whether buying or selling.

In brief, here are four key reasons to perform category searches:

- Gain familiarity with eBay category headers and subheaders. (They're subject to change, you know.)

- Recognize buyer and seller tendencies in where items are sought and where items might be categorized (or miscategorized).

- Locate hidden treasures that could lead to a bargain purchase (a purchase that, by the way, could serve as inexpensive investment in goods to resell later in a more profitable position).

- Discover items that are akin to what you'll buy or sell to better understand complementary goods that you or your buyers might desire.

Searches Made Simple

Most often, folks who regularly visit eBay have specific goods in mind and are interested in quickly determining if such items are currently (or were previously) available. The good news here is there's hardly a page on the eBay site that doesn't have some sort of handy search tool. These tools range from the very simplistic to the considerably complex, allowing you to customize your queries as you see fit. Although you'll probably defer to a certain search tool during most of your site time (I make significant use of the search box on the home page), expect to likewise use each of the tools being described here to help you best slice and dice the tens of millions of listings as well as to ensure that your expertise of the site remains up to date at all times.

The General Search

Look to the eBay home page and recall the search box labeled What Are You Looking For? (see Figure 6-1). This is a simple *keyword search* in which you'll type words ("laptop," "teapot," "hen's teeth," or whatever) and poll the item descriptions to see whatever matches might be out there.

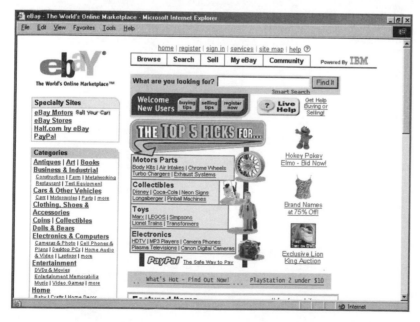

figure 6-1

The simplest general search tool is found right on eBay's home page.

Okay. For fun, I've entered a search for "hen's teeth" in the home page search box. Upon clicking the Find It button, eBay chugs off and then returns a list of items whose descriptions include my keywords (see Figure 6-2).

The results of my search deliver mixed results: I've found a music CD using the term, two copies of a book titled *Hen's Teeth and Horse's Toes* (a favorite phrase of mine), and an unrelated item that uses the term as a sort of rarity

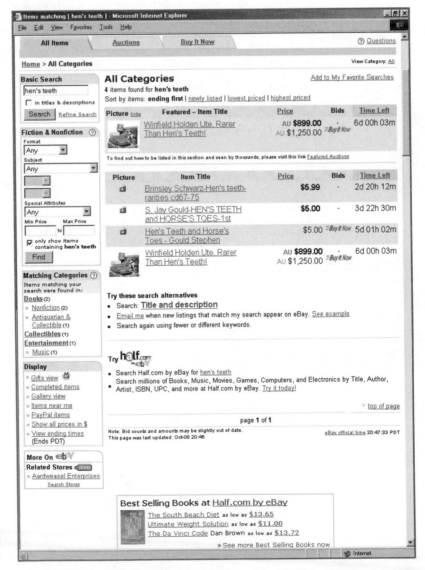

figure 6-2

Hen's teeth truly are rare, as none of these four items appears to be the real deal.

indicator. More interesting than the eclectic results of this search are the additional search options now made available to me.

Notice the box labeled Basic Search in the left column of the screen pictured in Figure 6-2; here's where I can enter refined keywords or entirely different keywords and run another general search. How convenient! There's also an innocuous little box within the Basic Search area where I can elect to search item *titles* as well as *descriptions* (the text on the item details page where sellers fully describe their goods, which is the topic of the next chapter); this can be useful if you are interested in digging deep, deep into the listings to see if you can root out hidden items that only make reference of your keywords within the descriptions.

 ALERT Beware. Searching item descriptions can become a wild goose chase because the terms you use, depending on how precise or unique they are, can return a list of hundreds or thousands of items that are nowhere near what you're looking for. Try it, though, if for no other reason than to become familiar with the method.

Before launching off into another search, notice further down that left column. See the area labeled Fiction & Nonfiction, and you'll recognize that eBay has linked the search terms with the item category of those listings more common to your search. (With two books in my results, eBay assumes I'm interested in reading material.) In this area, if it's truly pertinent to my search (in this case, it's not, but it gets points for trying), I can refine my search parameters on the spot. Further down the column, eBay reports item categories that seem to be associated with my keywords. Finally, notice the little area centered below the search results that invites me to peruse eBay's Half.com listings (a fixed-price venue I mentioned during the registration process) to see if I can find the book I seek there. Unfortunately, what I was seeking was real hen's teeth, and those seem to truly be as rare as . . . well, you know.

Before leaving the general (or Basic) search, recognize that the Basic Search box and another similar box that is usually positioned on the upper-right side of a page display will be available for use on nearly every eBay page you'll encounter. These are quite handy and help prevent the need to navigate back and forth inefficiently.

chapter 6

In Search Of . . . Anything and Everything

NOTE Be ready to use these handy basic search tools at a moment's notice. Often, search ideas will suddenly come to mind, only to vanish just as quickly. The moment you consider, "Hey, I ought to see if I can find . . ." you're best served to execute that search immediately than risk being momentarily delayed, unable to recall just what it was you thought you might hunt. It's not a sign of old age; it's the effect of tens of millions of items vying for your attention.

The Refined Search

If you've been particularly attentive, you noticed that beneath each of the basic search tools is a subtle colink that reads Smart Search, Refine Search, or Advanced Search. These links, as well as the more prevalent Search button on the main toolbar, all lead to the same place: eBay's search screen (see Figure 6-3).

The main eBay search page offers several search types (each with its own tab, as you can see in the figure). The default tab is curiously titled eBay Basic Search and is your window to specify more narrowly defined search criteria. Here, you can customize how your search keywords will be used by specifying which additional words to exclude (to restrict close but unwanted

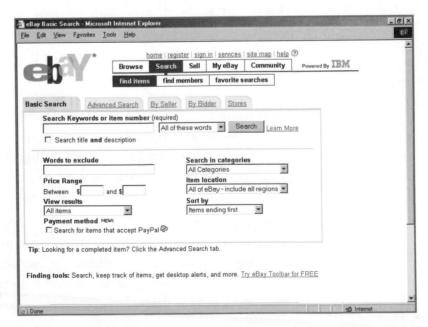

figure 6-3

The official eBay search screen is the hangout of choice for site data miners.

matches), which specific categories to search, which geographic locations to consider, and what price range is of interest to you. Additionally, you can sort the results of your search. With the objective to zero in on a certain item or type of item, these additional search delimiters help you perform more efficient searches and avoid needlessly wading through those "close but no cigar" search hits.

The Advanced Search

Click on the second tab, labeled Advanced Search, to find a slightly different search criteria screen, as pictured in Figure 6-4.

Honestly, the Advanced Search isn't all that advanced. A quick comparison between this and the Basic Search offerings reveals only a few additional check boxes plus sort and display options. Much of what you see on the Advanced Search can be accomplished from the Basic Search tab. Despite its promising name, the Advanced Search doesn't offer significantly more than the previous search screen; therefore, whether you use it becomes a matter of personal choice.

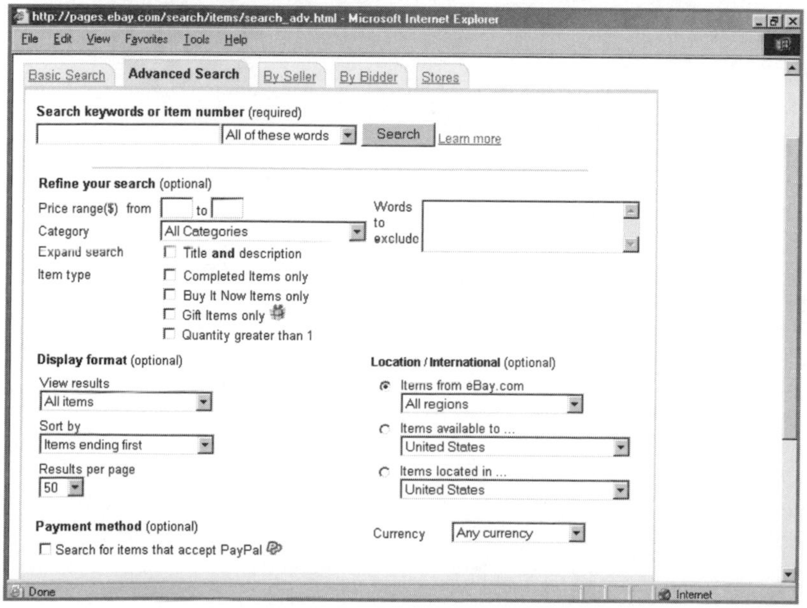

figure 6-4

The Advanced Search tab offers a few more criteria to help you in your quest for a specific item.

Searching by Seller

The next tab is labeled By Seller. Clicking this tab will provide a new window of search options, as shown in Figure 6-5.

Searching by seller is the quickest way to see what your favorite seller is selling or even to see how the items you might be selling are attracting bids. When you find a seller who seems to offer the sorts of items that most interest you, either as the provider of goods you desire or as a potential competitor to the goods you'll sell, this is the easy way to keep up with what the person is offering. A look at past auctions from the seller also provides an indication of the volume of sales the seller has been managing, what prices the seller has been getting for goods, and how many of the seller's auctions have been successful. As Figure 6-5 shows, it's easy to enter the seller's ID, select whether completed items (closed auctions) should be queried, and choose how the results should be sorted. Also note that a hybrid search exists in the lower half of the screen: a keyword search box coupled with a field to list multiple seller IDs for which items should be searched or, conversely,

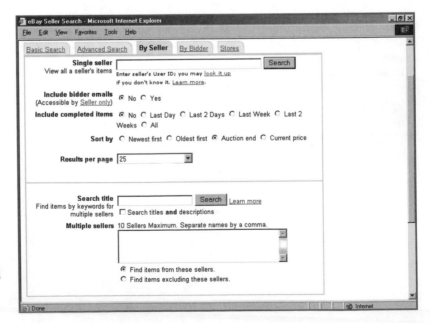

figure 6-5

Search by seller to find only those
goods offered by a single user.

from which results should be excluded (by selecting the radio button below the Multiple Sellers field).

Searching by Bidder

The fourth tab, By Bidder, is similar to the seller search except here you'll find a listing of current and previous goods a particular bidder (identified by user ID) has bid upon (see Figure 6-6).

 NOTE Don't overlook the usefulness of performing bidder searches using a seller's ID. To get a better feel for whom you're dealing with and what sorts of items these folks are buying as well as selling, look at their activity on both sides of the virtual sales counter.

Often, searching by bidder is a fast and simple way to monitor *your own* bidding activity but is equally useful in determining what others might be bidding on, especially those who have a propensity to outbid you on certain items. (You'll learn more about bidding strategies in Chapter 11, "Expert Bidding Strategies.")

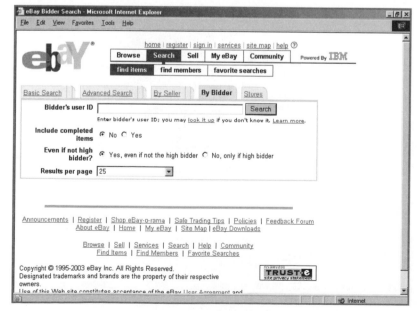

figure 6-6

Searching by bidder allows you to investigate what another user has been bidding on.

Searching by Stores

Finally, the last tab, Search Stores, provides a way to restrict your search results to those items listed for fixed-price sale in eBay Stores (shown in Figure 6-7). EBay Stores are direct sale outlets where sellers can offer items for immediate sale, at a designated price, outside of the usual auction method.

Notice how the search fields for eBay Stores are nearly identical to that of the Basic Search tab, with the minor addition of the View Results field. Naturally, the search results for this smaller division of eBay will be far fewer than if you had searched the entire site for both fixed-price and auction items.

The Keys Are in the Keywords

Before moving ahead, take a moment to consider the importance of the keywords you use when you perform an item search. Keywords are just that: *keys* to unlocking the vault of treasures within eBay. Well-constructed keywords help you uncover exactly what it is you seek and avoid laborious sifting through thousands of results that might or might not match your wants,

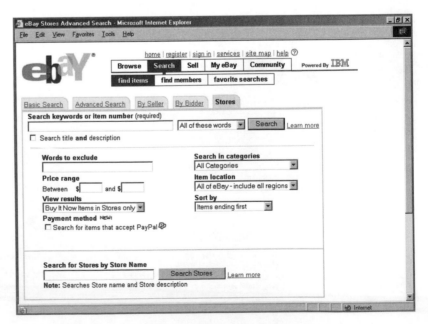

figure 6-7

Search eBay Stores to find only those goods offered in the fixed-price sales format.

needs, or expectations. Your success here comes from knowing the best keywords to use in searching for items, which you can do by observing how sellers seem to be crafting their item descriptions for these goods. Here are some quick tips for utilizing keywords in your searches:

- Use specific names and brands.
- Use common terms associated with the item you're seeking.
- Use associative terms (that is, genre, era, and so on).
- Use proper spelling.

As you sort through the listings that match your keyword search, take special note of any additional terms that seem to be commonly used with these goods and consider including those (or excluding them if they're not *exactly* what you're looking for) in future searches. Remember these commonly used words later when you are selling your own goods.

Using Superior Search Commands

Besides utilizing good keywords in your searches, recognize that there are several character commands you can incorporate to further refine your search results. This is an aspect of eBay searching that many users overlook but which can have a significant impact on your search successes. The most successful character commands you can include in your keyword searches are as follows:

- Use quotation marks (" ") around your keywords to return only items containing the words in a grouping in the order you specified [Example: "my mother the car"].

- Use the minus sign (–) to exclude words that might commonly accompany items that contain your keywords but in which you aren't interested [Example: spider-man –movie].

- To exclude multiple words, place the minus sign before a parenthetical listing of words to exclude, separated by commas but no spaces [Example: harry potter -(movie,toy)].

- Use the asterisk (*) as a wildcard to match items that contain a partial keyword string you'll enter [Example: sac* kings to find "sac kings," "sacto kings," or "sacramento kings"].

- Use the plus sign (+) to specify a particular word that appears along with multiple other words. [Example: (Wedgwood,Lennox) +cup]

You can utilize these search commands in any item search box on the site.

Other Ways to Uncover Hidden Treasures

Even with all the search tools just described, great items can still slip between the cracks. Although you've tried mightily to extract all the goods you can find using the various tools, some will still elude you (and other shoppers) and, if found, can often result in great finds at great prices. You can become a bona fide treasure hunter by turning over the virtual stones on the site to find those items that have been mislabeled, misfiled, and, if you're not careful, will be incredible deals on which you'll miss out.

To begin, review the results of your usual searches carefully. Identify the categories in which these items seem to be referenced and take a bit of time to search through all listings in that category to determine if there are any other terms you've yet to consider. Look to see what other goods appear in the category of listings and whether the sorts of things you're seeking have been titled or described in a way you hadn't considered or expected. More important to the treasure hunt, this is also how you'll determine if there are any common misspellings used in association with these items (as in "Beanie" versus "Beenie" versus "Beany"), which you'll likewise want to make note of so that you can ferret out the mistitled, and thereby passed over, treasures.

Another hunting method to employ frequently is to review the eBay listings that have moved into the Ending Today and Going, Going, Gone links found at the top of every category page. Although it isn't feasible to review these listings in all categories, it is worthwhile to scan these listings in the categories you might typically review. Whether you missed an item in your various search effort or there was yet another variation or oops on the seller's part in titling or listing the item, this is another proven method to unearth potentially lost goods.

Finally, keep an eye open for completed auctions (in your various searching and browsing activities) where the item perhaps didn't sell. If the item never received a bid and essentially slipped by you during its run, it's still possible to inquire of the seller about the item to see if a sale is still possible. Oftentimes, sellers will elect to relist their item and give it another go, yet many are highly motivated to make the quick sale upon receiving your inquiry.

Save Time by Saving Searches

You might have noticed that each search results page has a text link labeled Save This Search, located at the top-right and bottom-left corners of the screen. Upon clicking the link, you'll capture the search criteria in your My eBay settings under the My Favorite Searches heading (see Figure 6-8), and your searches will be much more efficient.

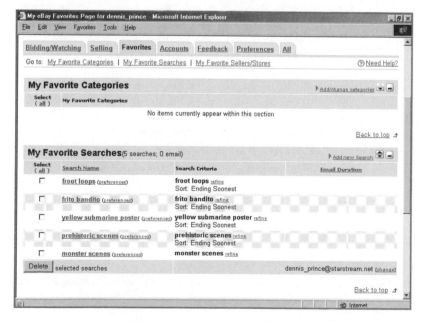

figure 6-8

Save your searches for easy reuse in the My eBay My Favorite Searches area.

Rather than try to recall what you've been searching for, the searches you save are readily available for another query just by clicking the Search Now link in the My eBay screen. Better yet is the check box labeled Email Me where, when enabled, an e-mail message will be sent to you whenever a new item is listed at eBay that fits your search criteria. Essentially, eBay is now doing the searching for you. What could be smarter than that?

The EBay Toolbar

One final search tool that's specifically designed for buyers is the newest feature: the eBay toolbar. Curiously enough, eBay designed a compact row of search functions that will grace your Web browser and File Manager windows (see Figure 6-9).

The eBay toolbar seems a bit superfluous given the many other search tools (especially the saved favorites) available for use. In a way, it's a bit annoyingly reminiscent of those banner areas that afflict free Internet access

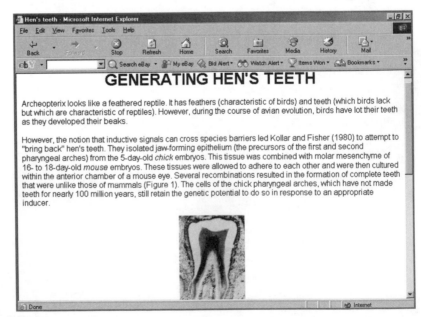

figure 6-9

The ever-present eBay toolbar allows you to perform searches even when researching other interesting Web sites.

providers. It can be useful, I suppose, if you want to perform ad hoc searches without having to visit the site's home page. It will add a bit to the clutter of your browser window, though.

You must download the eBay toolbar from the site (visit the Site Map page to find the link); then it will be enabled on your Web browser and File Manager windows. If ever you want to disable the toolbar, simply click on View, Toolbars and uncheck the eBay toolbar from the list of selections.

With these superior search skills at your disposal and so many results to sift through, the next task is to tame the information available on the individual item pages.

chapter 7

Item Details and Bidding Basics

Undoubtedly, your searching prowess has yielded numerous items that deserve deeper analysis. Whether you're looking to bid or sizing up the marketplace, now comes the time to get into the details of the items offered every day at eBay. This chapter offers the explanation of the various components of an item details page and gets you ready to bid more confidently if that's your desire.

Surveying an Item Page

So, thanks to my precise and uncanny search abilities, I've found an item that has been high on my want list: a print of dogs playing poker. With my velvet Elvis seeming so lonely above my mantel, this will be the perfect companion piece. Maybe you don't care for dogs playing poker and would prefer cats playing canasta but, for the sake of illustration, this irresistible piece of "shabby chic" will serve purpose to become better acquainted with the elements of an item detail page at eBay.

Looking at the example in Figure 7-1, you can see the usual eBay toolbar at the top of the screen and the eBay logo that links you back to the home page. Beyond those elements, here are the unique and key elements of an item page:

- **Item Title and Item Number.** In the header stripe is the item title, the same you would see in your search or casual browsing results as well as the item number at the far right of the banner. (In this case, it's item number 3546338897.)

- **Item Image.** Many listings include a small ("thumbnail") image of the item up for bid to provide immediate enticement to would-be bidders. (And who could resist fine art such as this?)

- **Current Bid.** As indicated, this is the current high bid for the item. Immediately below this, you'll see a handy button to leap into a bid, but not just yet.

- **Time Left.** Here you'll find out how much time is left before the auction ends. In smaller print, you'll see the original duration of the auction (this example showing it was a 7-day auction) as well as the exact date and time the auction will close. Note that, as the close of the auction encroaches to being within hours, not days, the minutes and seconds left are added to the countdown clock.

- **History.** Here you'll see how many bids have been placed on an item, the number shown being a link to allow you to drill further into the specific bidder details (a useful bit of information that you'll learn to skillfully utilize in Chapter 9, "Key to Success: The Educated Bid"). Also, in small print, you'll see the original starting bid for the item, that value having been set by the seller at the time of listing.

- **High Bidder.** Here's the user ID and feedback rating (the number in parentheses) of the current high bidder. This will also be useful information to mine and will be covered fully in Chapter 9.

- **Location.** Geographically, where is the item?

- **Seller Information.** More prominent in the shaded box to the right of the screen, here's where you'll quickly learn about the seller offering the item. The seller's user ID (in this case, the rather cryptic 19407) and feedback rating leads the information listing. Below, in smaller print, is an aggregate overview of the feedback profile and information regarding when the seller first registered with eBay. The three text links that follow are self-explanatory yet of significant use in reading feedback comments, posting an e-mail question, and reviewing other items this particular seller has listed concurrently.

By scrolling down the item detail page (see Figure 7-2), you'll find additional item information:

■ **Description.** Here are the details of the item you're considering bidding on, hopefully thorough and understandable enough to instill confidence that this item is everything you hope it will be. In this example, you see a larger image of the item up for bid and can even see a counter the seller included that tracks how many times this particular item has been viewed by prospective buyers.

figure 7-1

An item detail page has plenty of information that you'll want to understand prior to placing a bid.

figure 7-2

Scroll down the item detail
page to review the seller-
provided item description.

Scrolling down further (see Figure 7-3), you'll find the following:

- **Shipping and Payment Details.** Here the seller has noted the types
  of shipping methods that will be used to forward the item, the cost
  of the shipping, and who will cover those costs. (In this case, as in
  most, the buyer is expected to pay shipping costs.)

- **Payment Methods Accepted.** Here the seller provides information
  regarding the types of payment that will be accepted, be it personal
  check, money order, or some form of online payment. (Note that
  the seller indicated PayPal payments are accepted in the text of the
  Shipping and Payment Details section.)

So, with this information understood and fully digested, what can we
quickly discern about the item? First, it's an affordable print (not any sort of
original piece of artwork) that appears to be new and unused. The seller has
an impressive feedback rating and bears the distinction of being a PowerSeller (which indicates consistent high volume of sales and customer satisfaction). The image provided is clear and representative of the item and the

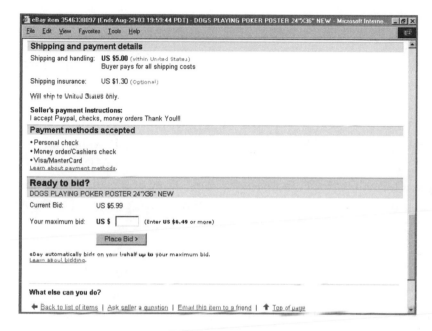

Shipping and payment details

Shipping and handling: **US $5.00** (within United States)
Buyer pays for all shipping costs

Shipping insurance: US $1.30 (Optional)

Will ship to United States only.

Seller's payment instructions:
I accept Paypal, checks, money orders Thank You!!!

Payment methods accepted

• Personal check
• Money order/Cashiers check
• Visa/MasterCard
Learn about payment methods.

Ready to bid?

DOGS PLAYING POKER POSTER 24"X36" NEW

Current Bid: US $5.99

Your maximum bid: US $ [   ]   (Enter **US $6.49** or more)

[Place Bid >]

eBay automatically bids on your behalf up to your maximum bid.
Learn about bidding.

What else can you do?

← Back to list of items | Ask seller a question | Email this item to a friend | ↑ Top of page

figure 7-3

An item detail page concludes with information regarding shipping and payment.

seller's shipping and payment costs seem reasonable. To me, this looks like a great item (velvet Elvis will be so thrilled) offered by an experienced and well-regarded seller. Yes, I think a bid is in order here.

A Quick Lesson in Proxy Bidding

EBay utilizes a proxy bidding system, a method by which bidders will enter the most they're willing to spend on an item at the time they place their bid. In the example used here, you can see that there is currently a high bidder. The current bid amount is $5.99 (that equals the minimum bid the seller would accept), but that might not be the maximum bid amount that the current high bidder offered up to the proxy system. If that bidder values the print at, say, $15.00, that would be the maximum bid amount he or she would have specified at the time of bidding. EBay's proxy system judiciously utilizes a bidder's maximum bid amount, using just enough to (hopefully) secure high bidder status. Being the first bidder, only $5.99 of the current high bidder's supposed $15.00 was used by the proxy system; the balance of that high bid amount will be kept in reserve to use if other bidders come along and bid. If I were to bid $9.99, eBay's proxy system would apply more of the first bidder's maximum bid amount to thwart my bid attempt. Naturally, I would be outbid because my maximum of $9.99 is less than the first bidder's maximum of $15.00. The current bid of the item, however, would rise to $10.49. (At this price level, the minimum bid increment is $.50.) The previous bidder would retain high bidder status and I would have to bid higher if I wanted to win the item (although, if achieved, I could likewise be subject to other bidders who might come along and outbid my maximum bid amount). If outbid, the former high bidder is contacted by eBay (via e-mail) and invited to bid again.

The key to the proxy bidding system is the critical element that supports the dynamic market: private information. Recall that I discussed this back in Chapter 3, "Entrepreneur Alert: Understanding and Applying the Auction Model to Your Business," when I mentioned how bidders maintain privacy over the price they're ultimately willing to offer for a particular item. EBay's proxy bidding system retains that privacy because others—including other bidders and the seller—are not permitted to see a bidder's maximum bid amount during the course of the auction. To make such information visible would be devastating to the dynamic model. If other bidders could see the current high bidder's maximum bid amount, they could swiftly outbid that bidder and thereby remove the back-and-forth competition of the bidding process. (Yes, even if by proxy where maximum bids are pitted against other maximum bids within eBay's programming, the competition is still waging.) Moreover, if the current high bidder's maximum is quite high (and visible), it might scare off other bidders and, if they don't bid, the seller would not benefit from a price escalation during the competitive bidding process. Finally, if the seller could see the bidder's maximum bid amount, that information could be used inappropriately to try to increase the item price (by an illicit term known as shilling; see Chapter 8, "E-Motions and Auction Affronts") or, conversely, the seller could decide to cancel the auction outright if not satisfied with what the potential price outcome might be.

Therefore, before moving on to actually bid, here's a brief recap of the proxy bidding process:

■ At the time you place your bid, eBay allows you to enter a maximum bid price, which represents the most you are willing to pay for the item.

■ EBay will only apply as much as is required (by minimum bid increments) to gain you high-bidder status.

■ If your initial bid results in your becoming high bidder, eBay will reserve the balance of your maximum bid value to apply, by proxy, when others bid for the item.

■ EBay will only bid on your behalf to the point that your maximum bid value is reached.

■ If your maximum bid value is surpassed by another bidder, eBay will notify you via e-mail that you've been outbid; you can elect to bid again if you like.

NOTE Many folks are perplexed, when bidding on an item, about how quickly they have been outbid. Upon placing their bid, they might immediately receive a message from the eBay system indicating, "You've been outbid." How so? Did another bidder just happen to be bidding at the same time? No, it was the proxy system that was utilizing the current high bidder's maximum bid amount. If not exceeded, eBay will utilize that maximum bid amount and will immediately report to a contending bidder that they've been outbid. That's not unfair; it's just the proxy system at work. The good news is that the proxy will perform the same battle for you when you're the reigning high bidder.

But why a proxy system anyway? Well, at live auctions, bidders in attendance will shout out, raise a paddle, tug an ear, or whatever else to indicate an additional bid yet, at eBay, such a system would be impractical, bidders having to remain in attendance and rebid every time a bid was placed. Because eBay auctions can run from 3 to 7 days, it is impractical to expect bidders to remain in attendance for such a duration.

DID YOU KNOW? If you do want to experience the live bidding process online, visit http://www.bidz.com. The site hosts live, 3-minute auctions where you battle against other bidders in a real-time setting.

The Simplicity of Bidding

If ever you believed spending money is much too easy, eBay is here to further bolster that sentiment. Bidding is easy at eBay. Here's what you'll need to do.

Figure 7-1 shows a Place Bid button just below the current bid value of the item. I click it to begin the bidding process.

NOTE Figure 7-3 also shows a Ready to Bid section at the bottom of the item details. It essentially does the same thing as the Place Bid button. You decide which you prefer to use.

After I click the Place Bid button, a new screen is displayed where I enter the most I'm willing to pay for this item (see Figure 7-4).

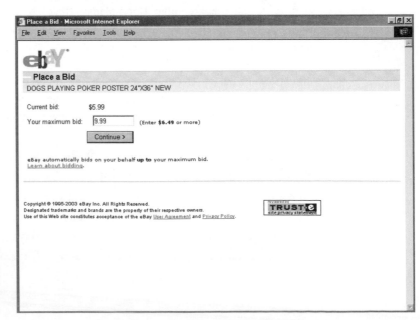

figure 7-4

The proxy system utilizes the maximum bid amount entered here to attempt to crown you current high bidder.

After entering my maximum bid amount and clicking the Continue button, eBay lets me review my bid one last time prior to submitting it (see Figure 7-5).

After I've clicked the Submit button, eBay's proxy system goes to work and pits my maximum bid amount against the previous bidder's maximum bid amount. Due to the private nature of the maximum, I won't know if my bid will be successful until the next screen is displayed (see Figure 7-6).

There, see how easy it was to spend money? The results in Figure 7-6 indicate I'm the new high bidder for this fine piece of dog art. The new current bid amount is $6.49; this indicates the former bidder only bid a maximum of $5.99 (the seller's minimum bid) and was easily outbid after the minimum bid increment of $.50 was applied. At this point, the proxy has my permission to use an additional $3.50 to ward off other bidders before my maximum is eclipsed.

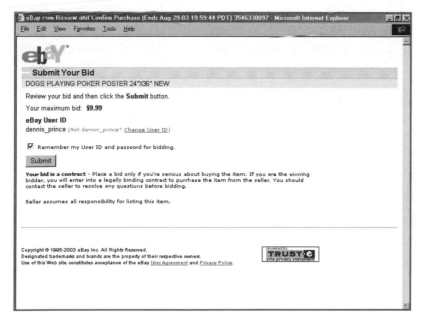

figure 7-5

One last look prior to launching the bid.

figure 7-6

I'm the new high bidder!

NOTE Understand that, as the current bid value increases, the minimum bid value will also increase. See Table 7-1 for information of minimum bid increment data.

Table 7-1 Minimum Bid Increment Index

Current Price	Bid Increment
$0.01–$0.99	$0.05
$1.00–$4.99	$0.25
$5.00–$24.99	$0.50
$25.00–$99.99	$1.00
$100.00–$249.99	$2.50
$250.00–$499.99	$5.00
$500.00–$999.99	$10.00
$1,000.00–$2499.99	$25.00
$2,500.00–$4999.99	$50.00
$5,000.00 and up	$100.00

After the Bid

After you place a bid that secures high bidder status, eBay sends you an e-mail confirmation of the bid. It's a simple text message that states the current high bid as well as your maximum bid. Now it's time to wait and see if you'll retain high bidder status or if other bidders will come along to challenge your offering.

If you're outbid (that is, your maximum is usurped by another bidder), eBay will send another e-mail message to indicate you've been dethroned and then go on to encourage you to visit the item details page again and place another bid. (That's the essence of competitive bidding, right?) Provided there's still time before the auction ends, you can revisit the page and determine if you're willing to offer up even more for the treasure you covet.

In the example here, I won. Now the exultant winner of the dogs playing poker print, eBay notified me once again via e-mail to congratulate me and to turn the transaction over to the seller and myself. At this point, eBay's work is done (they're just a venue, remember?) and it's up to the high bidder and seller to arrange payment and delivery. Later, in Chapters 12, "Exercising Control, Imposing Your Will, and Seizing the Moment," and 16, "Easy Money: Hassle-Free Payment Collection," I'll go into the best practices to ensure a smooth transaction for both buyers and sellers. For now, I've paid for my enviable win via an online payment service, and it's just a matter of time before velvet Elvis has a new pack of hound dogs to keep him company.

At this point, if you've been surfing about eBay and have begun bidding on items, you'll probably agree it's a rather compelling and intoxicating experience. The thrill of the competitive bidding and the anticipation of the ultimate win is oh so alluring; it's also the stuff of compulsive behavior. Read on to the next chapter to get some perspective on where unchecked bidding and buying might lead.

chapter 8

E-Motions and Auction Affronts

After all this talk of searching for goods, surveying the competition, learning about seller's wares, and launching bids, it's time to pause briefly and assess this bustling marketplace. Although I'm showing you the ins and outs of eBay and revealing the tools and techniques of expert auctioning, it becomes just as important that I discuss the *experience* of auctioning and the effect it has on you and your behavior. As a buyer, you'll undoubtedly become entranced at the multitude of goods that entice you to bid. As a seller, the sight of others who make daily profits will prompt you to grab hold of your own wares to turn a similar gain. The auction place is alluring, and it's wise to keep close tabs on your own behavior and your ever-changing moods and motivations as you find yourself getting caught up in the action. This chapter serves several purposes. First, it provides a glimpse of the different personalities you'll encounter as you rub elbows in the marketplace. Then it helps you assess your own behavior to determine if you're keeping your wits about you, even when the bidding and selling reaches a fevered pitch. Last, it offers insight into some of the gotchas that are inherent to auctioning, those scams and schemes that could catch you off guard if you're not vigilantly on the lookout. The true skill in mastering the auction place is achieved when you're able to recognize how the activity goes beyond keystrokes and mouse clicks and elicits good and not-so-good behavior from you and others with whom you share the cyber-market.

What Are the Other People Like?

When you're engaging in online auctions, the *e-motions* go 'round and 'round, and just about everybody experiences them—the thrill of victory, the agony of defeat. Some users are intense; some are indifferent. They come from all over the world, from all different personal and business backgrounds, and they all have their own particular motivations. Each user brings a unique personal flavor to the auction, making for one of the most interesting social forums you'll ever encounter. But, if you're determined to master the business, you'll need to become adept at managing the personalities, too.

As you interact with others, you'll detect certain *styles* of folk along the way.

 ALERT Okay, before I start here, I should issue a disclaimer: These are *my* opinions and *my* assessments of the different types of folks I've met during my years at eBay. These aren't rigid categorizations, and they aren't meant to be unjust stereotypes. I offer my view here just to let you know whom I've encountered at eBay and the behavior trends I've noticed. Maybe you'll agree. Maybe you won't.

The New Users

These new arrivals just came from the registration page and, boy, are they happy to be here. They're so wide-eyed and enthusiastic that you can practically hear them giggling as they search through the pages and pages of stuff up for auction. These new users might be a bit overzealous, though, the kind who contact sellers just seconds after an auction ends, exclaiming they've won and desperate to know what to do next. They're usually pretty even-tempered, if not a bit cautious. They don't want to make waves for this new ship they're sailing. They'll have many questions to ask and might make some *rookie* moves. It's okay, though. As long as they're polite and respectful, do what you can to help them along. (Who knows—maybe someone helped *you* when you first joined.) New users often bring a bunch of money to spend or a bunch of cool stuff to auction. Everybody starts out here. How do you quickly tell who the new users are? They'll have the feedback rating of 10 or less.

The Casual Users

These folks have probably been using eBay for a while. They cruise in from time to time, poke through the listings to see what's around, and occasionally drop a bid. They bid quietly, generally without asking too many questions. When you interact with them at the end of a deal, they're typically somewhat curt and concise in communication. They're not rude by any means, but they're also not overly excited about the auction. After all, it's just some junk that someone's selling. Why give it more credit than it's worth? These users typically have a moderate feedback rating (around 50 or so).

The Professional Users

These users have found eBay to be just what they hoped for: a veritable gold mine of business opportunity and one they've been actively mining for years. They've seen the eBay population and have carefully evaluated who's buying, who's selling, and how the best deals can be had. They might be those professional buyers who seek out and find the goods people are wanting. They hunt up the sleeper auctions and nab 'em while no one else is looking. (They're experts at the search.) They sell items like pros. They always seem to come up with that rare or hot piece that everyone is clamoring for. How do they do it? Well, they're probably making a respectable income doing this, and, therefore, put in an appropriate effort to buy and sell the things that will keep them comfortably in business. They have a professional style when interacting with others. Customer service and satisfaction are usually high on their list; if not, they know they'll soon be losing business. They're typically not the kind of user you can cut a deal with. They have to maintain a profit margin, but they can frequently be good sources for finding the things you're looking for. Their feedback rating is usually quite high (into the hundreds or thousands) as proof of their commitment to quality and customer satisfaction. These might be self-employed individuals or bona fide businesses that have expanded into the realm of online commerce.

The Elite

These guys are *really good*. They're the ones who can bid behind their backs, using a mirror and clicking with their big toe. They've absorbed eBay and assimilated with it to become one perpetual auction organism. They're smooth, clean, and sometimes a bit cocky. They're typically easy to deal with but won't put up with nonsense or shenanigans. Give these users the utmost respect; they've earned it. They usually have an amazingly high feedback rating (sporting the coveted shooting star of 10,000 feedback points or more). They're usually pretty helpful to the other users and will frequent the chat spaces to drop pearls of wisdom. Their area of interest is probably more focused, and they have become experts at what they buy and sell.

The Not-So-Nice Users

Then there are the occasional bad apples. You won't encounter this sort very often, but they are out there. They're not often outwardly mean, but they can be blunt and a bit cutting. They might be your professional Web rats from the age-old cyber-underground. They sometimes bring the old Internet attitude with them, believing all is fair game in cyberspace. They might not have come to grips with the fact that, even though eBay is in the Internet, it's still a social forum where people need to conduct themselves with common sense and restraint. These users might insist your prices are too high. As sellers, they might try to overcharge you shipping and handling costs and then verbally berate you if you dare ask, "Why so much?" They might just be in a bad mood. Maybe they've been burned in some online transaction in the past and (maybe subconsciously) seek a bit of revenge. Maybe they just weren't brought up with very good manners.

Maybe they're just mean people. Their feedback ratings could include 10 or more negative comments. Check their temper ahead of time before you buy or sell with them.

Now, no matter how much I generalize, there is still gray area when it comes to the different users you'll meet at eBay. The users' styles are all over the chart, and they're most often a Neapolitan mixture of many of these characteristics. Overall, the really fine users stay for the long haul, and the stinkers tend to get bagged and discarded. (Most of the original kooks and creeps from way back have been summarily run out of town.) The real key to a prosperous eBay experience rests in how you handle *your* e-motions. Remember the rules of netiquette and use them every time you participate.

The E-Motion Heats Up

When you get into a bidding confrontation, you're going to get excited. You can't see your opponents, but they're there and they're primed for an auction battle to win that whatever-it-is that you've also set your eyes on. In the beginning, you might feel it as an affront, almost offensive, when someone else bids on something you want. Bidders can repeatedly outbid one another in a tit-for-tat slap-fest to see who has the stamina to stay the course. It's not personal. Two people just want the same thing. So, lesson one is to understand that this is not a personal attack. No one is out to get you. Most often, they don't even know you.

But you decide you won't back down. Come Hell or high water, you're going to stand triumphant. Now you're on a crusade. This isn't just a bid for some silly item in an auction. This is a bid that represents all the unfortunate ones who were struck down in the battlefield of bids. You will restore honor to their names and dignity to their quest. You shall be victorious! (Getting a little carried away, aren't you?)

You will get impassioned from time to time when you work the auctions. But, when you're in the midst of a bidding frenzy, check your e-motions by stopping and asking yourself, "Do I really want this item, or do I just want to win?" Again, this is where the sport of the auction comes in, and the bid-battle is enough to make you bounce in your chair excitedly enjoying the virtual tug-of-war. But what if you win? Well, hooray! Right?

There's a concept in auctioning known as *winner's curse*, the dread that overcomes you once the jubilation of winning subsides and the realization that now you're beholden to pay for what you've just won. Caught in bidding frenzies, some folks have unwittingly tallied up some impressively high debts to one or more sellers. It's the curse that can befall you when you least expect it. You win the auction, and you are the master. You've fought the good fight and to you go the spoils—just as soon as you pay the bill. "Oh . . . right . . . the bill." Check your wallet and your ego at the home page before you jump into the action. Everybody gets overextended at one time or another. Know when to let it rest.

One other thing to watch for when you're in the midst of competition: Don't outbid others just because you can. I know it sounds a little far-fetched, but it has happened. Some users might be skilled in their bidding, and they might zap an auction just because they saw some excited bidders bidding and decided to go kick their marbles. These would probably be those not-so-nice users, and sometimes they don't even intend to honor their bid. They just wanted to win the auction. "It's not any kind of agreement you can hold me to. It's just the Internet." Yeah, beat it, Charlie.

Personality Swings After the Auction

Okay, but how does this competitive playground affect the moods and attitudes of the folks involved? Good question. Here's what I've seen.

The Euphoric Winner

Hey! Here comes Happy Dan, and he's grinnin' from ear to ear. He just won an auction, and he's ready to tell the whole world about it.

It's fun to win an auction. You see those words, "You are the high bidder." It feels good. If the item is something you really want, then you're the one who just grabbed the brass ring. It excites you to the point that you want to go out and win another, and another, and another. Enjoy the happy moment. It's probably what you'll experience most of the time, and it's the reason why eBay is so popular with Internet users. Incidentally, I'm happy for you, too.

The Disgruntled Loser

Then there's the user who doesn't win, and he's sometimes not very happy about it and might decide to let you know. He might be more than disappointed; he might have delusions of rightful restitution due him. Call him a poor sport or maybe someone who just wasn't ready for the competition.

In extreme cases, some disgruntled losers had tried to mail-bomb the winner's feedback file, posting line after line of negative feedback. You've heard of road rage; this is auction animosity. It's not good, and it's best not to get caught up in it. Thankfully, eBay put a stop to this by restricting feedback to only the high bidder and the seller of an auction. Before that, feedback bombing was the usual retort of sore losers.

When you lose an auction at eBay, just let it slide off. It's going to happen, and you'll move on. Of course, if you really want something bad enough, be sure you've put down a maximum bid to cover it. It might cost you a bit more, but maybe you'll avoid the disappointment of defeat.

How Do You Rate?

So what will your auction attitude be? Think about it: Your attitude will both follow you and precede you. Part of what makes the eBay community so powerful is the candor that the community members bring to their interactions. If you're being a creep, they'll let you know. If you're a real jewel, they'll let you know that, too. They give credit where credit is due, which is the core of what makes the eBay community effective.

Decide, then, what your motivations at eBay will be. Are you just a looky-loo? Fine. Are you going to be a casual user who pops in from time to time? That's fine, too. Are you going to be a die-hard who really wants to make a strong statement and amass a high positive feedback rating? Super cool. You'll need to work for it, though. Whatever your reason for being at eBay, conduct yourself in a way that will ensure the welcome mat is always there to greet you when you return.

Does it really matter? Does anyone really care online? In cyberspace, can anyone hear you scream? Yes, they can. eBay is a big deal to a lot of people. It's a hobby to many, but it's also a way of life to many more. If you've been around the Internet long enough, you'll know that people start to develop a sort of *virtual lifestyle*. eBay holds high importance to several million people. They're all working hard to make sure the site doesn't sour. Join them in preserving and improving the way the site works, and you'll see the gains to be had.

Auction Scams

Sometimes bad things happen to good people and bad things happen at good places. EBay is not immune to the misdeeds and misconduct of the few and, as such, has endured its share of online scams. Most likely you've read or heard about some of the more infamous auction crimes and, perhaps, you've wondered if venturing into the auction space is really a safe experience. Relax and know that 99 percent of the time, your transactions will go off just fine, whether you're the buyer or the seller. However, here are the 10 most commonly attempted scams and a quick but effective education in how to detect the major scams and protect yourself along the way.

Shill Bidding

A dishonest seller will make use of multiple user IDs or will enlist bogus bids placed by associates to unfairly raise the number of bids received or the price of an item. This scam is perpetrated by sellers who are looking to artificially increase the bidding activity and increase their final sales price.

Detection

Here's what you can do to detect shill bidding:

- Watch for recurring user IDs that are used to place bids on several of a particular seller's auctions.

- Watch for a recurring pattern where the same bidder or bidders place last-minute bids on a particular seller's auctions.

- Watch for bidders and sellers who regularly bid on each other's auctions.

Protection

If you think you've been victim of a shill, report the incident to eBay's Safe-Harbor immediately. (You'll find the link on the site map page where you can report such problems; be sure to provide any supporting evidence such as other auctions where you believe the seller employed shilling.) Your best bet for prevention is to make note of an apparent shill seller's/bidder's ID and avoid those auctions in the future.

Bid Shielding

This is a bidder's scam in which a ring of dishonest bidders (or a bidder using multiple user IDs) can target an item and inflate the high bid value to scare off other potential bidders. At the last moment, the high bidder or bidders will retract their bids, thus allowing the lower-bidding ring partner to win the item at the once again low—and dishonest—price. The innocent seller has been cheated out of a higher price and other bidders have been falsely steered away from a potential win.

Detection

Here are some ways to detect bid shielding:

- Watch for a bidder who seems to have a pattern of bidding and then retracting near the end of the auction.

- As with shilling, watch for patterns of apparent partnerships or use of multiple user IDs that tend to bid on the same items or one another's items.

Protection

As with shilling, report a suspected shield to eBay's SafeHarbor immediately. Make note of bidders who appear to be involved in repeated shielding and cancel their bids.

Fake Photos and Dishonest Descriptions

Another of the sellers' scams, some auctioneers falsely embellish or distort the presentation of what they're auctioning. Borrowed images, ambiguous descriptions, and falsified facts are some of the tactics a seller will employ when lacking confidence, knowledge, or good judgment in listing goods. The eventual buyer will typically receive an inferior item that doesn't match what was promised nor is worth the price paid.

Detection

Afraid of being scammed with fake photos and dishonest descriptions? Look for these signs:

- Watch for item descriptions that seem too good to be true.

- Watch for disparities between a written description and an embedded image of the item.

- Watch for ambiguous or incomplete descriptions.

- Watch for seemingly "borrowed" images (something that appeared in another auction just prior or concurrently, or something that looks as if it were lifted from a commercial advertisement).

- Watch for heavily touched-up photos.

Protection

Be informed about the items you'll bid on. Carefully scrutinize all descriptive information, including images. If you have questions or hesitations, contact the seller to inquire. If the seller seems evasive, avoid the auction and the seller.

Final Price Manipulation

This is another seller's scam in which final prices might be quoted inaccurately (*exact* bid for a Dutch auction purchase; see Chapter 10, "Mastering the Auction Variations"), might be quoted as your maximum bid due if a previous high bidder retracted, or might be quoted with superfluous "additional charges" that were never previously disclosed or don't make much sense.

Detection

Price manipulation doesn't have much prewarning because the costs requested by the seller come after the auction is over. However, be on the lookout for sales policies that ambiguously refer to odd or potentially excessive costs and end-of-auction prices.

Protection

Your best protection is to quote the seller's policy back to him. If the seller seems confused in the proper calculation of a final high bid (as in the case of Dutch auctions), refer the seller to eBay's rules. Do not pay if you believe price manipulation is occurring, and report the seller to eBay immediately. Avoid the seller in the future.

Inflated Shipping and Handling Costs

This is akin to some aspects of final price manipulation, although it can be somewhat more subtle. Perhaps a seller requests $6.00 for postage, but the item is something small and light that wouldn't cost more than $3.85 to ship. Sellers sometimes inflate postage and handling costs to garner a few extra dollars for themselves.

Detection

How do you know if shipping and handling costs have been inflated? These are the warning signs:

- Watch for sellers who charge a "handling" or "supplies" fee, especially when they utilize free packing supplies from the major carriers.

- Watch for sellers who charge flat rates for shipping and handling that seem beyond the acceptable norm (more than $7.00).

- Watch for sellers who charge high flat rates regardless of the actual item's size and weight.

- Watch for sellers who are evasive or unwilling to clarify their shipping and handling fees in advance.

Protection

Start by being sure you understand all fees you'll be asked to pay and question any fees that seem excessive. Politely ask the seller to clarify fees and how those fees were derived. Request specific carriers (such as USPS) and quote *to the seller* what the cost should be for shipping and any other services. Avoid the seller in the future.

Failure to Ship Merchandise

Probably the most feared yet most enraging of all scams: The buyer has paid up front in good faith and then is left to wait and wait and wait for an item that never arrives. A dishonest seller might claim the item was shipped and has since been lost, but most often, the seller fails to respond or communicate at all with the buyer even though the buyer's money has already been taken.

Detection

You typically aren't aware that you're about to be scammed until after you've sent your payment. But, here's the modus operandi of most nonshipping sellers:

- The seller is quick to make contact and request payment.

- The buyer sends payment but doesn't get a confirmation from the seller that payment has been received.

- Even after repeated attempts to contact the seller, there is no response.

- The buyer acquires the seller's contact information from the hosting site, and often it proves to be bogus.

- The seller might auction the same item again at the auction site, at a different auction site, or under a different user ID.

Protection

The bottom line is that this is classic mail fraud and is high on the list at investigative agencies as well as at eBay. Keep complete records of all correspondence, including messages received from the seller when payment was requested. Be sure all correspondence you send to the seller is professional and nonthreatening. Make a final request to the seller and advise him that you will turn the matter over to the proper authorities. (Start with eBay and your Attorney General, if appropriate.) When you're paying for items, try to use a credit card whenever possible: You will be able to dispute the charge and the card issuer will help you sort the matter out. But let justice take its course and be on the lookout for this seller around the auction places.

Selling Fakes and Reproductions

Knock-off, reproduced, and copycat goods make their way into the online auction marketplace every day. Sellers might claim it's real or might hedge a bit to authenticity, but these scammers know they're selling a cheap imitation and are hoping to catch a high-paying buyer who doesn't know how to spot a fake.

Detection

How can you tell if a product is a fake? It's simple:

- Watch out for truly rare and hard-to-find items suddenly appearing in pristine condition.

- Watch out for scarce items that are suddenly plentiful and just like new.

- Watch out for roundabout descriptions where sellers say they *think* it's the real thing or got it from another source that said it has to be authentic—no it doesn't, and it probably isn't.

- Watch out for descriptions that give little information about the provenance of an item.

Protection

It's a *caveat emptor* world at online auctions, so buyers need to know their stuff. Study up on the items you'll consider bidding on, especially if they have the potential to become quite expensive.

Improper Grading Techniques

The seller states the item is "definitely in excellent condition. A real '10' here." The item the buyer receives is less than perfect, might be flawed or damaged, and could even be incomplete. The seller has painted a rosy picture to bring in the bids even though he or she never really had the top-quality goods to command a high-end price.

Detection

Here are some tips for detecting whether a product might have problems with grading:

- The seller claims the item is in "100-percent mint condition." Even newly manufactured items carry some sort of imperfection.

- The description fails to offer full disclosure of the item's condition or completeness, especially when it's a well-known item and highly desirable.

- The seller has omitted critical details that are key to accurate grading of the particular item.

- Embedded images seem to show signs of being altered, selectively photographed (only one side is displayed), or unnecessarily cropped where damage might be concealed.

Protection

Your best protection in cases of gratuitous grading is to understand the item well, be able to spot potential problem areas quickly, and ask specific questions about an item's condition. Grading can be subjective depending on a seller's experience, expectations, and methods of comparison. If an item is less than stellar, although it was billed to be exquisite, send it back. In fact, if you're concerned about purchasing an item based on its grading, ask if the seller offers return privileges. If not, then it's caveat emptor all over again.

Phony Loss and Damage Claims

A buyer contacts a seller to state that an item never arrived or was seriously damaged. The buyer requests a refund and asks the seller to work out the details afterward. The item might have arrived just fine, but the buyer's hoping to ice the cake by getting his money back to boot.

Detection

To prevent phony loss and damage claims, keep an eye out for these warning signs:

- A buyer contacts you weeks or months after the item was shipped to claim loss or damage.

- A buyer demands a refund immediately before you've had sufficient time to assess the situation or involve the carrier for resolution.

- A buyer offers to throw a damaged item away for you since it won't be worth anything and is in such "bad" condition.

- A buyer is on record of having signed for or otherwise received an item that is now claimed to be lost in the mail.

Protection

This is another classic example of mail fraud. The best protection from phony claims is to insure or otherwise utilize tracking methods for all your packages. Be sure the buyer is aware of his responsibility for loss and damage if insurance or tracking is declined. (Remember: The buyer should pay for these services.) Keep all receipts and tracking numbers until you have confirmed with the buyer that the package arrived safely and the contents are in the same condition as when shipped.

Switch and Return

Some buyers will purchase an item, receive it, claim they're dissatisfied, and return it for a refund. The scam: The item they return is *not* the same item originally sent. This is a method where unscrupulous buyers attempt to upgrade their items for free, sending back an item of lesser quality or condition.

Detection

To detect the switch and return scam, watch out for any of the following:

- A buyer might seem overly interested in your return policy before he has bid or has won.

- A buyer is vague about his reason for wanting to return an item.

- A buyer wants to return an item after a significant elapse of time (weeks or months).

Protection

Unfortunately, this scam is the key reason why many sellers do not offer return privileges. You can still accept returns, but indicate that all items must be inspected prior to issuing a refund. Your clear description and good images will serve as proof of intrinsic details of your item, which helps identify a swapped item that was dishonestly returned. If the return is an attempt at a switch, notify the buyer that the item is not the same one shipped and return the bogus item back to the buyer (accompanied with clarification of points of dissimilarity). Bar the buyer from bidding in any of your future auctions.

Misdeed or Mistake?

With all that having been explained and with the exception of a few of the more blatant frauds noted, understand that some scams are really not scams at all—they're the result of an inexperienced buyer or seller. Take a first step to inquire and clarify; you might end up helping another auction user get a grip on the ways and means of auctioning. You have a scam on your hands if the other person becomes evasive, erratic, or irascible, indicating his original intentions were never designed to be honorable.

And with all this having been said—user personalities, personality disorders, and personal affronts—it's time to hone your bidding skills and perceptive prowess. Part 3 will show you how to become an expert bidder, one whose skills are to be reckoned with.

Now, before you hastily exit eBay, shut down your computer, and tuck tail and run, understand that I've taken you through the veritable Chamber of Horrors of eBay in this dissertation of auction scams. No doubt these tales will raise an eyebrow and perhaps elicit concern on your part whether this whole auction thing is safe; rest assured, it is safe. Remember that scams occur less than 1 percent of the time and, given the tens of millions of items being traded, that's a clear indication that plenty of good business takes place at eBay every hour of every day. As for me, I've never been scammed (I offer that as positive testimony, not as a challenge), largely thanks to my understanding of eBay and auctioning and good, safe transactions. To help you be better informed and better able to be certain of your eBay transactions, I have offered this information of some of the worst of the worst. Armed with this information, you're ready to enjoy all that is good at eBay and able to deftly side-step any misdeeds of others.

part 3

Becoming a
Savvy Bidder

chapter 9

Key to Success:
The Educated Bid

In the previous chapter, I subjected you to my dime-store psychoanalysis of user personalities. In this chapter, I'll help you analyze the items you'll bid on to ensure that every bid you cast will be placed with complete confidence. Again, true eBay expertise consists of equal parts of mastering the site mechanics, mastering the dynamic marketplace, and mastering the practical methods and philosophies that will make you an astute buyer or seller. At this point, *anyone* can place a bid on stuff, but it's the experts who can do so in a calculated and confident manner. Here's what you'll want to consider as your prepare to place your bids.

Understanding Buyers' Motivations:
Collectors, Resellers, and Investors

Whether you're here to find long-lost treasures or to turn a profit on your purchases, you'll see there are several driving motivations that goad buyers in their quests. Just as you learned of the many personalities of eBay users, here is a similar rundown of the potential reasons folks are turning to online auctions. Whether collectors, resellers, or investors, people purchase goods at eBay for different reasons: to have and to hold, to buy and resell, or to realize a healthy return on investment.

So, first consider what drives the reason for purchase.

Collectors might buy because of any of the following reasons:

- They had an item (or remember one like it) as a kid and it brings back fond memories of simpler times.

- They would be pleased and proud to display the item as unique decor in their home.

- They need it to complete an existing collection.

- They know the inherent value of the item although they would never part with it for any amount of money.

- They have a *passion* for it and, regardless of the cost, simply must possess it.

- They just can't help themselves—it's too cool to pass up!

- They dream of someday opening their own little collectibles shop.

Resellers might buy for these reasons:

- They know there is a strong demand for the item in the current market.

- They believe it's the kind of "merchandise" that their customers will appreciate.

- They have customers who have asked to be informed as soon as one becomes available.

- They can buy it at a reasonable price and resell it at a reasonable profit.

- They might be speculating that it's the next craze, fad, or retro trend.

- They can move the item quickly without having to incur storage costs or tie up their money for any lengthy period of time.

And here are the reasons that investors might buy:

- They're confident that the 5-, 10-, or 15-year return on investment is sizable with little chance of depreciation.

- They anticipate a quick sell at significant profit, although it's only a temporary window of opportunity. They must buy and sell quickly.

- They view the item as desirable only in its ability to generate significant profit.

- They might choose to keep the item (for a while) to display proudly for its inherent value—and a bit of bragging rights, too.

- They've studied the origin and association of this item and know it's a rare find.

- They're financially capable of investing in the item now and keeping it for any number of years until it "matures."

Before You Bid

As with most purchases you're considering, it's always best if you fully understand the product, determine how it will suit your needs, and assess if it's the best value available. The same sort of analysis is needed when bidding and buying at eBay, maybe even more so. Here's where you'll need to be diligent in "kicking the tires," so to speak, to ensure that the item you're buying won't wind up a lemon offered by some grinning shyster in a plaid sport jacket.

Analyzing Item Descriptions

Recall the print of the card-playing canines that I won back in Chapter 5, "Seeing the Site, Learning the Rules, and Getting Started." Remember how the seller provided descriptive information telling me the item was a "print," not an original, and that it was brand new? Therefore, when it shows up on my doorstep, that's exactly what I'll expect to receive. If, however, I'd purchased some rare piece of china or an authentic piece of movie memorabilia or whatever, I'd want to understand all the details of the item before I decided to bid. To that end, I'd be expecting the seller to have provided a comprehensive textual description that proactively answered my questions about the item. Some lazy sellers include an image of an item with the stingy text of, "See image; item as pictured." That's hardly compelling enough to encourage my bid and I'd probably pass, left to wonder if the seller would also be as stingy about sparing the time to actually ship the item after I've paid.

The wordier descriptions might also bear serious scrutiny, particular attention to be paid to whether what is described rings true with what is being offered. Some sellers misstate (or blatantly attempt to misrepresent) items by dolling up the description beyond the item's actual presence or conveniently omit key details that knowledgeable bidders (collectors, perhaps) consider critical in making their decision of whether or not to bid.

Therefore, study item descriptions closely, comparing them to the item title and any accompanying images. Use that information to compare and contrast what you already know about that sort of item (either through past experience or recent research), and then decide if the item is worthy of a bid.

Inspecting Item Images

Seeing is believing, but at online auctions, can you believe everything you see? We're talking about the images of items that are up for bid; some sellers provide terrific photos of their great items, whereas others seem to provide them as something of an afterthought. Sometimes you'll need to be especially diligent to be sure that what you see is what you'll get.

Although you should never suppose the worst from any seller at the outset, you should cast a critical eye on poor photos. Most cameras these days (be they digital or conventional) can help even the most incompetent shutter bug produce decent pictures. But, be aware (and maybe wary) of these poor-picture situations:

- **Excessively dark photos.** These could be hiding critical details of an item's condition or completeness. A photo that's a bit dark is understandable, but a seriously dark image might have something lurking in the shadows.

- **Excessively bright or color-saturated photos.** Some sellers like to "clean up" their images before posting them at the auction places. Typically, that's fine, but some cleanup might also misrepresent an item as being cleaner or brighter than it truly is.

- **Excessively sharpened photos.** A little bit of sprucing up is fine, but watch for images that show unnaturally sharp edges or details as well as the "blockiness" quality that indicates an image has been overly enhanced beyond the item's true appearance or otherwise overly reworked and overcompressed during multiple saves.

- **Cropped photos.** It's understandable that many items are cropped when they won't fit on a flatbed scanner, but you should always understand what tell-tale details might have conveniently been left out. This is especially pertinent when you're trying to determine corner or edge wear on items.

Learn to compare photos from auction to auction (as well as to photos you take yourself). Learn to spot the visual digital residue that comes with most image enhancements and compare what you see with other photographs you might find elsewhere. Again, your goal is not to incriminate a less-than-stellar photographer, but it's still your responsibility to watch out for your own interests and to deduce which images seem "augmented" and why.

What Can *You* Change About Images?

If you come across an image that's too dark, too light (overexposed or over-saturated), or possibly overly sharp, you can take a few simple steps to draw out some of the details hidden in the poor photography. Take a copy of the image and open it using any of the common image editors (such as Photo-shop, Picture It!, or Paint Shop Pro). Using the editor's filters, fiddle with brightness, contrast, hue, color saturation, and edge softeners. Often, you can elicit critical details that were otherwise obscured. Just remember that the image you've downloaded is not rightfully yours to make further use of. Unless you have the seller's permission to repurpose the photo, it's best to delete it from your PC's storage.

NOTE Another good graphics viewer that you can download for free is IrfanView. Get it at http://www.irfanview.com.

It Ain't No Big Thing?

That's the problem: If the image is too small, it's often impossible to get a good look at the item. Understand that small photos will conceal moderate wear or damage just because they're a compressed size. There's not much hope for enlarging the image using an editor because the image doesn't contain the inherent detail that would be visible upon resizing; it will just be a blocky mess. Don't risk the eyestrain or the chance that the little image is masking a bigger problem.

Back to the Item Description

Remember: One of your best tools in inspecting images is the written description that accompanies it. Read descriptions carefully and look for text that speaks to the details that you can (or possibly can't) see in the resident image. If the written facts don't support the visual clues, there might be reason to question what you're seeing or reading.

Researching a Seller

As important as the details of an item up for bid are the style, policy, and reputation of the seller offering it. Although most sellers you'll encounter at eBay will be reputable and trustworthy, it's still up to you to ensure you feel as comfortable bidding on the seller as you do about bidding on the item.

Check the Seller's Sales Policy

Before bidding on any seller's item, be certain that you fully understand the cost of shipping, the payment methods accepted, the timeliness of delivery, guarantees or return privileges, and so on. An experienced seller will recognize the need to provide all of these details and will do so in a comprehensive manner, usually within the body of the description text. Check these terms carefully and bid only if you agree to the methods and additional costs that might be incurred when the auction is over.

Check the Seller's Feedback

Always click on that parenthetical rating number to the right of the seller's user ID and read what other users have to say. Be sure to look for comments related to other sales and determine how recent the comments are. (Has the seller been away for a long time for some reason?) Be especially mindful of negative comments and try to assess their pertinence to your potential transaction. All registered eBay users are granted the ability to respond to feedback comments, so check those follow-up remarks to any negative comments that might have been posted.

Check the Seller's Response

If you have questions, eBay always provides the Ask Seller a Question link on the item details page that gives you easy access to pose a direct question. Of course, use this privilege responsibly; contact a seller only if you're serious about his auction. Don't waste a seller's time. And, having said that, understand it's always better to ask questions prior to placing a bid, not after. Not only does this help clarify any questions you might have before committing yourself to a transaction, but it also gives you an indication of a seller's promptness and reliability. If sellers fail to respond to your e-mails within a reasonable amount of time, then you have cause to doubt their professionalism or commitment to follow through after the auction has ended.

Check the Seller's Other Items

Don't forget to see what else the seller is selling. Often times, you'll discover a merchant that deals in the sorts of items that interest you most. You might find opportunity to deal with this seller directly, outside of eBay, after a first successful transaction (that being up to the seller's discretion).

Becoming a Comparison Shopper

Now, thanks to those fine searching skills you've been honing, you'll typically uncover a nice selection of similar items from which to choose; go ahead and be discriminating about which item you'll consider *bid worthy*. First, look at the items and determine which ones appear to be in the best condition, the most complete, and the most desirable overall. Of course, choosing the cream of the crop likely will put you in potential competition with other discerning bidders like yourself. Don't ignore, then, the possibility of picking up a slightly lesser quality offering (but still acceptable to your tastes) for a possible lower price. Rank all the items and determine in descending order which might be worth the gold and which might serve as reasonable runners-up.

However, don't overlook the other dimension of choice: choosing among the sellers who are putting the goods on the block. Here's where bidders have found much more bidding power than ever before, as the growing population of sellers must now compete for bids. Cast a critical eye on sellers' policies as well as their forthcoming item descriptions, images, and customer guarantees. Then, match those factors up to the item itself and decide which seller best deserves your business.

Make the Sellers Come to You

It bears repeating: Take your time in your bidding and be selective about with which sellers you'll do business. Gone are the days when you have to jump with all your effort and all your cash at the first item you see. (Recall the discussion in Chapter 1, "EBay and E-Commerce: How We Got Here and Where We're Going.") Knowing that most items can be found regularly at the auction sites, you have the luxury of being able to decide not only what you'll bid on but also *when* you'll bid. That is, if this month isn't the best time for you financially, chances are you'll find similar or even better pickings next month or the month after that or even next year. The sea of sellers is growing with each passing week, and all are jockeying their wares, their terms, and their prices. You easily can bide your time while you shop comparatively until the deal that best suits you comes along (and it *will* come along).

Think Outside the Auction Box

Finally, remember that eBay isn't the only place to shop online. Once seen as the alternative to mainstream shopping, bartering, and deal making, eBay's auctions have evolved into another option you can exercise before you commit to a purchase. If an item in which you're interested seems to be getting a bit pricey or carries a potentially risky or unfriendly sales policy, then investigate other marketplaces to see whether the item can be purchased outright from a commercial site or from another private party's Web site that could be offering the same or similar item—without the competitive bidding and without having to wait for the auction's end. While other buyers are caught up in the heat of the bidding, you sometimes can find a better deal away from all the action when your fellow bidders aren't looking.

Knowing When to Buy It Now

There's nothing more satisfying than finding an item you want and—boom!—buying it at first sight. No fuss. No muss. You find it, you buy it, you own it. And although this relatively new option of fixed-price purchasing at online auctions tends to buck the true "auction" experience, shrewd buyers should know a good deal when they see it and snap up an item immediately if it's well priced, well timed, or both.

But is there a secret to taking advantage of fixed-price offerings? Check out these scenarios to help clue you in to when the eBay Buy-It-Now price is the price you should buy it at—*now*!

Fast Sale for Tight Times

Timing is an element that makes a big difference in the auction market—to both sellers and buyers. Sometimes, when a seller needs to unload some items quickly—either to make fast cash or to clear out some storage space—there's a motivation to find fast sell-through. The *buy-now* approach is often adopted, along with pricing that is usually enticing enough to hook the speedy exchange. Alert buyers should keep their eyes peeled for such offerings, not to necessarily take advantage of the seller's situation, but then again, why not?

On the other hand, sometimes it's the buyer who's in a bit of a pinch, perhaps looking for a certain item to be given as a gift or whatever other reason where time might be running low. If, as a buyer, you need an item in a hurry, look for those *take it* opportunities where the fixed price you pay might not be as potentially low as possible but could be well worth it in easing the stress of a ticking clock.

Fill the Hole, Fast

Consider this: You're a collector who's been working on a collection for years (or maybe just months) and you've found just about every piece you need—except one. It might be that the one elusive piece is the most desirable, rare, or hard-to-find of the lot and whenever one does happen to show up, so does an army of competing bidders. Then along comes the *buy-it* offering where, yes, the price is a bit steep, but there it is ready for the taking. What do you do?

Here, it all comes down to nonmonetary expense—the expense of your time, the expense of passing this one by and waiting for another, the expense of the valuation of the item that might fluctuate up or down in the competitive marketplace. If you talk to other collectors in this situation, the majority will say, "Buy it the moment you see it." Check the fixed price, and if it's in the median to high end of the accepted market range, you're smart to pull the trigger and grab the goods. If the seller's price is too steep for you, then at least place a bid on the item via conventional auction style and try your luck against the other bidders. Of course, you'll be kicking yourself if the item goes for *more* than that original fixed price, won't you?

Buy It Below the Market

And then there's the good old-fashioned bargain. Whether the seller is motivated to make a fast sale or isn't aware of an item's present or future market value, there are plenty of below-market value items to be snatched up in a fixed-price sale. There's not much more to say here except that when you find those bargains, grab 'em while you can before someone else does.

That's a Wrap

The thrill and anticipation of bidding on auction items can sometimes cloud your good reason, instincts, and judgment. The point of this chapter is to help you establish a method and deliberateness to your bidding. Although the next chapter will unleash a host of effective bidding strategies for your use, remember that a key strategy to employ every time you bid—or *consider* bidding—is to be certain that the bid you'll place will be well founded and grounded in good judgment. And, forgive me if I appear repetitive here (I've heard too many first-hand horror stories from bidders who wished they hadn't bid), here's your checklist of tasks to complete before bidding:

- Carefully review the item description to be certain you know what you'll be receiving *before* you cast your bid. Remember: At eBay, the rules of *caveat emptor* ("let the buyer beware") apply; you can't actually hold and tacitly inspect the goods for sale.

- Look closely at images of the item and make sure that what you see matches what is being described.

- If you're unclear about anything, use the link Ask the Seller a Question. A good seller will respond via e-mail to answer all your questions clearly and completely.

- Research other items the seller is currently offering as well as what has been offered in the recent past (using eBay's Search by Seller function).

■ Review the seller's feedback rating and read the comments that others have left regarding their experiences.

■ Compare and contrast the item you're interested in with the same or similar item(s) being offered by other sellers. Look for description consistency, condition, and price.

■ Be certain that you understand and agree with the seller's terms, including postage and handling costs and options, insurance, accepted payment methods, and refund and return privileges.

chapter 10

Mastering the Auction Variations

When thinking of how auctions work, most folks envision the fabled exchanges of a gaunt and suited auctioneer with an impossibly motorized monologue that sounds something like, "Who'llgimmefive, gimmefive, gimmefivedollars, gimmefive, five! Gimmesix, gimmesix, gimmesix-dollars . . ." The auctioneer, in his rapid-fire dissertation, is working to excite the crowd to get them to increase the bid, using what is known as the ascending-price auction, which is the most common format for auctioning at eBay—minus the high-speed, dramatic dialogue. However, several other formats are actively in use at the site, and it's important to understand the variations as you sharpen your bidding skills. Here's your quick lesson in the formats you'll encounter at eBay.

The Ascending-Price Auction

Historically known as the *English auction* or the *straight auction*, the ascending-price auction is the most widely used format at eBay. After the first bid is cast at an opening bid value (as established by the seller), further bidding ensues in an ascending-price manner, where each additional bidder has to offer the appropriate bid increment.

NOTE Remember: Minimum bid increments are preordained by eBay based on an item's current price. Refer back to the bid increment table in Chapter 7, "Item Details and Bidding Basics," to review the escalating bid increment breakdown.

Reserve Price Auctions

The reserve price auction is a slight variation of the ascending price-auction. Here, the seller establishes a minimum price at which the item will be sold. That is, if the competitive bidding fails to reach or eclipse the seller's reserve price, the seller is not required by eBay's rules to sell the item. This variation is especially useful to sellers who are uncertain whether competitive bidding will return a price that either suits their needs or ensures recovery of the original investment.

Bidding in a reserve price auction follows the same rules as straight auctions. The bidders place their bids on the item and proceed to outbid one another either by way of minimum increments or by beating each other's maximum bids. Bidders are informed that they are bidding in a reserve price auction immediately when they enter the item details screen (see Figure 10-1).

figure 10-1

Reserve price auctions flag bidders whether the seller's minimum sales price value has been reached or not.

Just as with other bidders' maximum bids, you won't be able to see the reserve price the seller has specified on this item. How, then, will you know when the reserve price has been met? Oh, you'll know. Let me show you.

First, notice the text link next to the current high bid in Figure 10-1. Clearly, it tells you Reserve Not Met. If you click the link, it will take you to an area of eBay that explains more about reserve price auctions. When you place your bid for the item, the bid verification screen (see Figure 10-2) will remind you again that you're bidding in a reserve price auction.

In the bid confirmation screen, you get a second reminder that the reserve price hasn't been met and that your maximum bid might or might not meet the reserve regardless of whether you're crowned high bidder. Most importantly, eBay is quickly explaining that, before you submit your bid, the high bid for the item might be advanced beyond the minimum increment and up to the seller's reserve price if your maximum bid meets or exceeds the established reserve. So, in this case, if your maximum bid amount is greater than the reserve price, the new high bid amount jumps immediately to that

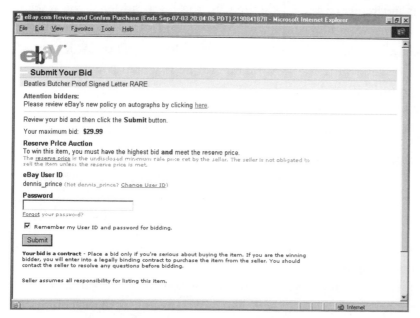

figure 10-2

In the bid confirmation screen, you'll be reminded that this is a reserve price auction.

reserve price rather than merely advancing to the next minimum bid increment. Bingo! You've just found out the seller's reserve price and committed to paying at least that price if you ultimately prevail as the winning bidder.

When the reserve price is met, it's open bidding from then on with minimum bid increments being all that are required—along with beating the high bidder's maximum bid—to win the auction. On the item details screen, the note next to the new high bid value will read Reserve Met.

But what if the reserve price wasn't met, not even by your maximum bid? If this happens, then the high bid will only increase to the next highest bid increment that would outbid any other bidder's maximum bid, if there were any. The Reserve Not Met note would remain next to the current high bid amount on the item details page. Other bidders would see the same text in the bid confirmation screen that they are bidding in a reserve price auction and their bid might be advanced to the reserve price as long as that price doesn't exceed their maximum bid.

Now assume that the reserve price is never met by the time the auction ends. Then what? In these cases, it can be treated as if the auction never happened. The seller is not required to sell the item to the high bidder if the reserve price was not met. The high bidder is not required to honor any bid if the reserve price was not met. The seller and high bidder can, however, contact one another to determine if a deal might still be reached. Maybe the high bidder would be willing to pay the reserve price after all. Maybe the seller would be willing to accept a little less than the reserve price now that it's turned out the bids just weren't there to meet the original expectations.

The key is that when the reserve price of an auction isn't met, everyone can walk away from the table without further obligation. The seller might decide to keep the item, work out a deal some other way, or relist the item, possibly at the same reserve price again or maybe at a lower reserve price.

Because you know so much about reserve price auctions now, you might have missed the keystone question (or maybe you think I missed it): Why not just make the opening bid the same as the reserve price and avoid the whole reserve price thing altogether? The answer is one with psychological roots: low opening bids will attract more bidders regardless of whether there is a reserve price or not. It's a universal truth and one you'll see proved again and again, especially when you step up as a seller yourself.

The Dutch Auction

Dutch auctions are a great way for sellers to auction duplicate items quickly in a single listing. They're also great tools for buyers to pick up a more plentiful item at what usually turns out to be a good price.

In a Dutch auction, the seller indicates that there are many of the same product and the whole quantity is available at the same time. The seller lists the auction as a Dutch auction, specifying how many items there are and the minimum opening bid for any bidder to stake a claim on one of the items.

When bidders come to a Dutch auction, they have to bid at least the minimum bid amount as set by the seller, but they can bid on as many units as the seller is offering in the lot. For instance, say a seller found an old case of Naugas (see Figure 10-3) and wants to move the whole box of critters in one fell swoop, thereby hosting a Dutch auction for the entire lot of 12 of them. Bidders are able to make a minimum acceptable bid to get into the competition but can also specify whether they want to bid for just one, two, five, or however many they would want to purchase.

When the auction ends, the qualifying bidders are notified and instructed to pay the lowest successful bid for whatever quantity of the item they bid on.

That's the rule of Dutch auctions: Regardless of what prices the winning bidders offered, they each are required to pay only the lowest winning bid amount when the auction is over. It's a bit confusing, but you'll learn the bidding strategy behind this format in Chapter 11, "Expert Bidding Strategies."

Dutch auctions, by ratio, are much less common on eBay than regular English auctions. Because they're a bit more complex to understand, many bidders avoid them. Don't let them scare you off, though. They're actually kind of fun, and you can get some great items at great prices. In the next chapter, I'll give you some strategies for bidding and winning in Dutch auctions.

figure 10-3

What? You don't know what a Nauga is? Well, where do you think Naugahyde came from?

NOTE Because of their format, Dutch auctions cannot be set with reserve prices. That would defeat the whole purpose of the auction because price variation—the main draw of a Dutch auction—would never occur.

Fixed Price and Buy-It-Now Listings

If sellers have a price in mind for which they'll sell their items outright, this format (which you have already seen termed as Buy-It-Now) allows a willing buyer to dispense of the competitive bidding and offer the seller's asking price, thus ending the auction immediately.

In some cases, sellers can offer items that are only made available for a fixed price whereas others might offer a traditional auction with a minimum bid amount and a simultaneous Buy-It-Now price. If no bids have yet been placed, a buyer could skip the bidding and purchase the item outright. If, however, a bid is placed, the Buy-It-Now option disappears and the auction follows standard ascending-price rules. The exception to this is that, when a reserve price has been established along with a Buy-It-Now price, the Buy-It-Now option remains in effect even if regular bidding has commenced so long as the reserve price hasn't been met. If regular bidding does meet the reserve price, the Buy-It-Now option disappears.

Private Auctions

What's the use of a private auction? Really, it's a means for a bunch of naughty buyers to bid on naughty things offered by naughty sellers, all of them rightfully ashamed of what they're doing and fearful their spouses, clergymen, or mothers might find them out.

Just kidding.

A private auction—a reasonable type of auction to conduct—provides anonymity to the bidders in an auction. In a private auction, the bidders' user IDs are suppressed from public view. Bidders' identities are revealed only to the seller after the auction has closed and only by way of e-mail. This way, bidders are able to bid on certain items without being subject to the public eye. Sellers recognize that, in some situations, bidders would prefer some additional privacy, the astute seller then electing to run a private auction.

Are there benefits to a private auction? Well, the main benefit is that certain bidders will feel more comfortable placing their bids in a private manner than if the auction had been posted publicly. A bidder whose identity is readily available to the public might not want to bid on—oh, I don't know—vintage inflatable sheep. Without ensuring bidders' privacy, the seller loses.

 NOTE All kidding aside, I've also seen sellers host private auctions for various collectibles and such, the sort that have attracted other would-be sellers into making unwanted contact with the active bidders. The seller, recognizing that his customers might be subject to such improper advances, has opted to provide privacy for his bidders.

Restricted Access Auctions

Okay. This is really where the naughty stuff is. Close cousin to private auctions, the restricted access format was designed to help users easily locate or summarily avoid erotica or other such adult-themed items. Categorized as "restricted access items," bidders who want to browse such goods must provide credit card information for age verification. Items of this sort, corralled in the Mature Audiences category, are not listed in general search results and require adult verification logon to access, thus shielding those of us who are easily embarrassed.

With the auction variations now understood, it's time to unleash the tried-and-true bidding strategies that will give you an edge in the online auction space. The details await you in the next chapter.

chapter 11

Expert Bidding Strategies

Here's where the real fun begins and the point at which the experts distance themselves from the novices. It's perfectly acceptable to place incremental bids on an item, hoping to ultimately get in the last winning bid before the auction ends; nevertheless, the good news is that winning can be much easier and less time intensive than maintaining an active presence in the virtual auction parlor.

A Quick Recap of the Proxy System

As a point of brief review, recall how eBay's *proxy bidding system* works. As previously described in Chapter 7, "Item Details and Bidding Basics," when you're bidding on an item, you're prompted to enter your *maximum bid amount*; this is the most you would ever be willing to pay for a particular item, your ultimate "drop out" price. EBay's proxy system will only consume as much of your maximum (by minimum bid increments) to maintain your high bidder status, incrementing the current bid value for you (bidding on your behalf) when other bidders come along and increase the price. You'll retain your high-bidder standing as long as another bidder doesn't eclipse your maximum bid value. When that happens, you will be outbid and another user will be proclaimed the high bidder. There's no trick to the proxy bidding system; it all comes down to who puts the most money on the table. There are few things you can do, though, to increase your odds of winning.

The Penny Principle

Would you laugh if I said you could win an auction with a mere penny? Here's how it's done. First, understand that whenever two bidders submit the same maximum bid value (say, $100), eBay recognizes the first to have submitted that maximum as the winner of the tie. At this point of incremental bidding, you would need to enter another bid that satisfies the minimum bid increment to become the new high bidder (in this case, an additional $2.50). However, if the current bid is $50, the high bidder having previously stated a maximum of $100, you can win this auction with a penny by bidding a maximum of $100.01. Your maximum will meet the minimum bid increment (that amount required while the current value was at $50) and, as eBay's proxy bidding system takes over to bid on behalf of you and the current high bidder, your bid will ultimately win out because you succeeded in bidding more than the previous bidder—*just a single penny*. Because you laid more money on the table, you walk away victorious. This principle works in reverse as well. In other words, your maximum bid of $100.01 will thwart other bidders who might come along long after you originally submitted your bid, they submitting a maximum value of $100. Your single penny will retain your high bidder status. To this end, it's good to be in the habit of bidding odd values such as $100.01, $25.37, and so on. Those few extra pennies might be all it takes to gain you the win without sending you significantly beyond your intended spending budget.

I Snipe; Therefore, I Win

Perhaps the most maligned bid practice of all is snipe bidding, or "sniping." Essentially, you lie in wait for an auction to approach its conclusion; then, just seconds before the time expires, you launch a stealth-like bid in hopes of supplanting the current high bidder while leaving no time for a rebutting bid. It sounds sneaky, but it's a perfectly allowable and widely used practice by many veteran bidders; only those who have been "sniped" are squawking about it. In essence, it's no different from traditional ascending price bidding; only the timing is different. But, beyond the prospect of winning, sniping has been a key draw, the truest and most intoxicating gamesmanship, to the bidding experience. In step-by-step fashion, here's how snipe bids are executed with all the suspense and excitement of which I'm speaking.

Why Snipe?

It's not just for sport or to add excitement to the bidding process. Long-time eBayers have discovered a strategic benefit to sniping. Having become a common practice among the seasoned bidders, here are some of the reasons that snipers swear by their approach:

- Sniping effectively eliminates the possibility of falling victim to a shill bid. If you bid late, there isn't time for an illicit shill to bid up the price before the auction ends.

- Sniping provides absolute anonymity, protecting you from "bid stalkers"—those who monitor what others bid on and bid against them in the final minutes of an auction.

- Sniping allows bidders time to consider their bid before committing to an item. When the end of the auction nears, the bidder can determine whether the item still is desirable and financially feasible.

- Sniping *can* result in better prices (averting a back-and-forth bidding war), although a majority of snipe wins come by way of some impressively high bids (and sellers love that).

- And, well, it does add that certain "thrill of victory" to the game.

Despite these pragmatic benefits, some users unfairly characterize sniping as a ruthless tactic. Recognize, though, that the snipe is to online auctions what the "jump bid" is to live auctions: An auction observer suddenly steps into a tit-for-tat bidding exchange, places a significant bid increase that *jumps* the high bid to a new level, and effectively eliminates the previous nickel-and-dime competition. Jump bidding, like sniping, is perfectly within the accepted rules of the auction and, like sniping, can deliver a high level of drama and excitement to the proceedings.

Getting Set to Snipe

So what is the secret to effective sniping? Well, contrary to what some might say, there is no secret to sniping at all, and there's little room for unfair advantage; anyone can snipe. Although there are a few different ways to monitor the final minutes of an auction (many folks employ the use of PC time-sync applications, whereas others actually make use of stopwatches), the easiest method I've found is to use side-by-side Web browser windows—one for monitoring the auction clock and the other for launching the snipe bid. In a nutshell, here's how I've found years of success in my sniping.

Fifteen to thirty minutes before the auction is scheduled to end, surf the auction site to get a feel for how well it's handling the current load. Watch for slow page refreshes and any other inconsistent behavior that could have an impact on how much time you'll need to get in that snipe bid. Slow response time might also be attributed to your Internet connection, although those of you who utilize a broadband connection shouldn't be hampered in your connectivity. Oh, and if you haven't already, be sure you're signed in at eBay before proceeding. Doing so prevents you from having to sign in as you're preparing to place your snipe bid. If you've forgotten, you can sign in quickly and easily by clicking the Sign In text link on the main toolbar.

Five minutes before the auction's end, launch two identical Web browser windows, both displaying the item you want to snipe (see Figure 11-1).

In the first window, refresh the page every few seconds or so to monitor the auction clock and, again, determine how well the site and your connection are responding. You'll notice that the Time Left on the item details page will count down with every refresh.

Now, toggle to the second screen and click the Bid icon. Enter your maximum bid amount and wait. Here's where it gets exciting.

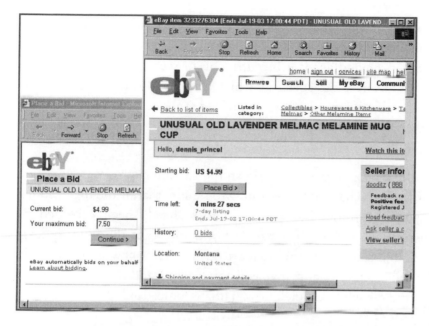

figure 11-1

Use two item screens when preparing to execute a snipe bid.

About two minutes before the auction will end, click on the Place Bid button in the second window. EBay will display a Confirm and Place Your Bid message with a button labeled Confirm Bid; don't bid yet! (See Figure 11-2.)

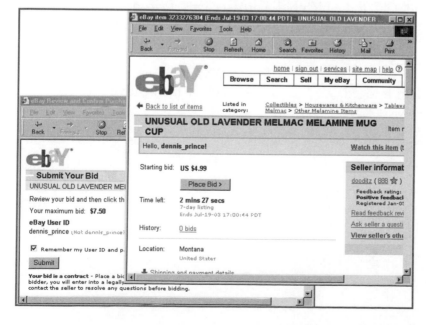

figure 11-2

At the two-minute mark, the snipe bid lay ready in wait.

Now, here's where it gets exciting. This is the final countdown. Keep reloading that item details screen. You're approaching the time to snipe. How is the eBay server responding? If it hiccups a bit or seems a bit slow, consider how that might affect the speed at which your final bid is received and processed. Usually, the speed of a screen reload is about half or one-third the time you can expect for the processing of your bid. Keep reloading the item details screen to get a feel for the response time.

As you continue reloading to count down the auction clock, keep an eye on the high bid. Has it changed? Check now to be sure that, if the high bid has changed, your maximum bid amount hasn't already been exceeded by another last-minute bidder. If it has, but you still want the item, quickly toggle to the bid screen, use the back arrow, re-enter a new maximum bid that you're willing to pay and that you think will stand a good chance of bringing home the win. Be quick now. Time is almost up!

One minute to go!

Bid now?

No, not yet. Wait. Reload that item details screen. There's still time, and you don't want to play your hand too fast. Reload. Reload. Check the response time. Reload. Check the high bid. Forty seconds. Reload.

Thirty seconds!

Bid now, right?

Not yet! Hold it together. Almost. Reload every moment you see the clock time redisplayed.

Twenty-five seconds. Twenty seconds. Eighteen seconds! Fifteen seconds! Ten seconds!

Quick! Move the mouse pointer to the bidding screen right over the Place Bid button and . . . hold your breath . . . count one, two, three . . . BID! Click on the button NOW!

Close your eyes. Say a prayer.

It's okay. You can open your eyes now. If you were successful in placing your snipe bid, eBay will report the results, either naming you the winner or informing you that you were outbid by the previous high bidder's proxy or possibly by another snipe bidder who was lurking. Here's the truth about snipe bidding: Recognize that a last-minute bid will *not* ensure a win because it is the maximum bid amount placed by any bidder that determines who will win, not just the timing of a bid. However, a successful snipe bid that does supplant a previous high bid is usually successful in that there is scant time left for another bidder to place a follow-up bid.

Again, there's nothing unfair about snipe bidding (if there was, eBay would prevent its use) because, in the end, no matter how late you wait to place a bid, if another bidder has offered more by way of a maximum bid amount, that amount will still win out.

You Need Not Be Present to Snipe

You've just seen a manual snipe in action requiring you to be present and interactive to deliver the late bid. For those of us who have been sniping for years, sniping often required getting up in the wee hours of the morning to snipe an auction ending at odd hours. Those sleepy-eyed days are gone, though. As exciting as sitting at attention to launch a snipe bid can be, sometimes you can't be present to monitor the end of an auction; you can still snipe, however. There are several automated snipe programs you can use to place your snipe bids for you. My personal favorite happens to be located at http://www.esnipe.com (see Figure 11-3).

This server-based sniping assistant allows you to enter your snipe bid information long before the auction ends and will then log on to eBay and place the snipe bid on your behalf. Although you'll pay a fee to use eSnipe, it costs only pennies on the dollar and often delivers big results. You're able to instruct eSnipe's sniping engine regarding how many seconds prior to the auction's end the bid should be placed. (I find constant success when specifying a mere six seconds.) Again, there's no manipulation going on here—just well-timed last-second bids done while you sleep, play, or work.

figure 11-3
Sign up with eSnipe and leave the sniping to them.

Winning Dutch Auctions

If you're new to the Dutch auction format (introduced in Chapter 10, "Mastering the Auction Variations"), you might be a bit confused about how the final price is determined, how the winning bidders are determined and, most importantly, how to increase your chances of winning. Recall that when sellers have multiple units of the same item to offer, the Dutch auction is one of the best methods to sell off the lot. As a bidder, your job is not only to understand the rules of Dutch auctions, but also to equally employ effective bidding tactics that can help you maximize your chances of winning while minimizing your final cost.

Dutch Pricing and the Winner's Circle

First off, let's review the rules for winning a Dutch auction. Remember: The winning bidders only need pay to the *lowest successful bid price* at the auction's close. Although you might have bid as high as, say, $30, in an auction for several nifty fountain pens, if the lowest winning bidder won at the price of $20, then *all* winning bidders pay only $20 for each item they've won.

To become a winner, though, you need to ensure that you're in the "winner's circle": the population of bidders who have successfully secured the right to claim some quantity of units up for auction. The highest bidders will be able to claim whatever quantity of units they had bid for, the second highest for their quantity of desired units, and so on down the line until all units have been claimed. If you're the lowest winning bidder, you'll only have claim to whatever quantity is left over, which might be less that what you originally desired. Still, you're in the winner's circle and you have claim to some quantity of the goods.

Bubble Economics

In Dutch auctions, the economics of supply and demand co-mingle with the concept of the auction "bubble." Simply put, when multiple bidders have accounted for the complete quantity available in a Dutch auction, they create a competitive coexistence that leaves one or more bidders precariously hanging on at the low end of the winner's circle. These bidders are deemed as being *on the bubble*. This means that another bidder who bids slightly more can negate the status of these "on the bubble" bidders, easily knocking them "off the bubble" and out of the winner's circle. Is that difficult to picture? How about a simple table like 11-1 to illustrate the bubble? Here, assume an available quantity of 12 units and a minimum bid of $25.

Table 11-1 Picturing the Dutch Auction Bubble

Bidder	Quantity Bid On	High Bid
1	1	$25
2	1	$27
3	4	$28
4	2	$28
5	4	$35

A quick look at the table shows that Bidder 1 is on the bubble; he's easy to knock out of the winner's circle with a bid of $26. Of course, if you decide that you want to bid that amount in this auction scenario, then you'll be on the bubble. The better strategy is to bid *outside the bubble*—that is, bid higher than the lowest bidders yet not as high as the highest bidder. (Remember that you only need to pay the lowest successful bid price.) Therefore, in this mock auction, your wisest bid (as new Bidder 6) would be for $29, resulting in the new scenario shown in Table 11-2.

Table 11-2 Results of a Dutch Auction Snipe

Bidder	Quantity Bid On	High Bid
2	1	$27
3	4	$28
4	2	$28
6	1	$29
5	4	$35

Notice how you've bumped Bidder 1 cleanly off the bubble but, rather than assume his vulnerable standing, your offering of $29 allows you to flank your bid by bidders 2, 3, and 4. In the best end-of-auction result, you might end up paying only $27 (the lowest successful bid) for the one unit you want. However, you also might end up paying the full $29, but only if additional bidders stake claim to all seven units behind yours. Chances are, your position outside the bubble should guard you from such an overtaking. This isn't failsafe, of course. A new bidder (or bidders) could come along to claim some or all of the units at a price higher than yours or Bidder 5's, but you see how this strategy gives you the best opportunity to win the unit you want without committing a bid at the highest end.

Sniping, Dutch Style

If the bubble strategy isn't enough of an edge for you, you can always snipe a Dutch auction. That's right—you can place your well-flanked Dutch bid in the closing moments of the auction for maximum effect. Again, the bidder(s) on the bubble will be knocked out of the winner's circle, and you'll still have the other bidders protecting your backside in case any other Dutch snipers are lurking in the shadows alongside you.

Yankee Doodle Dupe

Finally, your best bet in ensuring that you pay the lowest successful bid price is by making certain you know exactly what that price should be. Some sellers, accidentally or intentionally, might ask each bidder to pay their *exact* bid price for the units won, regardless of whether the lowest successful price is lower. This is wrong! That approach is used in *Yankee* auctions. Each bidder in the winner's circle pays his exact bid price. (And, yes, the winning bidders could all be paying different prices.) Yankee auctions are not supported at eBay. Remember that in Dutch auctions, you only pay that lowest successful bid price. And, because Dutch auctions can be a bit confusing to some sellers, your winning bid is ultimately protected if you understand the Dutch rules better than the seller.

The Strategy of Not Bidding

It sounds crazy, but it's true: Sometimes it's more advantageous *not* to win an auction. It's easy to get caught up in the excitement and competition of winning an auction, losing sight of the price being paid, with a win resulting in an undesirable final cost. Always consider the following when you're tempted to get caught up with "winning" the auction:

- If the item offered is at a price equal to or higher than that which you could pay elsewhere, there's no reason to bid.

- If an item isn't in the condition you would prefer, wait for another item to show up.

- If the seller's feedback rating is low or the sales policy is suspect, consider skipping this auction.

■ Consider avoiding an item in which the bid history reveals that two bidders have been active in back-and-forth bidding through the course of the auction. This might be a *bidding war* in the works, and you'll likely not fare well between the two impassioned bidders.

Additional Strategies That Give You the Edge

Just as not bidding can be a valid and effective strategy, not being seen is also an effective approach to gaining success at eBay. Here are a couple more methods to employ to help you achieve your bidding goals.

Dealing with Bidding Rivalries

They say all's fair in love and war, and that includes bidding wars. If you hang around eBay long enough, you might begin to recognize some of the other bidders who frequently compete for the same items you're after. Are they rival bidders? You bet they are, and they're riding in your wake, ready to leap out of the pixels and snare the goods you've been actively hunting and bidding on.

Whether you're hiding below, behind, or just off in a dark corner of the virtual parlor, you need to identify when particular bidders seem to be haunting the same auctions that interest you. Although there's nothing unfair or necessarily underhanded about others bidding against you, there are some who will ride your coattails as you uncover some great treasures, intent on snatching items away from you after you've surfaced the goods.

This adversary, as previously mentioned, is commonly referred to as a "bid stalker," and that's just what bid stalkers do: stalk your activity in the auction places, searching on the items you're currently bidding on, and even researching the items you've bid on in the past. If you appear to be adept at locating the things that bid stalkers also seek, they'll consider you to be a terrific—and unwary—ally in helping them acquire the items they covet (thanks to *your* efforts).

Your best defense against rival bidders is a good offense. It stands to reason that your bids can't be stalked if you haven't yet placed them. Going stealth at the auctions, then, means utilizing protective techniques such as auction tracking, watching, and (here it comes again) sniping.

Watching is made easy thanks to eBay's own Watch This Auction program. Notice on the item detail page (as pictured in Figure 7-1 in Chapter 7) the text link titled Watch This Item, located to the right just below the item title. Click this link, and the auction item will be added to the Items I'm Watching tab on the My eBay page. Then, 36 hours prior to the end of an auction you're watching, eBay will send an e-mail message alerting you to the pending completion of the auction. In addition, if you downloaded the eBay toolbar, it can also provide easy review and alerts of items you might be watching.

If you've ever find yourself surrounded by familiar faces at the auction sites—you know, the ones who seem to jack up prices with their penny-ante bids or snipe you on each item you've dropped a proxy on, then it's high time that you strategically cloak your bidding intentions by electing to watch first and bid later.

Using Multiple IDs

Just as you might have multiple bank or investment accounts or separate personal and business credit card accounts, so too might you consider having multiple eBay user IDs. No, this isn't registration abuse, and it's also not the crooked use of numerous auction disguises to pull off assorted schemes and scams. Although it's true that misuse of multiple user IDs is prohibited at eBay, many longtime users—buyers and sellers—understand that responsible use of multiple IDs at eBay is not only permitted but is key to efficiently managing auction activity while adding a bit of homegrown fraud protection.

Are You Sure It's Legal?

Well, of course it's legal, when done with proper intent. EBay's own spokesperson Kevin Pursglove had previously conceded to me, "Many of our users have determined that it is useful to have multiple user IDs for their businesses."

If you run your own auction business but also dabble in personal sales or bidding outside your business dealings, it's smart to clearly separate the two. To that end, creating a business user ID (perhaps designated as a business name) and a personal ID will help to ensure that your business and personal worlds don't overlap in a way that blurs the clear division between the two. (This is especially important in terms of tracking tax liabilities and business expenses.)

Then again, some business owners create multiple IDs within their business structure, potentially allowing business partners or employees to conduct auction sales and purchases concurrently. This can effectively manage different product portfolios or commodities within a business, allowing the business owner(s) to easily assess the costs and profits associated with each commodity they might manage.

Be Your Own Crime Buster

Many seasoned auction users have learned how susceptible their lone ID can be to the misdeeds of others. Burned by bid stalkers (those who specifically seek out what *you're* bidding on then bid against you), some users have used one ID to place initial bids on items of interest, later to come back to place final bids (even snipes) using a different ID. The same approach can be used to thwart bid shills, using one ID to essentially "stake your claim" on an item but at a low maximum (just in case a shill is lurking). Using a secondary ID to make a final bid will prevent the artificial and illegal inflation of an item's final price.

How Many IDs Do You Need?

Although the decision of how many IDs to have is up to you and depends on how you want to run your business and personal affairs, practice the method of "less is best." Some users are well served by just two IDs—one for business and one for pleasure, or one for buying and one for selling.

Others like to use the fraud protection ID that is available to misdirect would-be shills and bid stalkers. And, as mentioned earlier, if you are involved in a business that has multiple owners or employees, it might make sense to obtain a unique ID for each.

Regardless of how many IDs you believe you need to best manage your online auction activity, be 100 percent certain that these IDs never become entangled in bidding or selling in a way that could lead someone to believe that you've joined the ranks of auction scammers and registration abusers. Again, less is more.

chapter 12

Exercising Control, Imposing Your Will, and Seizing the Moment

Armed with so many bidding strategies and auction approaches, it's time again to assess your ability to use good judgment and apply your knack for bidding and buying as you establish your bidding expertise. Here's where you'll determine just how savvy you really are, knowing when it's time to buy and when it's time to bow out. Likewise, here is where you can use your shrewd analysis and acquired information to get what you want, avoid what you don't, and ensure that you're in full control every step of the way.

Resisting Impulse Buys

Whether it's raining outside, there's nothing to do, you haven't bought anything for days, or you're just plain bored—whatever your situation of unease or dissatisfaction—there's always a quick fix to your restlessness: Hit eBay and start bidding.

But, as you're gleefully surfing, looking, and bidding, are you sure you're buying things you really want, things you can really afford, and things that won't leave you muttering, "Now why did I buy that?" It could have been an impulse bid, and it might mean you're falling into the trap of bidding and buying for all the wrong reasons. Here, now, is a bit of insight into what might lead to impulse bidding, where it might lead you, and what you can

do to avoid those pangs of remorse when the winning bid announcements start piling up in your e-mail Inbox.

It's All in the Mind, Y'Know

We've all heard of compulsive shoppers and compulsive gamblers. Online auctions have emerged as an equally addictive activity, providing a combination of the thrill of buying an item and the excitement of doing so in a sort of high-stakes gaming environment. Some people actually experience a euphoric sensation during the act of buying and definitely in the striving to gain a "win."

Psychologists have documented the chemical reactions that take place in the human brain that provide the euphoria: A chemical dopamine is released during these activities, which provides the individual with a euphoric sensation, albeit short lived. That feeling actually can become addictive and is often cited as the reason some folks shop compulsively or gamble excessively or maybe even bid irresponsibly at online auctions: They want that high.

Who Says You're an Impulsive Bidder?

Often, no one has to say a word; your actions will speak volumes. Although I'm not about to practice amateur psychology here, if you're wondering whether some of your bidding could be impulsive in nature, see if any of the following might apply:

- Do the items you win hold little interest to you after they've arrived at your home?

- Are you disappointed if days pass without a new package landing on your doorstep—to the extent that you'll quickly buy something else to get the deliveries coming again?

- Do you love the thrill of winning auctions, yet delay paying for the items you've won?

- Has your personal debt increased significantly within a short period of time (especially credit card balances)?

- Do you keep your auction spending a secret from friends and family?

- Do you ever feel guilty about the amount of money you're spending online?

Although a "yes" answer to any one of these questions isn't necessarily a sign that you've developed compulsive behavior, it could signal the beginning signs that you're caught up in impulsive bidding, which could eventually lead to compulsive buying. Therefore, it might be wise to consider some preventive action.

A Good Defense

It's your financial well being and online reputation that we're talking about here (failure to pay for items in a timely manner can bring about negative feedback from sellers), so take a long hard look at your bidding habits and, if you feel you're losing a bit of self-control, consider one or more of the following remedies:

- **Take control of your time.** Consider all the other activities you need (and want) to complete in a day, and then allot a more reasonable amount of time to be used for surfing the auctions. If it helps, set an alarm clock to tell you "time's up."

- **Log off after each use.** It's too easy to plop into the chair and impulsively surf for stuff when the PC is always warm and running. Log off after each sitting. The fact that you'll need to wait for the PC to boot up later is usually enough time to reconsider a bidding binge.

- **Set a dollar limit.** Regulate your bidding by establishing a strict spending budget (and sticking to it). You don't have to entirely sign off from online bidding, but by allotting an affordable amount of spending every month, you'll satisfy the desire to bid without jeopardizing other financial commitments.

- **Make a shopping list.** Look for the items that are truly of interest or importance to you and search only for those.

- **Avoid browsing.** Use specific searches to find the items you want, freeing you from the temptation to bid on something just because you happened to come across it.

- **Don't fall for fads.** It's all the rage today, but no one will care tomorrow. Try to avoid hype and trends that often lead to impulsive bidding. Ask yourself whether you'll still want it a month from now.

- **Do something else for a change.** The Internet and eBay are exciting new forms of interactive shopping, but do you remember what you did before they arrived on the scene? Take time to rediscover an old hobby (or an old friend) and balance your online and offline time.

A Little Help from Your Friends

In case you're worried that you've gotten a bit too caught up in all the bidding and winning, don't keep it a secret—tell someone. Whether it's your spouse, partner, family members, or friends, if ever you doubt your control over your online bidding, let someone know. You might need to hear another point of view on your activity, have someone else point out alternative activities to pursue, or need someone to help you gain a more professional assessment.

Don't panic, but don't take impulsive bidding too lightly. Take control instead.

Playing the Waiting Game

Okay. So you have control over your bidding, but you're still impatiently awaiting your latest win, that item that seems to be taking forever to arrive. Although no one enjoys the wait, there are some things you can do to help get your item sooner.

Some of the best ways to speed the arrival of your item begin with you, the buyer. Hopefully, the seller contacted you quickly via e-mail to congratulate you on your win and to instruct where payment should be sent. Here's where you spring into action: Send an e-mail reply quickly to acknowledge your intention to follow through. Provide your mailing address when you reply; most sellers will begin packaging your item in anticipation of receiving your payment. Then get that payment in the mail right away. Most snail mail will reach its destination within two or three days.

If the seller is a bit slow in contacting you (more than 48–72 hours after the auction's end), take the initiative to make first contact. (You won't appear to be an overzealous newbie if you've waited two or three days.) Request the final tally and the manner in which payment should be sent. If you need the item for a special occasion (a birthday, Christmas, and so on), let the seller know so that you can both work toward a speedy transaction. Most sellers will try to accommodate special situations.

Easy Payment, Quick Service

Naturally, sellers need to verify the payment they receive. If you pay via a money order or cashier's check, the seller knows it's as good as cash and will often state that such types of payment get immediate shipment service. Personal checks are fine, but expect to wait an additional week or two for that check to clear (and hopefully not bounce).

Along with your payment, be sure to identify who you are and what you've won. Many sellers complain that they receive payments without a description of what item was won, or they receive an ambiguous note that reads, "Send my item." Which item? Which auction did you bid in? Who are you? It takes the seller additional time to cross-reference who you are and what you've won, and it's especially tedious for sellers who list at multiple sites (auctions and otherwise). Give sellers the right information up front, and you'll help them get your item out more quickly.

Track Your Goods

A good seller will send an e-mail informing you when your item actually ships and which carrier will be delivering it. (If you aren't given this information, ask for it.) If your item is traveling via Federal Express, UPS, or USPS Express Mail, get the tracking number for the package. These carriers (and others) have Web sites where you can enter the tracking number and determine where your item is during the journey. This is a fun little diversion that helps anxious buyers pass the time while also assuring them that the item is truly in transit.

How Long Should You Wait?

Many variables come into play in determining how long it will take to receive your item. Of course, the carrier used and the service requested play major roles in determining this. UPS Ground Service takes at least a week, whereas USPS Priority Mail often takes only two to three days. Different carriers have different timetables at different rates, so understand the typical delivery lead-time before you worry about foul play.

Next, consider the location from which the item is being shipped. International shipments can take up to six weeks if traveling via surface (the literal "slow boat"). Also, don't forget to consider the time of year. If it's the holiday season, for example, expect the increased volume of packages to affect your item's eventual arrival. And sometimes a package just takes a wrong turn but will show up eventually. Although it happens infrequently, some packages take the scenic route, and many carriers will state a standard waiting period before investigating the whereabouts of the parcel. Give it some time before you call out the bloodhounds.

Communicate, Communicate, Communicate!

If the item still seems to be taking too long to arrive, then what? Have you been scammed? Before you jump to conclusions, jump to your e-mail first. The best way to ease anxiety you might have about your item's arrival is to maintain open communication between you and the seller. Confirm when your payment was sent and when the seller received it. Confirm when the seller shipped your item and which carrier is delivering it. (Don't forget that tracking number if one was issued.) Most sellers are just as interested in seeing the deal come off as smoothly as possible, so team up and work together to unravel the mystery.

When your item arrives, send a final e-mail to the seller to confirm receipt, especially if the package went a bit wayward during its trek. The seller will want to know that the case is closed and that, hopefully, you're a satisfied customer. Always indicate that you'll be posting positive feedback—that's a good way to wrap up the deal.

Establishing a Bidding Budget

With those tens of millions of items up for auction every day at eBay, it's hardly far fetched to consider the risk of auction-goers spending a king's ransom on the items they find. Although the searching, bidding, and buying can definitely pay off, have you been minding how much you might be paying?

Talk to any financial counselor, and he'll advise you to spend within your means. The same holds true for bidding. Not only is it deceptively simple to commit your money with the click of a Confirm Bid button, but there is also the added element of competition, which easily can blind you as to how much money you ultimately will spend as you fight for the "win." In the passion of the final bidding, many folks end up spending more than what they originally intended to bid—often more than an item's true worth. It happens all the time.

To avoid this adrenaline-induced high bidding, set a dollar limit on how much you'll spend for an item and stick to it. If the item is relatively common, bid a "maximum bid" and don't look back. If you lose, wait for the next one to surface and bid on it. There are plenty more fish in this cyber-sea.

Next, closely monitor the cumulative effect of your concurrent bids. At eBay, you can 10- and 20-dollar yourself into financial straits. Therefore, consider setting a monthly cap on your bidding and be vigilant about monitoring how much is left in your coffer after placing each maximum bid.

If, however, it's a rarer-than-rare item that you absolutely must have, and if money is no object (yeah, right), be sure you can afford whatever you might pay and prepare for the purchase by curtailing all other bidding. Focus your attention and funds on this choice relic, whatever it might be. Not only will your focused attention gain you a better chance to win, but you'll also be better able to recover from the purchase financially and, later, resume your treasure hunting.

Just Look Away

Despite your best efforts to establish and adhere to a bidding budget, there might be times when you'll need to go "cold turkey." If your bidding is getting a bit carried away (or you anticipate it's about to), then stop looking. It's rare that browsing can be totally harmless; you'll almost *always* find something you want. If you continue to look, you'll most likely continue to bid. It might be wise to give your budget—and your will power—a breather.

Keep in mind that the majority of items you'll find at eBay will become available on an almost regular basis (a topic I'll discuss at length later in this chapter). Even those vintage, rare, and out-of-production items regularly make the rounds in a virtual elliptical stream of availability. Turning your back for a while doesn't mean that all the good stuff will be gone, never to be found again. Online auctioning has blossomed into an economy all its own, and folks are buying and selling many of the same items over and over.

So, when your spending has reached or surpassed a comfortable limit, settle up with the sellers and take a break from the auctions. There will be plenty of goodies to tempt you upon your return.

Help Your Hobby Pay For Itself

Of course, one of the best ways to afford and even justify your auction spending is if the money you spend is strictly "off the top"—that is, it doesn't take away from your regular living expenses. The best and easiest way to do this is to become a seller yourself. If you have a bunch of stuff on which folks will bid (and people bid on just about anything), consider listing those items and use the income you receive to pay for your later bidding. Build up several hundred dollars from your auction sales and turn it into bidding bucks to get the stuff you want. In virtual terms, you're "trading" your stuff for other stuff, with a bit of money exchanging in the meantime. In essence, your hobby has begun to pay for itself.

Enjoy What You Have

The final point is to appreciate the items you've already won. Auction bidding can become addictive and habitual to the point that you toss your winnings on some stack of stuff without enjoying them. In these cases, it's probably the bidding, not the item, that is the sole target of your effort. Take time to enjoy what you've won. Allow your bidding budget to build up again. Then, when you've got the funds and have an item in your sights, go get it and bring it home to be equally enjoyed. *That* will be money well spent.

When to Buy (and When to Consider Selling)

True buying prowess and self-control comes from knowing the marketplace and being able to determine when is a good time to make your purchases. The key, of course, is to know when the best buying and selling opportunities are about to present themselves.

Recognizing the Best Times to Buy

We would all like to think we can spot buried treasure from a mile away, although many of us wouldn't recognize it if it bit us on the nose. Because there are different reasons to buy, there are also different definitions of the "best time to buy":

- **Buy when you can afford to.** What better time is there?

- **Buy when you see the item you crave.** I'm not promoting impulse buying. However, if you merely make a mental note of where you spotted some treasure, exercising admirable control to buy a little later, you need to figure that treasure will have since been discovered by someone else; that's a missed opportunity for sure. Collectors know that when you spot a rare item, you should grab it when you see it.

- **Buy ahead of the curve.** Stay tuned to coming trends, events, or celebrations (perhaps tied to world history, holidays, movie releases, award presentations, or whatever) and buy related items or investments at lower prices *before* the public hype (and subsequent demand) is high.

- **Buy *after* the dust has settled.** Hype and trends are funny in their fickleness. And, with more and more of them being fueled by a hyperactive marketing mentality, today's gold might be tomorrow's mica, quickly replaced by "the next big thing." Sometimes, you can pick up inexpensive booty after the looters have dropped it in pursuit of the next treasure.

- **Although it's often uncertain, you can sometimes prosper when buying the stuff that no one's paying attention to.** That goes for stock, collectibles, artwork, or whatever. Sometimes you might have a true sleeper on your hands that will be limited in supply when it finally takes off—and your supply escalates in value quite nicely.

- **Finally, although it isn't truly a *when* scenario, buy whatever it is that you like, and buy it when you like it.** It has value: the personal value that you assign to it for your own uses.

Recognizing the Best Times to Sell

If you buy with an intention to sell (whether right away or after some period of time), you'll want to be attuned to some of the better selling opportunities. Selling doesn't always mean you'll rake in the big bucks (that depends on your personal situation and motivation for selling), but here are some of the better times to consider liquidating your assets:

- **Sell when demand is at (or near) its peak potential.** This can be a gamble sometimes because sellers wait for the highest profit potential before offering their items. If you wait too long, the wave might have passed and the spike in demand might have passed as well.

- **Sell when the bottom is about to drop out.** If Beanie Babies are about to fizzle out and your collection was purchased for their profit potential, then sell, sell, sell! Do it quickly before the news spreads and everyone dumps theirs on the market.

- **Sell when a good offer is made.** It's the old "bird in the hand" thing; the two in the bush might never really materialize.

- **Always sell whenever you can at least recoup or improve on your initial investment.** If you've had funds tied up in stuff for a long time and need to free up some cash, sell the stuff and call it even. Remember that there was probably the value of ownership that you had enjoyed over the years, and that was worth something, wasn't it?

Understanding the Elliptical Marketplace

Does it ever amaze you when you seem to see the same items changing hands right in front of your eyes? Not the same "sort" of item, but the *exact same pieces*. So many times I've seen items I had previously sold coming up for bid again, months or years later. (I recognize them by certain markings or possibly disclosed imperfections as the items I once owned and auctioned.) Others have expressed the same, proclaiming something they once possessed is making the rounds, from owner to owner, state to state, country to country. How come? The Elliptical Marketplace is in operation. Here's how it works.

What's in the Stream?

Valued goods, typically those in finite supply, are regularly traded in the resale market. Whether by a private individual or by an auction house, goods enter the "supply stream" whenever they're offered for sale, and usually on more than one occasion. Here's how it works:

- Certain commodities have inherent value and resale potential; it is what draws many folks to buy and sell them.

- Large and small collections are sold off every year at auctions (online or off), estate sales, or wherever, often causing the original collection to be fragmented among multiple buyers.

- The buyer might choose to sell at a point when a profit can be realized or he no longer wants to keep the item; it goes back into the supply chain.

- A new buyer spots the item and "pulls" it out of the stream.

- When the buyer decides to "put" the item back into the stream, the cycle repeats itself, time and time again.

So How Is This Market Elliptical?

The ellipse is oval, right? That means it has a length that exceeds its height. See the image in Figure 12-1. Put your finger in the center of the oval or ellipse, and you'll notice that the two points or ends of the oval are farther away from the center than the top and bottom. It sounds unrelated at first, but here's how the analogy applies:

- At the two distinct points, which are either end of the oval, supply in the stream is farthest away from the buyer. The outline of the oval represents a supply line of goods.

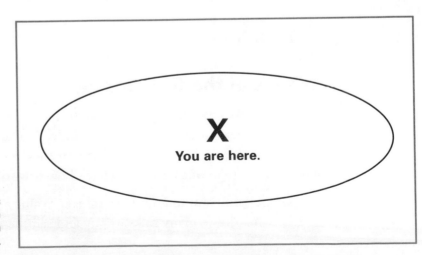

figure 12-1

The elliptical market is represented by a simple oval. Place your finger on the X in the middle.

- When at the farthest points of the oval's outline, supply seems nonexistent, hard to find, and incredibly rare. (The items are, in essence of time and space, farthest away from your position in the middle of the oval.) Do the items still exist?

- The stream is usually in steady motion as people sell their possessions (for whatever reason).

- The sell, if it's at a significant price, can arouse the attention of other people who own the same or similar items. That could prompt them to sell their items.

- If demand supports it, all such items could be wrested out of the woodwork and put into the stream, vastly increasing the previous limited (or seemingly nonexistent supply).

- Now there are several items to choose from, and buyers are poised to make their purchases. (This is analogous to the sides of the ellipse that are closest to the buyer.)

- If the supply is depleted and the buyers choose to hold their purchases for a period of time, the supply is again at the farthest points of the ellipse . . . until the next wave of trading hands takes place.

This elliptical marketplace isn't a true economic science, and it's doubtful whether you can look this up in a college textbook. The idea is based on my experiences and observations of the auction market. It is real, and the point is to understand that when there is a drought, it might only be a temporary situation. As a buyer, it's necessary you keep this in mind as you choose the time you'll buy. If prices are incredibly high, even though you know more such items are still out there (somewhere), bide your time and watch the market. A high-priced sale might be just the keystone to bringing down an avalanche of supply. *That's* when you can take your pick among the offerings.

Your Personal Power at the Auction Place

Well, by now you've seen some of the most common scenarios and situations in the buying market. And with so many options available to you, that translates to purchasing power that can work in concert with the funds you can commit.

The advent of the Internet and eBay has made it easier to buy and sell goods like never before. That means more choice, selection, and leverage for you as a buyer. With selection comes competition as sellers work harder for your money, now understanding that you have the power to say no to one seller and yes to another who is offering the same (or better) item.

The activity of buying and selling is wonderfully documented in auction sales. Buyers can analyze selling trends and track the rise and fall of item demand. This allows buyers to compare prices and overall shifts in accepted market value, allowing them to choose the best time to make their purchases.

The next power you'll want to harness is the power of selling. The next section is your soup-to-nuts review of selling at eBay, from the simple listing to bulk sales. You're an expert bidder and buyer now; it's time to extend that expertise as you advance to the ranks of expert seller.

part 4

Selling at EBay:
For Fun and Profit

chapter 13

Immediate Success with Your First Listing

Now that you have a solid understanding of how eBay works, how bidding strategies help you become a better buyer, and how to determine if a deal is on the up and up, it's time to take the next step and become an auctioneer yourself. Listing items at eBay is quite easy, and the site does a good job of providing guidance along the way. If you're new to listing at eBay, this chapter will offer a crash course in how to put an item up for bid, quickly and easily. By no means is this the end-all instruction on listing items, however. On the contrary, the single listing method I'll show you here will get you familiar with the listing process and the options and opportunities available to you when you offer items for bid or sale. However, if you have visions of conducting high-volume business, there are additional methods and short-cuts I'll explain in the coming chapters. For now, here's an overview to getting your feet wet as an online auctioneer.

First Things First: What Will You List?

The listing process begins with the question of "What will you offer for bid?" Surely, there are plenty of items at your feet (figuratively or possibly literally) that you would like to rid yourself of or cash in on. The best news here is that you can sell practically *anything* at eBay. Provided that you've priced the item reasonably, there's generally a buyer out there for everything.

Without a doubt, while you were searching the site, you encountered several pieces that likely caused you to muse, "Someone's really trying to sell *that*?" Moreover, you also might have been shocked that those quirky goods actually received bids. It's true—practically everything is worth something to somebody. Therefore, I work by this motto: Don't throw it away; throw it on eBay! I can practically guarantee you'll find a bidder for nearly anything you might offer up.

To that end, start your listing adventure with some simple items. The best ones are things you might have already seen up for bid and which you also have laying around the house. You don't need to necessarily strike it rich on your first sale; your goal is to become accustomed to the listing process. (Recall my first listing of the California Raisins premium; this was a great first sell based on the fact that I saw active demand before deciding to list it.)

Remember your search activities and recall items you might have seen that seem to be in demand. Check the high bids on these items and determine how many bidders have been vying for the sorts of things you have at your disposal and which you would be ready to dispose.

DID YOU KNOW? I usually advise newcomers to gather all the clutter in their homes and run some quick searches to see if those items are being bid upon. That includes everything from old books to videotapes to calendars to posters and whatever else in between. Work from the perspective that, to make a go of auctioning, you'll need to clear out your living space—soon to be your *workspace*—to become efficient. Everything you see that needs to be cleared out serves as your first lot of auctionable goods. If you don't absolutely love it or need it, auction it.

The point is that there's certainly something of interest that you're sure to sell and which likely isn't near and dear to your heart at this time. Do some quick rooting around, find an item or two, and get to listing.

Using EBay's Single Item Listing Forms

With your item in hand, here's a quick review of eBay's single item listing process. I'll assume that you already created your seller's account at the time you registered with eBay. If not, you'll be required to do so as you begin the process to list an item. (Refer to Chapter 5, "Seeing the Site, Learning the Rules, and Getting Started, for step-by-step instruction.)

From the main toolbar, click on the Sell button to access the Sell Your Item pages. You'll likely be prompted to sign in with your user ID and password (see Figure 13-1). This is also where you can complete your seller account creation by clicking on the Create a Seller's Account text link.

After you're signed in, the listing process begins with a first screen that asks you to choose your selling format (see Figure 13-2).

Your format options begin with the traditional auction format but also include the ability to list an item for a fixed-price sale within the auction space, similar to listing items at Half.com and eBay Stores. (This eliminates bidding in deference for offering at a fixed sales price; you'll learn more about those options later.) Because it's traditional auctioning I'm discussing, select the first radio button and then click Continue.

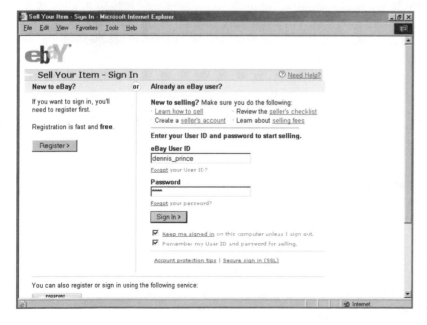

figure 13-1

You'll need to sign in before you can list an item.

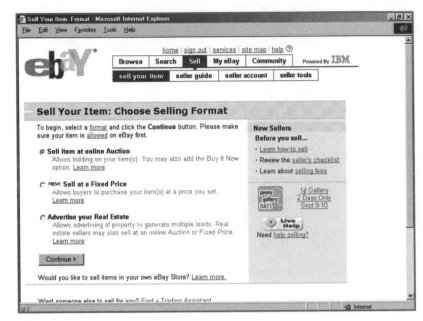

figure 13-2

Listing an item begins with choosing a selling format.

NOTE Throughout this process, you'll see text links embedded within the screens captured here that can go deeper into the details of the listing process. I encourage you to explore those links and the information they'll lead to if, after completing this chapter, you still have additional questions. What I'm presenting is all you'll need to do, but I certainly don't want to misdirect you away from eBay's own instruction if that will help you along your way.

Next, select a category header by clicking the appropriate radio button from those offered in the following screen (see Figure 13-3). Make your selection and click Continue.

NOTE Again, rely on your findings during item searches to determine which might be the best categories and subcategories as you list your item.

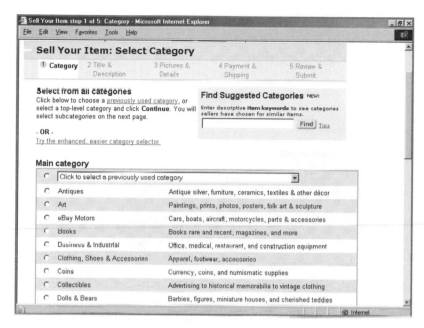

figure 13-3

Carefully select a main category header that will best represent your item.

ALERT Look out! EBay allows you to select a second category for your listing (at the bottom of the category header screen) based on the notion that two category appearances will improve your sales results. I'm not convinced that's true. Choosing an additional category incurs additional listing fees that will eat away at your eventual profit. I'll describe the fee structure later in this chapter but, for now, forget the second category option.

In the screen that follows, refine the category for your item as shown in Figure 13-4. Clicking on the subcategory title in each of the tiled windows will allow you to zero in on the final subcategory for your item. Click Continue to move along.

Incidentally, notice that eBay has just about everyone and everything covered in this category I've chosen: Everything Else > Weird Stuff > Slightly Unusual. What's so odd about what I'm listing? Wait and see.

Now it's time to create the title and enter the full description for your item. The two windows in which to do so are clearly labeled (see Figure 13-5).

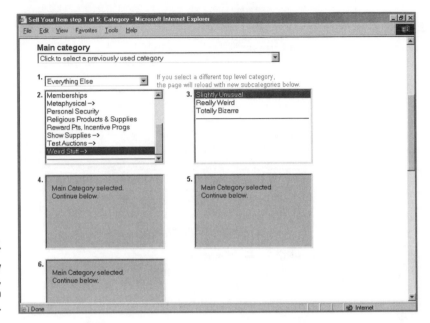

figure 13-4

As you click in the subcategory titles in the successive windows, you'll complete the categorization process for your item.

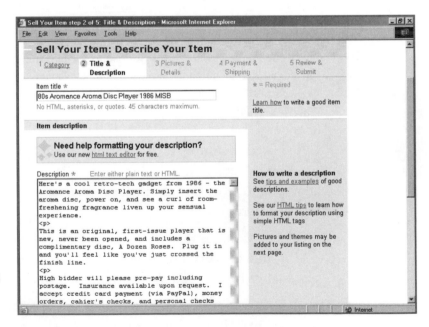

figure 13-5

In the third listing screen, enter your item title and description.

You're limited to 45 characters for the item title, so you'll need to be selective in your verbiage. The item description field, however, is virtually limitless.

 NOTE If you're handy with Hypertext Markup Language (HTML), you're free to enter your custom code within the item description window. (You'll see my <p> paragraph break tags in Figure 13-5.) Look to Chapter 17, "Managing Your Auctions: Sell More, Earn More, Work Less," for a deeper discussion on the best ways to utilize HTML in your listings.

Complete the title and description portions and then click Continue to move to the next screen.

The next screen, Pictures and Item Details, gets a bit more involved. (The conditions you'll be entering going forward will be subject to various listing and selling strategies that will be discussed fully in Chapter 14, "Supply, Demand, and Proper Positioning.") In the first section of this screen (as shown in Figure 13-6), you specify the following:

- The **duration** of your auction (how many days you want it to run)
- The **start time** of your auction (immediate upon saving or delayed)
- The **quantity** of units being offered (in case you're running a Dutch auction)
- The **starting price** or opening bid amount
- A **reserve price**, if you elect to specify one
- A **Buy-It-Now** price if you want to offer the option of an immediate sale
- A check box to list this as a **private auction** (bidders' IDs will be visible to the seller only)

Next, scroll down a bit to enter the details of the physical location (city, state, and country) of your item. Then continue scrolling to specify images to accompany your item (as shown in Figure 13-7).

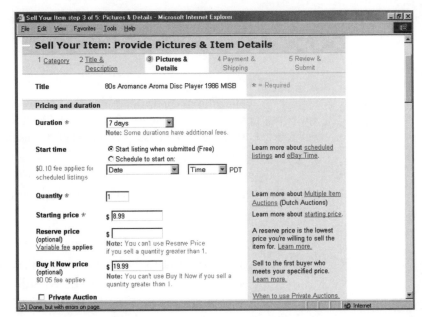

figure 13-6

The first part of the item details screen allows you to specify time and price parameters for your auction.

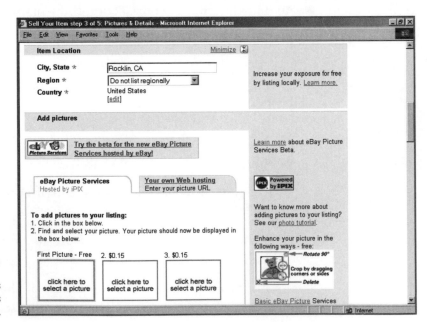

figure 13-7

Images are critical to sales success; specify them in this portion of the listing screen.

If you're new to eBay and listing auctions, you're likely harboring a bit of anxiety over the perceived difficulty of adding the all-important item image to your listing. Really, this is a simple task and one easily accomplished in one of two ways: Let eBay host the image for you, or tell eBay where you're hosting the image yourself.

In the first scenario, you can easily utilize eBay's own iPix image-hosting service in which you'll offer up a digital image of an item from your computer. Notice in Figure 13-7 under the Add Pictures area the exposed tab labeled eBay Picture Services. All you need to do is click on the first picture box. (The first picture is free; additional images will add 15 cents each to your listing fee.) Then, when prompted, tell eBay where on your computer the appropriate image can be found. If I were using this option, I would indicate the image of the Aroma Disc Player I'm listing (a high-tech sort of incense burner from the nifty 1980s) could be found in my PC's computer folder path of C:\AuctionPics\aroma_disc.jpg. EBay will locate the picture I've specified and upload it to its hosting server for use in my listing.

 NOTE The first time you use iPix, expect a small program to be downloaded to your computer. This enables eBay's host system to access and retrieve the images you'll select.

As simple as that, your image will be ready to use in your listing.

The alternative and, in my opinion, preferable approach is to direct eBay to images I have stored at a host of my own. Most likely, when you obtained access to the Internet, your ISP provided a certain amount of free Web space for you to use (usually 10 MB). All you need to do is upload item images to that Web space and direct eBay to that location. For this sample auction, I'll specify the URL (the Web "address") where I've previously uploaded my image of the Aroma Disc Player. The good news here is that, whereas iPix will crunch and crush your item image for minimal host storage (sometimes degrading the image quality and detail), specifying an alternative URL will leave the image unaltered. Better yet, by hosting my own images, I can specify additional pictures in my listing without paying image fees to eBay by including additional URLs within the description portion of my listing. (We'll discuss that topic more in Chapter 17.) So, having specified my item image, I'll scroll further down this long screen where I can select additional features for displaying the images, graphical themes, additional listing features such as bold titles and gallery images, and graphical counters. Some of these features are free and some are not. And don't worry if this seems overwhelming at this point. For your first listing, just get used to the various screens and selections. I'll discuss the best way to use these item accoutrements in Chapter 17. When you're finished with this screen, click the Continue button at the bottom.

The next screen is where you select the payment methods you'll accept, who'll be responsible for shipping costs, plus any additional shipping instructions you would like displayed with your listing (see Figure 13-8).

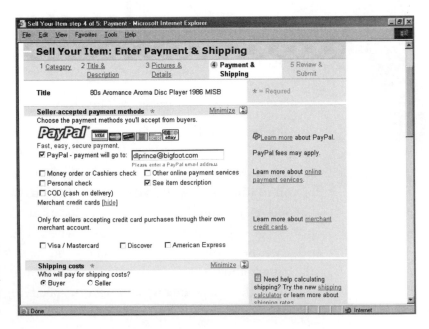

figure 13-8

Using the various radio buttons and text boxes, establish your preferences for payment method and shipping instructions.

For more information on these different methods, see Chapter 16, "Easy Money: Hassle-Free Payment Collection." Click Continue to proceed.

At last, it's time to preview your listing. Carefully reread your item title and description, be sure your image(s) display properly, and review the various other listing conditions and features you specified. Figure 13-9 shows how this example listing will appear.

Be sure to scroll down to the bottom of the screen and review the insertion fees that will be charged when you list the item. This is where individual listing fees for your selections of starting price, reserve or Buy-It-Now prices, additional images (if using iPix), and special features are tallied. Take a look at Table 13-1 to understand how your listing choices will affect the cost to post your auction. In Chapter 17, I'll further explain these listing features and show you how to control these costs without adversely affecting your profit potential.

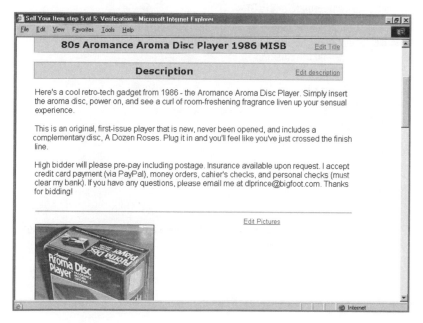

figure 13-9

The preview screen gives you a last chance to verify your item before submitting it for auction.

Table 13-1 Index to EBay Fees

Starting Price, Opening Value, or Reserve Price	Insertion Fee
$0.01–$9.99	$0.30
$10.00–$24.99	$0.55
$25.00–$49.99	$1.10
$50.00–$199.99	$2.20
$200.00 and up	$3.30

Reserve Price	Reserve Price Auction Fee
$0.01–$24.99	$0.50
$25.00–$199.99	$1.00
$200 and up	$2.00

Closing Value	Final Value Fee
$0–$25	5.25 percent of the closing value
$25–$1,000	5.25 percent of the initial $25 ($1.31), plus 2.75 percent of the remaining closing value balance ($25.01–$1,000)
Over $1,000	5.25 percent of the initial $25 ($1.31), plus 2.75 percent of the initial $25–$1000 ($26.81), plus 1.50 percent of the remaining closing value balance ($1000.01–closing value)

Listing Upgrade	Listing Upgrade Fee
Home Page Featured	$99.95
Featured Plus!	$19.95
Highlight	$5.00
Bold	$2.00
Gallery	$0.25
Gallery Featured	$19.95
List in Two Categories	Double the insertion and listing upgrade fees (excluding Scheduled Listings and Home Page Featured)
10-Day Duration *The longest listing duration available*	$0.10
Scheduled Listings	$0.10
Buy-It-Now	$0.05
Gift Services	$0.25

If you're not satisfied with what you see, either graphically or within the listing selections you've chosen, use the active links across the top of the listing page to navigate back to the previous screens to make necessary adjustments. If all looks well, click the Submit Listing button at the bottom of the screen to launch your auction. Upon doing so, eBay will provide you a new screen that contains the active link to your item page (see Figure 13-10).

With your listing submitted, the auction clock is now ticking. Upon selecting the link shown in Figure 13-10, you can jump to the item details page that bidders will soon be reviewing (see Figure 13-11).

NOTE Although your auction is immediately active, it won't appear on search results right away. Results pages are updated about once every hour at eBay, but soon you'll be able to search on a keyword and your item will show up in the search results. However, you will be able to find your item immediately if you (or your customers) search by seller by specifying your user ID; that type of search lists every item you have available the moment the listings are submitted.

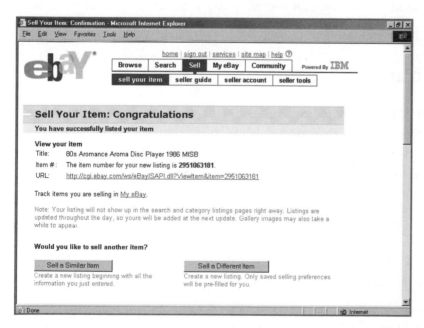

figure 13-10

Your listing is live! Follow the text link to view the actual listing page.

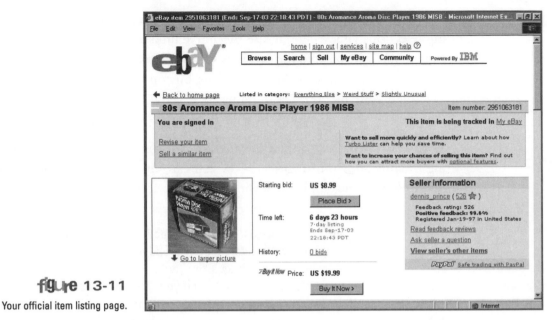

figure 13-11
Your official item listing page.

EBay will send a confirmation e-mail message to notify you of your successful listing. As simple as that, you're off and selling.

Listing at Half.com

Recall that I promised to explain listing fixed-price items within eBay's Half.com site. Luckily, that process is much quicker and more straightforward than listing within the auction realm. Remember that when you registered to sell at eBay, you were simultaneously enabled to list at Half.com, too. How convenient.

Half.com is designed to simplify the fixed-price listing of items bearing the famous UPC symbol (the bar code that beeps when you're checking out at your favorite retail establishment). Of course, you can list items without bar codes, too, but this example will utilize an item that has a UPC.

For this example, I'll list a used DVD that I want to sell. Begin by venturing to http://www.half.com. As you can see from the home page image

figure 13-12

The Half.com home page provides an opportunity to sell at fixed prices similar to eBay auctions.

captured in Figure 13-12, the site is similar to Amazon.com and offers the opportunity to buy books, music, videos, and much more. Because we're here to sell, I'll select the tab Sell Your Stuff.

The Sell Your Stuff page offers categories similar to eBay. For this example, I chose the Movies/DVDs category. Upon doing so, I'm shuttled to the next page where I merely enter the item's UPC number (see Figure 13-13).

After I enter the UPC number and click Continue, most of the work is already done. The next screen reveals a successful recognition of the UPC number with an item image and description being automatically loaded by Half.com (see Figure 13-14). At this point, all I need to do is establish the item's condition by choosing from a drop-down menu of choices and then entering any additional text of my choosing. I click Continue to proceed.

The final step is to establish a fixed selling price. Half.com offers information regarding other items like yours and at what prices they're currently listed and have recently sold (see Figure 13-15). You're free to establish whatever price you like. Upon doing so, click List Item, and the job is complete.

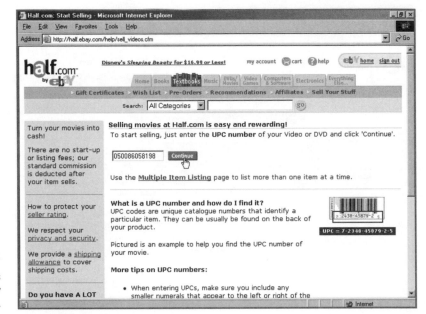

figure 13-13

figure 13-13

Listing items with UPC numbers is the fastest and easiest way to post items for sale.

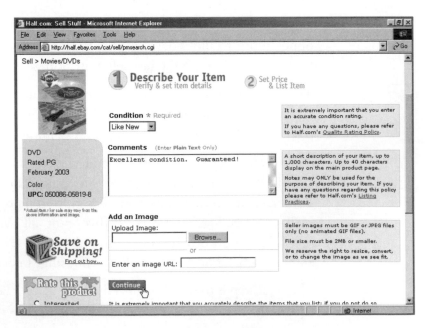

figure 13-14

The valid UPC number identifies the item via description and image.

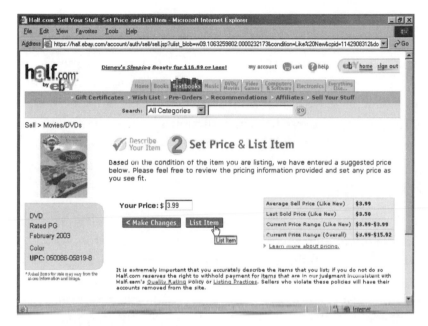

figure 13-15

Set your price and list the item.
It's that easy.

The main difference in listing at Half.com versus eBay is that no fees are levied at Half.com *until the item sells*. Moreover, Half.com collects the buyer's payment for you and then notifies you to ship the product. (You're behaving as a drop-shipper, of sorts, for Half.com.) Half.com also suggests that you ship via media mail (for music, books, and video) and allots a fund to cover those costs. Fees, then, are levied after the sale and deducted from your balance (see Table 13-2). The money you collect, then, is automatically transferred to your registered bank (checking) account around the 15th of every month.

Table 13-2 Index to Half.com Fees

Selling Price + Applicable Shipping Costs	Half.com Commission
< $50.00	15.0 percent
$50.01–$100.00	12.5 percent
$100.01–$250.00	10.0 percent
$250.01–$500.00	7.5 percent
> $500.00	5.0 percent

Although I'll discuss the benefits of using other venues outside of eBay, the immediate benefit of Half.com is the ability to virtually store your inventory in a manner that does not immediately incur fees, is not subject to aging off, yet is always visible to any buyers who might come searching for an item like yours. Know that active links to Half.com are provided on eBay search result pages, guiding potential buyers from the auction space to the fixed-price offerings.

Less Than Half?

With all this having been said about Half.com, be aware that eBay has been actively pursuing integrating the features of the fixed-price site, purchased by the auction giant in 2000, into eBay's own space. The integration is scheduled for completion for the fourth quarter of 2004 at which time, eBay reports, Half.com will cease to exist, the functionality having been completely absorbed and available within eBay. As proof, eBay has now made available the *Pre-Filled Item Information* feature (launched in October 2003), where sellers can make use of "stock" information for items such as books, CDs, videos, and video games. By providing predefined information regarding production credits, song lists, and more, eBay hopes to speed up the listing process for sellers while enabling greater levels of details to be provided in listings. The caveat: The "stock" images of the items might be a cause for question, especially when actual item condition (appearance, completeness) comes into play. The onus will be on you, as seller, to ensure that you're completely thorough and forthright in providing details of the item you're actually selling (the same as you would at Half.com) to ensure that your buyer isn't unpleasantly surprised by the item that ultimately arrives. To this end, you might want to forgo the use of stock photos and provide an actual photo of your own.

The Pre-Filled Item Description is optional and is being made available (initially, at least) at no cost.

Before You List Again

Chances are, seeing your items listed will motivate you to run off and find another of your treasures to offer up; that's the spirit! Before you grab more goods to offer, take time to read through the next several chapters so that you'll have a greater understanding for presenting yourself as a seller in the eBay realm and elsewhere. With matters of online payment, sales policies, and pricing considerations understood, you can successfully tinker with listing more items for bid. Of course, the subtle nuances and selling strategies that the pros use can be found within the chapters to follow; that's where you'll truly hone your auction expertise. For now, though, dabble with the listing process.

chapter 14

Supply, Demand, and Proper Positioning

Seeing that there's no mystery to the tactical listing process, what is the key to successful sales at eBay? I'm glad you asked; from this point forward, this heftiest section of the book will guide you through the various elements, attributes, and approaches to ensuring you greater success in your auction endeavors. Forget others who have tried to convince you they possess mythical enlightenment and I-can-tell-you-but-then-I'll-have-to-kill-you "secrets" of super selling. There are no secrets, and there is no danger of demise in applying the methods to improve your eBay sales. The only key ingredient, really, is your willingness to learn and try to think "outside the box."

Online Sales Mining

The old adage states, "Good business is where you find it." The trick to that little euphemism, though, is actually knowing where to find such good business. Although the implication seems to be that anyone can stumble onto a business oasis, it makes better sense these days to leave nothing up to chance. When it comes to knowing what to sell, how to sell, and where to sell, it becomes imperative to actively drill deep into the online sales market and let the cyber-statistics guide you on your way to better results. When you're starting out, see what others are doing and how they're doing it, and then strive to emulate the best.

Data at Your Fingertips

Perhaps one of the greatest contributions of the eBay marketplace (next to the ease with which we can all buy and sell goods) is its volume of real-time sales data, readily available 24×7. This is the core of the data mining potential, enabling sellers to seek out products similar to theirs and determine the mood of the marketplace for such goods.

What's easiest to mine are the current listings at eBay. In an instant, you can take a quick pulse of buying and selling trends. Start this analysis by finding out who else is selling the sorts of items you'll offer. First, check their minimum bid prices as well as their "Buy-It-Now" prices and determine which sellers' strategies seem to be attracting the highest bids or fixed-price sales. Next, check the bidding activity to see which items are commanding the most active bidding. When you zero in on the listings that are generating the greatest "buzz," take note of the listing categories being used, which is an indication of where most buyers might be congregating. Beyond price and category, take a careful look at the effectiveness of the listing title (a full discussion of which is upcoming in this chapter), the listing description, the images presented, the seller's sales policies, and the seller's feedback. (Remember: Much of this is the same information you studied when you were searching to bid; this time you're reverse searching.) In short order, you'll be able to quickly ascertain which sellers are successful, which products are drawing activity and garnering the best prices, and what overall sales style seems to attract the most customers.

When you're ready to do some deep, deep mining, I heartily recommend that you investigate a tool called Deep Analysis as offered by HammerTap. Visit http://www.hammertap.com (see Figure 14-1) and navigate to the information about Deep Analysis, which is a downloadable program that can provide you with the sorts of detailed eBay sales statistics that help you make better decisions regarding what you'll sell and at which prices you

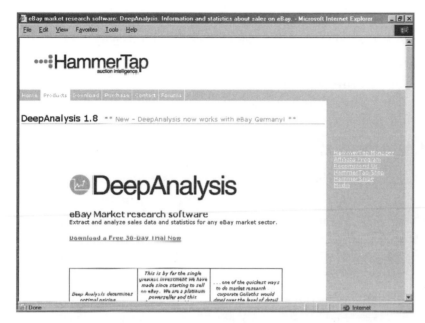

figure 14-1

HammerTap's Deep Analysis tool is ideal for culling the millions of eBay listings as you mine the marketplace.

should offer it. Hardcore sellers have been using this tool for some time, many telling me they simply wouldn't want to live without it; I agree.

NOTE Incidentally, HammerTap offers many more tools besides Deep Analysis. It also offers cool tools to help you better investigate other eBay sellers, bidders, and more.

But what about other sales venues on the Web? Is eBay the end-all for your sales analysis? No. Be sure to expand your data mining to the various retail venues (such as at Yahoo!, Amazon, and others) and search those listings, too. Then perform a search engine query to comb the entire World Wide Web so that you can locate merchant sites run by folks just like you. Standing in the customer's shoes, ask yourself how well each destination you encounter motivates you to inquire further and possibly compels you to buy. Check carefully to determine if the site is being updated regularly or if it appears to have been overrun by virtual cobwebs. Don't be bashful about contacting the shop owner via e-mail to ask specific questions about his operation and his merchandise. Throughout this exercise, take notes of the elements of your various experiences and how they impact your desire (or declination) to buy; this is the sort of information that will help you determine how to best position and promote your own sales.

Don't Overlook the Past

Next, look carefully at eBay's completed listings, seeking out final selling prices as well as determining if prices are holding steady or are experiencing either upward or downward trends. Be particularly attentive to listings that seem to appear as "spikes" in the market (with a final price being either noticeably high or low); these are the listings to closely scrutinize as you seek to determine what contributed to the spike. (Was the item miscategorized, priced too high at the outset, poorly presented, or was it marketed brilliantly and thereby gained a high final-bid price?)

This sort of sales history data is a bit limited in that it's only available from eBay (and thereby HammerTap's Deep Analysis) for the past 30 days. Nonetheless, if offers a tremendous amount of "live" information that will serve you well if you study it closely.

Counter Culture

Another way to gauge the appeal of products and sales strategies is to quantify the public response by way of a counter. Recall the option to select a counter when I listed the single item back in Chapter 13, "Immediate Success with Your First Listing"; look for counters in the auctions you're reviewing to determine the popularity or attractiveness of an item up for sale. Although these auction counters don't necessarily indicate unique page views or site visits (one person can tally up multiple counter hits on repeat visits to a listing), they are a good indicator of whether the seller's style and strategy seem to be successful with potential customers. If the counter numbers are low, then something in the seller's methodology could be amiss.

Mine Your Own Business

While you're actively sifting through the items and actions of others around you, don't forget to carefully examine your own offerings as well, presuming you've already begun listing your own items. Keep close track of your sales history, determining which items sell best, when they seem to be in greatest demand, and which transactions encouraged a customer to make a return visit. By regularly watching others while monitoring your own results, you'll have the conclusive data that will help you successfully navigate the ever-changing online marketplace.

Item Titles: The Key Is in the Keywords

What's in a word? Well, when it comes to the titles of the items you offer at eBay, your eventual success often depends on how carefully you choose your words. If you haven't given much thought to this aspect of marketing your goods or you wonder if you're making optimum use of your item titles, consider these "keys" to keyword usage—why they're so important to your sales success and how to make every word count.

Hit Me

Your first order of duty is to ensure that your items can be found easily. Keywords serve as the virtual beacon that leads to your goods. When you're listing in the vast sea of offerings at eBay, you're immediately challenged to be seen among the tens of millions of other items up for bid. Many shoppers make near-exclusive use of the search tools to locate those goods they seek (who has the time or patience to painstakingly scroll through pages upon pages of listings, right?), and your effective use of keywords will better ensure that your items are represented in keyword hit lists.

Begin by including as many pertinent keywords that shoppers are likely to search for as you can. Knowing your commodity well helps you understand which words are typically searched for, in which combinations, and to what level of detail. As a rule, you'll want to include brand name, origin, year (or period), and manufacturer of the goods you're offering. Depending on what you sell, anticipate that color, size, and other such attributes might also be elemental information to include in your listing titles.

DID YOU KNOW? The online search performance analyzer, Overture, is one cool tool you shouldn't overlook. Essentially, it has a function that reports the most popular search terms for the previous month relating to any word you query. Enter "tiffany lamp," and Overture provides a listing of the most popular search terms and combinations used by Web surfers the world over. This translates directly into how eBay searchers might be sifting through the site for certain items. Find this invaluable tool at http://inventory.overture.com/d/searchinventory/suggestion.

Check Your Spelling

Here, more than anywhere else, is where spelling counts. Buyers and sellers continually lament lost sales and missed purchasing opportunities due to misspelled keywords. Be sure to spell correctly, especially when items like yours feature intentional spelling variations or are identified by words that are commonly misspelled. Many sellers go so far as to include common misspellings in their item titles to better ensure that their listings will be included in a greater number of search results. Buyers, too, search for these commonly misspelled words to ensure that desirable—albeit misspelled—goods don't get away. (The Overture tool can help you discover these grammatically incorrect goofs.)

Don't Get Cute

Don't waste valuable title space (you're limited to 45 characters at eBay) on words that do little to describe the item or properly identify it to the discriminating buyer. Words like "cute," "adorable," "desirable," and the like often do little to help attract let alone convince a buyer. Words like "rare," "hard to find," and so on are not only superfluous at times (especially when buyers are often already aware of the scarcity of an item), but they sometimes work to expose a seller's attempt to justify a higher price. Subjective words like "awesome," "unbelievable," and "must see" might seem to be enticing but usually just succeed in wasting space. Finally, visual come-ons like "L@@K" and its ilk are nothing short of obnoxious and should be avoided.

Abbreviated Angst

Again, it goes back to search functions and the kinds of words your buyers might be searching for. Abbreviations might make sense to you—and might even be recognized among purveyors of certain products—but they might cost you a sale if they fail to show up on keyword search hit lists. Unless the abbreviations you employ are commonly used by your buyers, it's best to avoid spontaneous contractions or concatenations whenever possible.

Writing the Perfect Item Description

With the need for good keyword usage understood, let's move on to the item description. You realize now how important good images are when buyers come poking through your listings, but don't overlook the importance of terrific descriptions that spell out all the vital details—those of your item and those of your business policy. Although many buyers have bemoaned the bad habits of lazy sellers—exhibited through ambiguous facts or littered with horrendous spelling and grammatical errors—here are the keys to presenting professional item descriptions that you'll want to master to put your items in the best possible light.

Get the Facts

The first order of business is to offer a full disclosure of your item. Although images reveal much, supportive text can confirm visual details and illuminate unseen minutiae. In brief, be sure that your descriptions include the following:

- All distinguishing and authenticating details
- Details of item completeness or lack thereof
- Any and all imperfections

■ Provenance of the item (where you got it, how long you've owned it, and so on)

These facts, accompanied by high-quality images (the topic of the next chapter), will paint the full picture that helps potential buyers determine the complete nature of the item as well as your knowledge and integrity in presenting it.

Moreover, as trite as it might seem, spelling and grammar do still count and can quickly alienate buyers when they struggle through sloppily crafted descriptions from apparently unskilled sellers. Use a computer-based spelling and grammar checker if you need, and dig out the dictionary when your electronic resources come up short. Although it can be a tough pill to swallow, your skills in the written language will have a direct reflection on you and your business.

The Hook That Helps

When writing your descriptions, go ahead and add a certain amount of "sales appeal" to your listing. Although you'll want to get to the point when presenting the facts, there's still enough room for a bit of pitch that could entice a sale. A good sales "hook," then, might incorporate the following:

■ A bit of nostalgic language or phraseology that's suited to the item's time period

■ A link to a current trend such as the revived interest in items like yours

■ A bit of humor that might invoke the sort of fun or whimsy that your item represents

■ Historical events or styles that account for the manner in which your item was designed or manufactured

You don't want to distract or annoy your buyers with excessive promotion or hard-sell verbiage, but recognize that the persuasive power of a good sales hook might be just the nudge to encourage a shopper to become convinced that your item is the one he simply must have.

Things to Avoid

As you gear up to get descriptive, here are few things you'll want to avoid as you craft your item descriptions:

- Verbal stinginess as found in maddeningly brief one-liners like "Item as pictured"

- Intentionally ambiguous language that side-steps or otherwise hides pertinent details

- Too much subjective language ("This is the best you'll find for sale anywhere" and "you'll probably not see another one in a long time") that often incites buyers to shop around

- Criticisms of other sellers' goods or derision of the seller's themselves; that's always in bad taste and always a bad idea

If ever you doubted the importance of good item descriptions, hopefully you'll recognize their key effect on your sales success as well as their impact on how well you are perceived. If you'll take a bit of time to carefully consider how you'll describe your items, you'll likely be serving up perfect descriptions every time.

Timing Your Auctions

Then there's the other old saying that proclaims "Timing is everything." Although that might be an overstatement when it comes to online auctioning, savvy sellers have found that strategic timing—in terms of when and how long an auction will run—can have a significant impact on their ultimate success. This topic then begs these questions: What is the best day of the week to list or end an auction? How long should an auction run? Is there a magical hour for ending an auction? If these are your questions, here are your answers.

The Long and the Short of It

Before listing, you'll need to calculate which day you want your auction to end (this, in turn, dictates your auction's starting day). At eBay, you can choose from several auction length alternatives, ranging from three to ten days.

 ALERT A quick word of caution: If an auction is too long (such as the 10-day epoch), it might be forgotten during its lengthy duration, whereas if it's too short (as in the 3- or 5-day quickie), it might not get noticed by the critical masses before it disappears.

In general, it's best to let auctions run for a 7-day stretch. Granted, this can be a long wait for sellers who are anxious to close a deal, and it seems increasingly evident that many buyers are also in more of a hurry these days; however, by enabling an auction to encompass a full seven days, you'll potentially reach people who browse the Internet and eBay only on certain days of the week. (Believe it or not, some folks still have limited access to a computer.) Most importantly, the 7-day listing will span both weekend days, when auction traffic is generally higher.

What a Difference a Day Makes

Although opinions vary, Sunday is still considered to be the best day to end an auction (and Saturday runs a close second). Start and end your auction on a Sunday, and you'll tap a full week and weekend's worth of exposure. Again, Saturdays and Sundays tend to bring out bidders, accommodating those who don't enjoy the luxury of surfing the auctions at their workplaces.

So, are there bad days to end an auction? Well, Fridays can be challenging because your listings won't benefit from the weekend surge. And folks who sneak off for early weekends might be away from their computers on Fridays and Saturdays. By ending an auction on a Sunday, though, you can still entertain those folks who've been away for most of the weekend yet are ready to go online upon returning home Sunday afternoon or evening.

How about those holidays? Most sellers agree that it's best to avoid ending auctions on a holiday (especially holiday weekends). Because many folks elect to travel or become otherwise occupied by festivities, the traffic at auction sites is typically light.

Rush Hour

Perhaps the most crucial consideration in timing strategy, though, is determining the hour your auction will ultimately end. By and large, the best time to end an auction (as dictated by the hour you start it) is during the early evening hours when potential bidders are better able to browse for extended periods of time, having better chance to notice your new listings, not to mention allowing them to be "in attendance" to bid during your auction's final minutes. Be sure to consider time zones in all this, allowing West Coast citizens enough time to get home from work without making East Coast citizens stay up all night (Hint: Ending an auction between 6 P.M. and 9 P.M. Pacific Time is the safest bet.)

 NOTE But what about our global friends, those across the pond and around the world? Well, that's the difficulty of applying timing considerations to your listings. Typically, sellers only consider their own geographic locations when timing options but, if you determine that the items you sell have a strong appeal to overseas bidders, by all means adjust the auction clock to best suit their diurnal schedules.

Enticing Pricing: Strategies That Work

No doubt about it, competition among auction sellers is stiff, but don't throw up your hands in exasperation, believing the only way to lure bidders is by offering your great stuff at giveaway prices. Truth is, high bids and healthy profits are still within reach provided that you're using sensible pricing strategies. Here are some of those strategies.

Know Thy Stuff; Know Thy Market

The preamble to proper pricing is understanding how your goods will measure up in the competitive auction marketplace. Therefore, consider these tenets of smart pricing: supply and demand, condition and completeness of your goods, your investment value in your goods, and your realistic sales goals. Research current and closed auctions to ensure that your pricing strategies will complement, not contradict, current trends in auction sales.

You'll find this to be the critical information to determine if what you want to sell is what the bidders want to buy—and at what price.

How Low Will You Go?

Naturally, bidders are looking for a bargain—it's the key draw of the auction experience. Your task, then, is to hook bidders with an opening bid that's well below current market value and practically screams "Take me home, cheap!" If you've done your sales research well, you'll find that you can attract those hopeful bargain hunters yet still wind up achieving market value (and sometimes beyond) in the dynamic marketplace.

And don't forget that half the fun of online auctions is the gamesmanship of back-and-forth bidding. Low opening bids effectively start the ball rolling. After a bidding volley ensues, thwarted bidders often return to reclaim the item they've likely taken "emotional possession" of; they'll frequently fight it out to bring home the win, often in disregard that market value has already been eclipsed.

Is Higher Better?

Some sellers avoid using the garage-sale price tactics of low minimum bids, yet find high success in obtaining high bids. Sometimes, higher-quality or highly desirable goods might be ill-represented by a low opening bid, one that conjures thoughts of "At that low a price, there must be something wrong." Higher opening bids, then, work well to effectively communicate that your item is the real deal: It caters to the truly discriminating buyers (especially those who search specifically for higher priced offerings) and showcases your knowledge and confidence in the fine goods you're offering.

However, keep that starting price well below market value; don't stall the bidding with too high of a price. Try establishing an opening bid price that falls between 50 and 75 percent of current market value. Bidders will see that you know your item's value but aren't opposed to encouraging their competitive bidding to set the final price. Savvy buyers rarely let a desirable item sell cheap.

Reserve Your Right

There's nothing wrong with a little protection, and if you're unsure that you'll recover your investment or get a reasonable price for an item, slap a reserve on it. Although certain bidders are put off at the mere sight of a reserve price auction, sometimes it's your best bet to prevent taking a significant loss. Use reserves wisely, though; don't get greedy or drop a reserve on every auction lest you gain a reputation of being a high-priced seller who has little knowledge or faith in the bidding market.

To wrap up this discussion, I encourage you to experiment with different price strategies, learning from how well some methods work for you and how some don't. Review the activity of those sellers and items around you to keep your goods persuasively priced at all times.

The Art of Product Rotation

Whether due to seasonal appeal, a sudden and unexpected peak in interest, or a premeditated hype intended to drive a new trend, items you'll consider selling will likely have a "best time" to be put in front of the community of bidders. To understand the ebbs and flows of product popularity and to shift attention to the various items in your inventory when the time is just right is what could be referred to as the art of product rotation. Although some sellers prefer to spill out every item in their inventory in one fell swoop, others have found that careful flow and selective positioning of their wares is a better way to attract buyers at peak periods and keep them returning to bid time and again, eager to see what might show up next in your auction offerings.

'Tis the Season

Naturally, seasonal items need to be given prominent prioritization in your listing duties, usually to appear just prior to their annual peak period. The same goes for trendy items or those goods that are "all the rage" at the moment. If you have goods that herald an approaching holiday or are affiliated with the current public frenzy, get 'em up for bid, fast.

Don't Be Afraid to Get Cheap

As you go along in your selling ventures, when you come to anticipate certain times of the year when your top-dollar items tend to languish a bit, consider increasing your offering of lower-priced goods. Although it's natural that folks will shy away from big purchases at certain times of year, they're generally always in the mood to purchase something, right? Be sure to bring forth your low- to mid-priced wares so that there's still temptation for bidders to find something affordable they would like to take home. (Remember that bidders can get caught up in bidding on something, anything, if the price seems compelling enough.)

Matchmaker, Matchmaker . . .

Sometimes, a lone item seems to never find a buyer. However, marry that overlooked piece with a complementary element, and you could find the fast path to a quicker sale. If that set of attractive napkin rings seems destined to house a family of dust bunnies, try offering a nice set of dinner napkins alongside them (within the same listing) to give those rejected rings more immediate purpose, function, and appeal. Whatever it is that's gathering cobwebs on your shelves, try to rotate complementary items along with the wallflowers and see if you can catch the eye of a bidder hoping to bring home a perfect match.

Getting a Win from a Loss

You've likely heard the term "loss leader." One good hook that reels customers in is the offering of decent items at fire sale prices. Establish and flow listings that appear at marked down prices (try to offer more than just a scant couple of items) and where shrewd buyers will coagulate to comb through the great deals. Then, after the buyers have ventured into your listings to claim a bargain, be sure to encourage them to review your other active listings that might also appeal to their tastes.

Position, and Then Reposition

Building on that last point, if some goods still seem to elude your customers' desires, that "virtual sales table" you might set up could do more than just hook the virtual passers-by. Sometimes applying the label "sale" to an item is enough to generate interest in an item yet without the need to drastically slash prices. (Make sure you don't sacrifice crucial keywords, though.) And, to that end, you might consider procuring and rotating items for the sole purpose of keeping such an offering of bargain listings available at all times. Again, the lure of the good deals is often enough to get customers into your own corner of eBay where they can peruse the rest of the listings after they've found you.

Learn a Lesson from Your Customers

Finally, your customers determine the key barometer of your overall product placement prowess. Although some sellers get caught up into thinking they know how to best market their goods, the truth is that actual sales serve as the irrefutable report card. Monitor your patrons, be attentive to their wants and needs (via e-mail questions they might ask before, during, or after a sale), and be ready to shift your featured inventory at a click of the mouse when you see what's really hot—and what's really not—in your auction offerings.

chapter 15

Photo Shop: Images Made Easy

In the early days of eBay, finding an actual image to accompany an item up for auction was a real treat; today, it's an absolute necessity. To attract more bidders and earn higher prices, you need to serve up quality images every time. Bidders aren't as prone to take risks on poorly presented items and, with the amount of items to choose from at eBay every day, bidders won't settle for items sporting low-quality pictures. In this chapter, you'll learn how to take better pictures and how to avoid having your auctions summarily dismissed for an apparent half-hearted attempt. Even if you're not a professional photographer, taking good photos is easier than you might expect, and the bids those photos will attract is well worth the extra effort.

Imaging Equipment

First things first: Good images are the product of good equipment. Before you concern yourself with *how* to take better photos, focus on how well-equipped you are for the task.

Digital Cameras

Digital cameras are definitely the tool of choice these days, thanks to their portability and versatility. When shopping for a digital camera, pay close attention to these features that contribute to better images:

- **Image resolution.** This is the most important factor in determining which camera you should purchase and how much you can expect to pay. Low-priced VGA cameras (offering only 640-by-480 pixels) are inexpensive but won't give the detail and clarity your bidders are looking for. Instead, aim for at least a 2.1-megapixel (1600 by 1200 pixels) model. Although it's true that a higher pixel count results in a sharper and truer image, you'll also find a commensurate increase in camera price as well as image size by means of consuming megabytes on your computer and photo image hosting service.

- **Lenses and focus mechanics.** Look for a camera that offers both auto and manual focusing, with a real bonus being zoom capability for illuminating tiny details with crystal clarity.

- **Ease-of-use.** The simpler, the better. Fighting and fumbling with a camera is not only frustrating but also usually results in less-than-stellar images.

- **Tripod mount.** Most cameras have these by default, but be sure. Mounting your camera on a tripod reduces blur caused by a shaky hand.

Digital cameras have gotten significantly less expensive than when they first appeared on the scene, yet a good camera will still cost between $150 and $300; that's still a bit pricey, but it's well worth the investment due to the camera's versatile nature.

DID YOU KNOW? Although the topic will be covered fully in Chapter 21, "On Becoming a Business," understand that some of the equipment purchases you make to support an eBay business might qualify as tax write-offs. If you'll be serious about conducting a "business for profit," the equipment and other necessities that support that profitable venture are often expenses that can be deducted from your annual taxable income. Perhaps that helps take some of the sting out of purchasing some of the imaging equipment discussed in this chapter.

Of course, camera prices vary depending on the extras you might desire as well as the camera's method of image storage and retrieval (internal memory sticks or 3.5" floppy disc storage). Try several different models before you decide to purchase.

Scanners

Digital scanners are generally the second-best choice for auction images unless you deal strictly with flat items (such as prints, photos, and the like), where the scanner actually becomes the preferred imaging equipment for its ability to deliver even sharper detail than a camera. Scanners are becoming better and better, while their prices keep dropping lower and lower. As with cameras, look for image resolution as your guide to which models will deliver the best results. (1200 × 2400 dpi is the lowest "dot-per-inch" resolution you should settle for today.) The bonus of scanners is that they serve multiple uses. Many scan direct from 35mm slides or negatives, allowing you to easily digitize pictures from last year's Disneyland trip when you're not listing auction items. As for prices, scanners are a great value with the mid-range models priced at about $100 to $175.

Traditional Cameras

And don't forget conventional 35mm cameras. Although they lack the convenience of photographing direct to a digital source, many film processors (online and off) can now develop your pictures direct to downloadable online files or to an easy-to-use CD-ROM. If you've photographed several auction items using a 35mm film camera, it's easy to convert those to digital images that are ready for auction use.

Setting Up a Simple Photo Studio

With a camera in hand, it's time to take a picture of the treasure you'll offer up for bid. Don't just plop an item on your desk or drop it on the garage floor, though, and start snapping photos—you'll likely end up doing the item a disservice by introducing background elements that will detract from the item's overall appearance, not to mention expose it to all manner of dirt or damage. Rather, find a spot in your home or apartment (or wherever else you'll be working) to create your own designated photo studio. Here's how cheap and easy it can be to create a simple shooting stage that renders surprisingly superlative results.

Setting the Stage

You don't have to commandeer the spare bedroom or begin renovating the garage to establish your private atelier. All you really need is a few feet of dedicated working space. A photo studio begins with a stage. Many folks begin with a chair over which fabric can be draped (for a seamless background—more on that in a moment) and the item safely situated. I've been successful with one or two parson's tables (the inexpensive kind you find in the bed and bath stores), which I use individually or situated side by side for a larger working surface. If you'll be photographing even larger items, get a piece of ½" plywood that can straddle the two tables or saw horses; it doesn't have to be fancy to be effective—just stable and sturdy. The best news about using these parson's tables, I've found, is that their little legs unscrew and the whole arrangement can be stored easily in a closet or under a bed.

Background Check

With your studio "stage" in place, you now need to establish a background that will best complement your items and provide a more professional appearance. The key to obtaining better photos is to establish a *seamless backdrop*. According to Hollywood sculptor and photographer Nelson Broskey, the trick is to photograph your items much the same way that curvaceous supermodels are photographed: utilizing a backdrop that complements, not upstages, the intended subject of the camera's eye and doesn't introduce lines or creases or anything else that would detract from the main subject. However, you needn't bother with the expensive scrims the professionals use, counsels Broskey; rather, be inventive to get the same results on a shoestring budget (only *you* know for sure).

Depending on the size of your item, a simple cardboard box could be all that's needed to host your backdrop. An oversized sheet of nonglossy construction paper can be used as a neutral base and backdrop color, curving upward without creasing (see Figure 15-1).

You probably have an old cardboard box laying about that you can quickly cannibalize for this purpose. If you're shy on the construction paper, visit your local craft or stationery store where you can find an oversized sheet for less than a dollar.

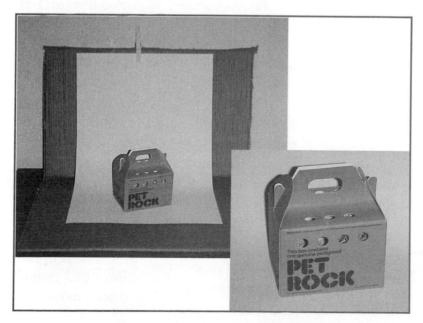

figure 15-1

A cardboard box and sheet of construction paper makes for the least expensive yet highly effective backdrop solution.

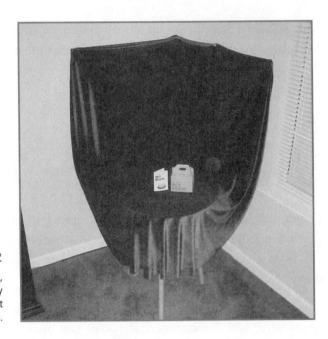

figure 15-2

An inexpensive parson's table, some dark velvet, and an empty corner make for a stellar but simple photo studio.

For a somewhat nicer yet still highly affordable alternative, purchase or otherwise locate a length of inexpensive material of a solid color (with off-white, black, or dark blue offering the best contrast results; no flowered bed sheets, please). Tack the material to a wall or in a corner to form a backdrop, then drape it over your work surface (see Figure 15-2). You now have a consistent background color that will show off the item without showing it up.

Light Source

A key consideration to any photography is lighting. Although it's not terribly difficult to establish good lighting, it's almost certain death for an image (and an auction) if the lighting is terrible. Here are a few of the best-used lighting tricks the professionals employ to get the highest-quality images on an amateur budget:

- **Go natural.** Photos that are taken in natural sunlight usually bring the best results as far as illumination of detail and truer color. If the sun is shining, photograph outdoors.

- **If it must be artificial.** Use incandescent bulbs (of no higher wattage than 60W) for best results. Higher wattage bulbs tend to oversaturate the item with light, giving it a washed-out look. Also, stay away from fluorescent lighting; it casts a yellow-green tint on your images and usually misrepresents the coloring of the item.

- **Control the light.** Aim the light where you need it to get the best results. If you're outdoors, use a reflector (something as simple as stark white poster board or a Mylar auto sunshade) to direct sunlight at your item. If you're using artificial lighting, purchase three automobile work lights (the inexpensive clamp-on sort) and suspend them above and on either side of the item (again, being careful not to blast too high a wattage at your item).

As simple as that, you have a professional-quality photo studio at a cut-rate cost. Experiment with the different elements and with your camera's settings until you have the perfect balance to gain consistently superlative results.

Touching Up Your Item Images

Although you're now equipped to properly light, accentuate, and photograph your items, it still might be necessary to do a bit of post-photography touch-up. Whether you need to crop, color correct, or just sharpen some fuzzy edges, here are some tips to help you decide when and how to polish up your pictures.

When Are Touch-Ups Necessary?

Try as you might, the images you shoot sometimes need just a bit of minor tweaking to properly represent your items. These should be minor adjustments, though, not wholesale reworking. If the image you're working with seems to require significant modification, you're better off photographing the item a second time. However, barring a complete restart, here are the sorts of attributes of an image that can be adjusted easily without scrapping the whole shoot:

- Images that are excessively bright, overly dark, or oversaturated with color

■ Images that do not properly represent the actual appearance of the item (usually related to coloring and brightness)

■ Images that include unnecessary or distracting background elements that should be cropped out

■ Images that are simply too large and should be resized prior to utilizing in an auction

ALERT Beware! If your image editing results in the concealment of blemishes or defects, stop immediately. You'll want to steer clear of those fabled "touched-up photos" that mask the item's true appearance, serving only to mislead bidders into believing they'll be receiving something significantly different from what you really have to offer. This is not to say that altering item images is an exercise in deception. However, many sellers have unintentionally misrepresented their items in their honest effort to provide customers with a clearer and more colorful picture. To avoid this accidental occurrence, always compare your final image to the actual piece and ask yourself if the image looks *better* than the item itself; if it does, you've edited too much.

Picture *Im*-Perfect: Eight Common Imaging Mistakes to Avoid

Although there's no denying that quality images will boost bidding rates and potentially increase your sales prices, it's equally true that poor photos can quickly undercut your best efforts, alienating and even angering potential bidders. Despite your efforts to create a fabulous photo studio and to have harnessed the best lighting to take the potentially greatest pictures with your nifty digital camera, there is still potential for trouble. To help you learn from the mistakes of others (namely, *me*), here are the eight most common blunders that tend to afflict sellers' item images, those of which you'll want to avoid at all times:

■ **Poor lighting.** This is usually the number one image offense. If the lighting is dim, the image detail can be grossly underrepresented.

Equally, an item that is too brightly lit will result in a severely overexposed image. Refer to the lighting tips to ensure that you'll avoid this malady.

■ **Blurry images.** Okay —tied for first place are fuzzy images, which are truly annoying to buyers and which reflect a lack of attention on the seller's part. Always check the focus before you shoot and, if you have a jittery hand, use a tripod for a true "still-life" image.

 N0TE When you have a three-dimensional object to photograph, you'll need to make up your mind about which part of the item you'll want to show in sharp focus. In this case, multiple images are typically your best bet.

■ **Excessive glare.** A close cousin to poor lighting, excessive glare can be the result of an overlit item yet is usually caused by improper flash usage. Shoot items from an angle (left, right, over, or under) or wait until you can photograph outdoors. If you're photographing shiny items (shrinkwrapped, chrome, and so on), try tilting the item forward a bit to deflect the lighting or the camera's flash to avoid *hot spots*, those blinding orbs of light that obscure the item's surface.

■ **Lack of cropping.** Few bidders are interested in scouring an image of your messy desk in search of the item you purport to be selling. Crop your images to cut out anything that distracts from the item—that includes the kids or the kitten, no matter how cute they might be. And, if you're photographing downward at an item on the floor, please crop out your toes (sheesh!).

■ **Reflective surfaces.** There's an infamous image that has made the rounds on the Internet of a chrome tea kettle reflecting a full view of its immodest proprietor (an *au naturel* shutterbug, if you know what I mean). If you've seen this picture, then you know why you need to take care when photographing reflective items that might reveal distracting or even embarrassing elements opposite them. Much like avoiding hot spots, shoot reflective items at an angle and across from a neutral background.

- **Bad backgrounds.** Forgo the overly fancy backdrops or the garish colors—they only distract from your item. As already mentioned, choose neutral or complementary colors to really make your item stand out.

- **Confounding combo-shots.** Some sellers think it's a good idea to photograph multiple items in a single image; they should think again. Other items that are adjacent to the one you're selling distract the potential buyer away from what you're really offering for sale.

- **Lack of close-up.** Ever looked at images of jewelry or small collectibles where the item is too tiny to clearly discern? Avoid this frustration by getting closer to the item (watch the focus) or by taking full advantage of your camera's zoom function.

Image-Editing Tools

Despite your best efforts, sometimes an image just doesn't turn out. Although you might simply reshoot, you might also be able to easily amend the image with some simple computer wizardry. Photo-editing software allows you to enhance your images quickly and easily and comes in a wide variety of prices and accompanying features. If you want the Cadillac of applications, look no further than Adobe *Photoshop*. It's the application that the pros use yet commands a professional's price of around $600. If a more economically priced application will suit you, look at Jasc Software's *Paint Shop Pro*, Microsoft's *Picture-It*, or MGI's *PhotoSuite*—each is generally available for $100 or less and can deliver the fundamental photo-editing features you'll need. The truly frugal among of us have found many *shareware* and *freeware* versions of these applications and others ready to be downloaded from the Internet right to your computer.

DID YOU KNOW? In case they're new terms to you, *shareware* and *freeware* are functional programs or applications that are free—that's right, free—for you to download from the Internet and onto your PC. By definition, shareware programs are of the sort you can download and try for free to decide whether you like it or not. For a nominal fee, you can then download the full-featured version to use (the shareware version of the program usually is missing some features of the fee-based version). Freeware is free to use and typically has all features that the programmer intended to provide. To find out more about shareware and freeware, as well as to find a ton of programs you can try or have free of cost, visit http://www.tucows.com; it's the preferred download destination on the Web that features safe (virus-free) applications that are easy to transfer to your PC. Now, if you're still wanting the full-powered features of a costly application like Photoshop, check into *The Gimp*; it boasts about 90 percent of the editing features as Photoshop but is free (yes, free) at http://www.gimp.org.

Although these free products might have a limited use period or are equally limited in their capabilities, free downloads are a great way to test-drive an application before you invest in it. And don't overlook decent image editors that might have actually come preloaded on your computer or on a CD-ROM accompanying the digital camera you purchased.

Fine-Tuning the Fine Details

So what exactly can you hope to correct if your image doesn't represent your item just right? Using one of the image editors previously mentioned, here are the most common image enhancements you can make with just a few clicks and drags of your computer's mouse:

- **Brightness and contrast.** If your image is too dark, washed out, or rather murky, work with the brightness and contrast controls to draw out details and brighten the color tones.

- **Color saturation/hue.** If the lighting you used cast an odd tint on your item's natural coloring, this control allows you to independently adjust the red, green, and blue levels. With only minor adjustments, you can deliver the actual coloring of your item that was otherwise misrepresented in your unretouched photo.

■ **Sharpen/edge enhance/smooth.** After making other adjustments, you might find that you need to add crispness to your image or, conversely, soften what might have emerged as harsh edges. Using these controls, you can bring out blurred detail or smooth out jagged edges. Be careful, though; this adjustment can often result in giving your image that dreaded "touched-up" look.

Too Big for Your Bidders?

Finally, don't overlook the importance of being equally attentive to the size of your photos. Online shoppers can be an impatient lot, and few are inclined to wait around while a "fat" image creeps onto their computer display. Rather than risk losing a sale, be sure your images load quickly by keeping the image file sizes at or near the 30KB mark. Start with your camera: Work image adjustments down from ultra-fine to medium quality (which still renders a nice photo).

You can also use image-editing applications to resize larger images (but watch out for image degradation). In addition, you can find image compression software (programs that essentially squeeze large files down to a manageable size without forsaking picture quality) like WinSoftMagic's Advanced JPEG Compressor that can get those files down to size and speedier to display. Of course, if you elect to utilize eBay's iPix feature, it will do the crunching for you, although the results are often less spectacular than if you had managed the compression yourself.

chapter 16

Easy Money: Hassle-Free Payment Collection

Let's not beat around the bush: All this auctioning is about money. As a seller, the great prices you earn in your auction exploits are only as fruitful as your ability to quickly and cleanly *collect* the cash you've been promised. Although you've likely considered conventional payment vehicles—money orders, cashier's checks, personal checks, and cash—dealing in the online realm provides you with the ability and efficiency to collect more quickly thanks to the next step in e-commerce: online payment. In this chapter, you'll learn what online payment is, where and how it's managed, and how it can help you gain even higher prices to help you close the deal, hassle free. Moreover, as a buyer, you'll learn about the ease and safety by which you can pay for your goods. For both buyers and sellers, online payment is just what the online auction ordered.

The Fear Factor: Is Online Payment Safe?

If registering at eBay gave you reason to pause, uncertain whether it would be safe to provide such sensitive credit card and bank account information online, then the consideration of sending and receiving actual funds through cyberspace and surrendering personal finance account information might send you into fits. However, take comfort in the fact that online payment services, the budding and sometimes bumbling cottage industry of a few years ago, has quickly evolved into a secure and increasingly preferred method for managing payment transactions. The payment sites have implemented additional customer safeguards and protections against unauthorized or otherwise illicit account tampering. And each site provides different levels of protection to put your mind at ease.

Likewise, your financial institution probably has also evolved in matters of online payment and has responded to your needs (and anxieties) for managing account-funded cyber-purchases. Most credit card issuers and personal bank account managers offer protections to their customers should something go amiss in an online transaction. Here again, check with your issuer and other financial institution to be clear about their safeguards and your responsibilities as an account owner.

ALERT Is that a credit card or a debit card? Many point-of-sale cards sport recognizable Visa and MasterCard logos yet are not credit cards at all: They're tapping your finite checking account funds as we speak. Be especially clear of the protections your issuer might (or might not) offer if you choose to use a debit card to make your online purchases and what recourse you might have, if any, should something go amiss.

The bottom line is that millions of online transactions are completed every day, the vast majority being completed as easily as those at your local department store. It's your duty, though, to ensure that you understand the payment site's protections as well as your card issuer's terms to guarantee that you're covered in case your card information is ever compromised.

The How's and Why's of Online Payment

Experienced bidders and other online buyers have embraced online payment as the fastest and arguably easiest method to quickly pay for a variety of goods, at eBay and elsewhere online. As easy as sending an e-mail message, online payments can be made in a few simple steps:

■ The buyer establishes an account with an online payment provider.

- The seller, also with an active online payment account, indicates the user ID to which payment is to be forwarded (separate from an eBay user ID).

- The buyer posts the agreed-upon payment amount and is provided verification of the seller's account that will receive funds.

- Payment is posted to the seller's account, deducted from the buyer's account, and a notification of the transaction is provided via e-mail to both parties.

Thanks to online payment services, an auction transaction can be completed in a matter of minutes, with many buyers and sellers indicating they've been able to close the post-auction deal in less than 30 minutes' time. (It's true; I do it all the time.)

But is time of such importance in completing an online transaction? Can't the sending of a traditional *snail mail* payment still suffice? Actually, traditional payment methods, as previously mentioned, are just as viable today has ever. Nevertheless, going hand in hand with the speed of the Internet and the access to vast goods and services at the click of a mouse, fast online payment simply makes sense and offers a truly integrated approach to selecting, purchasing, and paying for goods, all made possible from the same computer.

DID YOU KNOW? Yes, faster sometimes *is* better. When dealing online, a speedy transaction is usually the best. The seller is able to quickly receive payment, thus developing trust in the buyer, via online payment. The buyer is likewise able to receive goods more quickly, thereby gaining confidence in the seller and the entire online bidding and buying experience. Both parties, who might be online concurrently when the auction closes, are able to complete the transaction quickly, which spells success for all involved.

Most compelling, though, is that the use of most online payment services enables buyers and sellers to transact via credit card. (This is *really* important, sellers, so listen up.) Without the cost and complexity of establishing a traditional merchant account, sellers can advertise acceptance of credit card purchase via an online payment venue. Likewise, buyers can manage their purchases via use of a credit card, no longer limited to funds in their checking or saving accounts alone. This really boils down to earnings potential. Sellers can proudly state that they accept payment via major credit cards without having to pay for a bona-fide merchant account. Buyers, statistics show, will far and away spend more money if they can float the purchase on their credit cards (while enjoying a higher level of purchasing power and being able to take advantage of terrific auction offerings they otherwise might be forced to bypass). For both parties, then, online payment serves as another convenient and lucrative option in buying and selling via online business transactions.

Who's Who in Online Payment Services

Where do you go when you want to sign up to utilize online payment? Actually, there are a number of sites and services available online today but, to free you from hours of analysis and cross-comparison, here are the major players I've used in the past and which seem to have gained the trust of the majority of buyers and sellers.

PayPal (http://www.paypal.com)

By and large, PayPal.com (see Figure 16-1) is the biggest player in the online payment arena. Like eBay, PayPal had arrived on the scene early (in October 1999, then known as X.com) and gained fast brand and service recognition. Many other sites have come and gone, but PayPal has stood fast. The site, boasting a registered user base of more than 30 million worldwide, was so successful it even supplanted eBay's former Billpoint payment site. In an about-face, eBay acquired PayPal for $1.5 billion in October 2002, making it a truly integrated tool in the eBay experience. PayPal is free for buyers and charges a sales commission to sellers (30 cents plus 2.2–2.9 percent of the total value per payment received), deducted from the amount of payment received. Account activation can be accomplished in a matter of minutes. Business and Premiere accounts are available to sellers, at a monthly fee, that give access to automated e-mail tools, an invoicing system, inventory management, and more. PayPal also enables transactions to 39 different

figure 16-1

PayPal, an eBay company, is still the front-runner in the online payment realm.

countries (no more fear and loathing over the mystery of dealing with foreign currencies) and allows payment for auction goods and nonauction-related goods and services.

BidPay (http://www.bidpay.com)

In a new twist on an old exchange, BidPay (see Figure 16-2) came along several years ago to allow buyers to purchase and forward actual money orders to sellers via an online site. Backed by Western Union, the long-recognized name in fund transfers, BidPay allows buyers to purchase money orders online using a credit or debit card (brick-and-mortar institutions typically accept only debit cards or cash). Sellers (recipients) need not be registered with BidPay to receive payment because the money order is printed and forwarded to the seller's snail mail address. The delay of awaiting receipt of the money order has been eradicated; sellers are notified via official e-mail when a money order purchase has been approved and is in transit, instilling confidence so that the item can be safely shipped prior to the actual money order being in hand.

DID YOU KNOW? Notice that using BidPay serves as a suitable compromise between the fast payment available via online payment methods without the need to offer credit card or bank account information as with PayPal. Although PayPal is genuinely secure for transactions, some buyers feel even more at ease dealing with longtime financial enabler Western Union.

International sales are also easily managed, as BidPay delivers to countries outside of the United States. As with traditional money orders, the buyer pays a fee for the service and can also elect to pay additional fees for quicker delivery to the seller.

But change is in the air for BidPay. Western Union has recently announced that it will be changing the service's name to *Western Union Auction Payments*. BidPay executives said that the new name will be phased in late 2003 to early 2004. In addition, in response to the nagging sentiment that Bid-Pay is too pricey to use when compared to the cost of traditional money

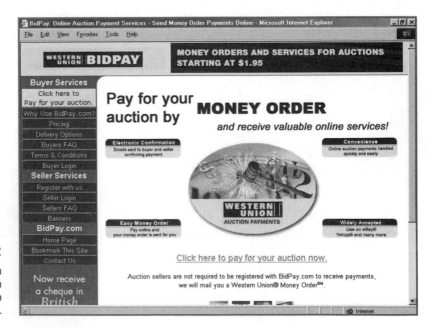

figure 16-2

BidPay, soon to become Western Union Auction Payments, offers an easy and secure way for sellers to collect money orders.

orders, BidPay has recently lowered its fees. With processing fees as low as $1.95, BidPay is still more expensive than money orders purchased at grocery or convenience stores. However, with the ability to purchase with a credit card and the ease of not having to deal with delays of snail mail delivery and confirmation, BidPay maintains itself as a competitive and convenient payment option.

Yahoo PayDirect (http://paydirect.yahoo.com)

As another of the suite of business and consumer tools offered by the online portal giant, Yahoo delivers PayDirect (see Figure 16-3) to support online payment activities. Unfortunately, the services fall dreadfully short of those offered by PayPal. PayDirect only supports transactions within the United States, charges a use fee to buyers and sellers, and delays account activation until the registrar receives a snail mail confirmation.

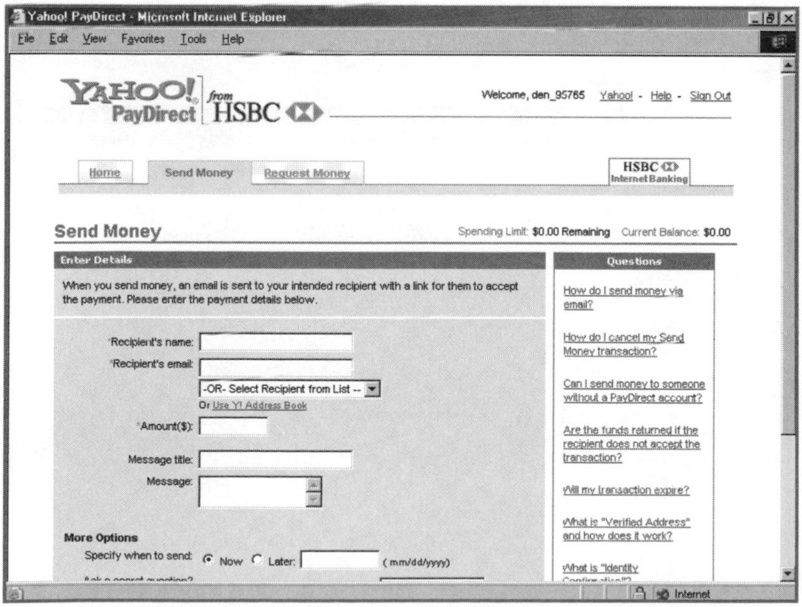

figure 16-3

Yahoo PayDirect is yet another low-cost, albeit limited, online payment alternative.

Escrow Services (http://www.escrow.com)

Another new service to spring forth from the evolution of online auctions and other forms of e-commerce is online escrow. Like a traditional escrow account, online escrow accounts serve to confirm and hold a buyer's payment, prompting a seller to send the item purchased. The buyer, upon receipt of the item, confirms delivery and satisfaction, thus prompting release of funds to the seller. If the buyer is dissatisfied, the funds in escrow are held until the seller confirms receipt of the returned item. If the buyer fails to confirm item receipt, funds are released to the seller within three days of the tracked delivery confirmation (per the package carrier's records). Escrow is typically expensive because it's generally used for high-value purchases (greater than $500). Buyers and sellers can negotiate who will pay the escrow fees or can agree to split the cost. Escrow.com (see Figure 16-4) is recommended for use with eBay. The site also lists several other escrow sites for use outside the United States.

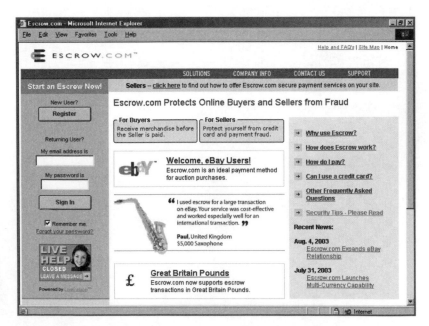

figure 16-4

Online escrow is a valuable service that helps ease the anxiety of high-value transactions.

Online Merchant Accounts

Although you might have your sights set initially on eBay activities alone, there might come the time when you endeavor to go beyond the auction space to further bolster your fortune-making opportunities. If you decide to create an online store or other such commercial Web site, you'll be glad to know that traditional merchant accounts are available online as well. Yes, I realize I risk self-contradiction, stating earlier that PayPal allows acceptance of credit card payments without the cost of creating a merchant account. The caveat, I'll now share, is that your buyers will *have to* establish a PayPal account of their own to pay you; some, believe it or not, are still resistant to registering many places online yet would gladly pay via credit card if able to do so directly. (Go figure.) Despite the cost of a merchant account (about $200 setup plus per-transaction fees, similar to PayPal), if you keep your business restricted to the virtual storefront, you needn't bother with a credit card terminal or clunky charge plate. Instead, online merchant accounts are usually accompanied with online "shopping cart" solutions, enabling shoppers to select items from your inventory, carry them in a virtual cart, and check out by paying via a credit or debit card. (This is a feature that makes the setup cost worth the price, believe me.) Again, this is probably a consideration to entertain a bit later down the road. (I'll discuss this further in Part 5, "Beyond eBay.") For now, just be aware that the option is available if and when you decide to expand your online horizons.

Why Bother with Online Payment?

The original question still persists: If checks and money orders are still suitable and acceptable, why bother with online payment? It's a good question that evokes several good answers. Consider these reasons why online payment is something you should embrace, especially when you're the seller:

- **It fits the bill.** In the early days of online auctions and cybershopping, it seemed clumsy to utilize the speed and convenience of online buying only to be relegated to the comparatively ancient process of actually *mailing* payment and waiting for checks to clear. Integration is what it's all about, and online payment fits seamlessly into this new way of doing business.

- **More options draw more customers.** As you'll learn in Chapter 17, "Managing Your Auctions: Sell More, Earn More, Work Less," when it comes time to create a sales policy, bidders and buyers crave options and alternatives. Specifically, the more choices you offer regarding terms of payment (especially the cutting edge of online payment), the better your ability to encourage more business to your online offerings. Buyers love choices.

- **Buyer profiling has concluded that consumers tend to spend more money when they can shop on credit.** Because online payment services enable you to accept credit card payment, you stand a greater chance of earning higher prices for your goods. The best part of all: Online payment services make the whole transaction transparent to you, ridding you of the cost and coordination of maintaining an actual merchant account of your own.

- **Online payment services are adaptable to your business.** Because they service all manner of transactions, at eBay or elsewhere, online payment can support all your business transactions no matter where or when you sell goods or services.

In a Hurry? Buy-It-Now with Pay-It-Now

Lastly, as I mentioned in Chapter 11, "Expert Bidding Strategies," about how the Buy-It-Now feature serves as an advantageous alternative for motivated buyers, here's a twist that likewise serves the seller. As the seller, you'll find a new eBay option that allows you to sell an item in the Buy-It-Now format *provided* that the buyer will agree to *Pay-It-Now*. Here's how it works.

When you're completing the Payment and Shipping portion of the item listing process (refer to Chapter 13, "Intermediate Success with Your First Listing," if you like), there is a text link that allows you to turn on the Immediate Payment Requirement (see Figure 16-5), summarily disabling and disallowing other payment methods.

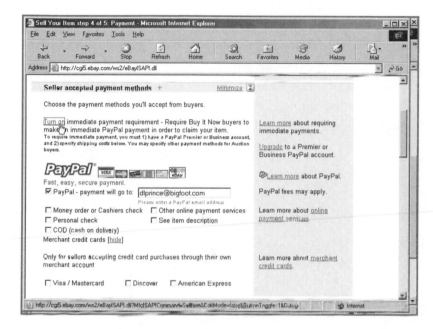

figure 16-5

It takes a sharp eye to spot the Pay-It-Now option on the eBay listing page.

Now, the only way a buyer can successfully purchase your item is to select the Buy-It-Now option and be able to complete the Pay-It-Now process via PayPal. The item will remain available until a buyer successfully posts a payment to your PayPal account; this, of course, requires that your buyer be a registered user of PayPal. As seller, you, too, have a few prerequisites to fulfill before being able to utilize Pay-It-Now:

- You must have an active PayPal Premier or Business account when you list your item.

- The Buy-It-Now price you specify cannot be greater than $2,000.

- You must specify complete shipping costs at the time you list.

- You must ship to a buyer's confirmed PayPal shipping address (unless you change your PayPal profile so that you'll also ship to unconfirmed addresses).

- You must maintain a positive record (feedback rating) on eBay at all times.

Although it might seem a bit draconian to force a potential buyer to pay exclusively through PayPal, it's another option you should consider nonetheless in attaining a level of effortless payment collection. Buyers have yet to fully speak out about their opinions of this option yet, with so many migrating to PayPal for the reasons previously stated in this chapter, this is definitely a good way to speed up the post-auction, post-sale transaction.

chapter 17

Managing Your Auctions: Sell More, Earn More, Work Less

Mo' money. Mo' money. Mo' money. You want it, and it's within your grasp if you're ready to reach for it. Don't expect that it will be easy, but *do* expect it to be completely plausible. By this point, you have most of your seller's tools in place, and you're ready to storm the auction place with your great offerings and savvy selling approach. That's good, but you also need to incorporate a few more elements to your seller's toolbox and then turn your attention toward how to get better results from your efforts. This chapter will round out your auction acumen and poise you to look toward efficiency to improve your selling results.

Establishing a Sane Sales Policy

At last—the moment of which you might have dreamed: *You're* in charge and *you* can make the rules. Free yourself from the anguish of working for someone else and having to toe the line of *their* directive. When you become an eBay seller, you become your own boss. (It's true.) But don't let that freedom cloud your better judgment; the rules you set down to serve your needs will also need to serve (and attract) your customers-to-be. Here are the key ingredients of a good sales policy along with some hints about how to make the stipulations of best use to you and your buyers.

Accepted Payment Methods

It starts with the money. Recall in Chapter 16, "Easy Money: Hassle-Free Payment Collection," that I mentioned how buyers like options, most often in the ways they can pay. Certainly, you would like to steer your customers in the direction of the quickest and most reliable methods to bring a sale to quick and clean closure. Accepting other methods of payment, however, will show you're interested in what makes the customer feel comfortable as well. Here's the quick rundown.

Online Payments

If it might seem I'm overly touting this one, it's because I am. Online payments have emerged to be the quickest and most convenient payment method for online purchases (at auctions and elsewhere) today. Credit the online auction as the impetus for the creation of online payment services such as those I mentioned in Chapter 16. Whereas just about everything else in eBay and the rest of cyberspace has been conducted in real time, at the click of a mouse, the method of paying for items by sending funds through the mail simply didn't follow suit. Eager auction winners (and the sellers who served them) wanted fast action and near-immediate gratification. Online payment has helped to compress the post-auction transaction cycle for both parties because funds can be received instantly and goods can be shipped immediately thereafter. Plus, don't forget that online payment allows credit card funding, and that typically results in higher bids for sellers.

Escrow

Although another form of online payment (thanks to sites like Escrow.com), escrow isn't invoked for routine transactions at eBay, those being of a modicum amount of money. If a purchase ventures into the realm of thousands of dollars or involves an item of significant importance that would require inspection prior to release of funds (as in cases of valuable art pieces or vehicles or such), escrow might be a good option to consider. The key to making escrow work, however, is to establish agreement on how the escrow fee (which can get pricey—into the hundreds of dollars in some cases) will be paid. Some sellers will pick up the tab, others will expect the buyer to do so, and still others will split the cost down the middle. Whatever approach you take in managing the escrow fee, make sure you and your buyer are in full agreement before proceeding.

Money Orders and Cashier's Checks

If your buyer wants to send payment through snail mail, that's fine. Encourage the use of money orders or cashier's checks in these cases because, upon receipt, they're as good as cash in your hand. Immediately, you can be confident in the payment and can ship the winner's goods to close a still relatively quick transaction.

Personal Checks

Despite the proliferation of ATMs and point-of-sale debit cards, personal checks have not yet gone the way of the vinyl record. Although I've seen a marked decrease in personal check use, some buyers still elect to pay with a personal check; therefore, you would be well served to accept these. The only stipulation here is to indicate that such checks must clear your bank prior to an item being shipped. This policy, of course, can be relaxed for your return customers in good standing; they'll appreciate your heightened display of trust.

Cash

It doesn't happen often, but sometimes a buyer will send good ol' greenback dollars. Most often, this is used to pay for low-cost items (in the $5–10 range) or as payment from an international customer. (Your local currency apparently is easier to acquire than international money orders.) I never encourage the use of cash for lack of traceability but, if I do receive cash, I ship the buyer's item fast, fast, fast.

Other Methods?

So what about bank transfers, wire transfers, and C.O.D. (which pretty much went the way of the 8-track tape and the "as seen on TV" Kitchen Magician)? Are these still viable methods of payment? Sure, payment can still be managed in any one of these ways but, with the options already offered, there's not much need or demand for these sorts of transactions.

Specifying the "When" of Payment

You've been conscientious in offering a variety of payment methods, but don't forget to likewise establish *when* you expect to receive the funds. Some buyers dally a bit or outright forget to pay unless they're prodded up front. There's nothing clever or mysterious about this condition: State that payment must be received within seven days from the close of the auction (or anywhere within four to ten days as reasonable). Unless you intend to offer some sort of layaway service, you have every right to expect payment quickly. Typically, this isn't an issue because the majority of buyers are eager to collect their winnings. Because prepayment is the *modus operandi* in online auctioning, the sooner the buyer pays, the sooner you can ship his item. Just provide the boundary for when you expect to be compensated or explain that the buyer's high-bidder status could rightfully be revoked and the item offered to the next-highest bidder or relisted for another go around.

Shipping and Handling

Then there's the cost of getting that item from Point A to Point B. You need to be clear up front on who will pay these costs but, if you're new to this, understand that the long-standing protocol has established that the buyer will pay such fees in addition to the actual item selling price. This, however, has sometimes been something of a lightning rod of heated debate as auction goers weigh in on exactly what is "reasonable" in such fees.

For starters, shipping and handling fees must be stated as an actual dollar amount and not a calculated fee as a percentage of the final selling price. (That's an eBay rule, folks.) That fee, however, is up to the seller's discretion and, for best results, should be clearly explained in your sales policy. Potential buyers will want to understand how much shipping charges will be so that they can calculate that into their potential purchase price; this often motivates a buyer to buy or fly.

So what's reasonable? Well, many sellers (myself included) prefer to set a fixed price up front based on the size, weight, and shipping method for the item upon sale. For instance, when I sell a DVD or videotape, I know that USPS Priority Mail charges will amount to $3.85 for destinations within the continental United States, and I can indicate that when I list such an item. (International postage will be extra, I explain, and will be calculated at the close of the auction.) In this approach, the shipping fee is based on the size and weight of the item and is often the most reasonable approach from the buyer's perspective. Other sellers pride themselves on advertising that they charge *exact* postage costs, which are calculated and specified at the end of the auction. Whichever approach suits you and is within reason, state as much.

 NOTE EBay offers a ready-made link to the UPS (United Parcel Service) rate calculator for inclusion in your listing. If you elect to utilize UPS, you can specify your ZIP code and specifics of the item to allow bidders to automatically calculate how much the charge will be to deliver the item to their address. Or, if you prefer to utilize USPS (United States Postal Service) as your carrier of choice, you can similarly add a link to your auction listing to direct potential buyers to the USPS rate calculator page. (It's at http://postcalc.usps.com.) Either way, help your potential buyers take a more interactive role in determining and understanding shipping charges.

Here again, buyers like choices, so consider offering a variety of shipping methods to suit your shoppers' needs (within reason). By far, I rely on the USPS method because it features static prices (until the next increase, that is) and quick service. Even so, I am amenable to offering other services besides my default Priority Mail delivery. Luckily, I can stay within the service structure of the USPS and offer lower-cost options of First-Class mail, Media Mail, or Book Rate if my buyers desire. Alternatively, I can offer expedited service via USPS Express Mail or international service via Air Mail or Global Priority. But you needn't settle on USPS; you might prefer UPS, which also offers varied delivery methods. In addition, the different carriers offer services such as package tracking, insurance, and delivery confirmation (often incurring additional nominal fees). Consider all these services and select those that will serve your customers' needs without twisting your efficient process all out of whack. Clearly state those service offerings in your sales policy.

DID YOU KNOW? In my opinion, USPS made notable improvements in their services during the UPS/Teamsters strike of 1997. Because UPS services were unavailable for the seemingly interminable 15-day walk-off, USPS jumped into high gear and re-established their "neither rain nor sleet" dependability with sellers like me, also allowing me to drop off packages at the in-store postal counter of my local grocery store. My customers have never been let down. (Repeat: *never.*)

Insurance and Tracking

I hinted at this in the previous section. For an additional fee (unless it's included in the carrier's standard fee), offer the option of insurance, tracking, and delivery confirmation to your buyers. Be clear to state whether you'll cover this cost yourself or, if not, if it will be a mandatory or optional service for your buyer. If the buyer elects to forgo additional costs of insurance and such, be clear about your liability and coverage in case of damage or loss. Although some disagree with me, I indicate that the buyer assumes full responsibility for damage or loss if such coverage is waived. (My packaging prowess, however, has helped me avoid any such troubles, knock on wood.)

 ALERT Okay, I lied just a bit. In some cases when I've sold a pricey, rare, or fragile item (sometimes all wrapped up in one) and the buyer has opted *not* to purchase insurance, I've graciously covered that expense out of my own pocket. Call me a bad businessman, but in these occasions, I've slept easier knowing the item was fully protected just in case the worst would occur. Thankfully, all items were delivered safely.

Guarantees, Refunds, and Exchanges

If the item isn't what the customer expected or that buyer simply isn't thrilled and overjoyed, you'll need to provide direction on what options are available in these cases, too. Your best bet is to be perfectly clear: You either support a "100-percent satisfaction guaranteed with no questions asked" policy or you don't. Actually, there is some middle-ground to be found when it comes to refunds, guarantees, and exchanges, but your first challenge is to decide whether you're willing to take back an item after it's been sold. If you're completely confident in your items and feel it best to offer total satisfaction (which includes absorbing the cost of buyer flubs and fibs), then proudly state that you'll honor all returns. However, you can be just as successful if you provide *conditional* refunds. You can state that if the item received is not as advertised, you'll gladly accept a return. It's okay to stipulate that all returns are subject to inspection and verification (recalling Scam #10 from Chapter 8, "E-Motions and Auction Affronts"). It's likewise your prerogative to state that all sales are final (which is especially applicable for the sale of items that are easily duplicated, such as music and video). You might need to experiment a bit with this portion of your policy, but it's most prudent to begin with the conditional return at the outset.

Summing It All Up

To wrap it all up, consider these examples of a sales policy you might include in your item descriptions:

> *High bidder will please prepay plus shipping costs (calculated at close of auction). Payment must be received within 10 days of auction close else transaction will be considered null and void. Payment by PayPal, money order, or cashier's check will gain immediate shipment of item upon payment receipt. Personal checks gladly accepted but will need to clear (approx. 10 days) before item can be shipped. All items shipped via USPS Priority Mail or ExpressMail. FedEx delivery is available upon request and for additional fee. Insurance and delivery confirmation are available at additional cost if not already covered in shipping method selected. If insurance*

is declined, buyer assumes responsibility for damage or loss. All items guaranteed to arrive as described with refunds cheerfully granted if item received is materially different than as listed. Items must be returned within 10 days of original delivery and are subject to inspection prior to issuance of refund. If there are any questions regarding these terms and conditions, please contact me via e-mail before bidding. Thank you for your interest in my auctions.

Or how about this . . .

High bidder to prepay plus $5.85 fixed shipping/insurance cost. Payment must be received within 10 days of auction close via PayPal, money order, cashier's check, or personal check (must clear). All items guaranteed to be as described and are offered on an "as is" basis with no warranties or refund privileges implied. If you have any questions, please contact me via e-mail before bidding. Thanks for your interest in my auctions.

Publishing Your Policy

With your policy ready to go, make sure to post it plainly for all bidders and future buyers to see. The easiest method of posting your policy is to include it in the body of your item descriptions. If, later, you decide you want to improve the visual appearance of your policy, consider utilizing HTML code in your item descriptions to offset the text, present it in a different (slightly smaller) font, or enable an offsite link to your own Web page. (See the discussion of simple HTML use later in this chapter.) However you decide to present the policy, be sure it's always available and easy to find. Go the extra step by encouraging potential customers to contact you directly *before* bidding if they have any questions, concerns, or doubts.

Review, Respond, and Revise

The final point about sales policies and a key to your ongoing success is to closely monitor how your policy is serving both you and your customers. There might be times when your edicts come under fire or are tested for reasonable flexibility. Here's where you'll need to listen and learn from your customers, determining which requests seem to make sense versus those which seem, well, ridiculous. (Some buyers will want the moon and stars, too.) Stay attuned to your customers' needs and be open to making revisions to your policy as the market continues to evolve and expand. Keep from being stodgy, and you'll keep yourself in a positive light with your current and future customers.

Establishing an End-of-Auction Routine

If you'll only be selling an item or two as the mood strikes you, there's not much to get excited about in the end-of-auction phase other than to make e-mail contact with the buyer, collect payment, and ship the item. By now, you've seen how that interaction will work with the listings you've probably already dabbled in. However, if you're looking to make any sort of significant income from auctioning (and I'm assuming that's your goal), you'll want to take the *busy-ness* out of your business to get more done in fewer steps.

When it comes to managing the end-of-auction phase, consider these tasks that you'll need to complete and the methods available to you in bringing the transaction to a successful fruition.

Buyer Notification and Invoicing

There was a time was managing multiple auctions (tens or hundreds of listings) became quite a chore when the auction ended and the seller (that's you) had to be anchored to his chair to send out numerous end-of-auction e-mail messages. This task alone was so time consuming to we early sellers that it sometimes challenged our resolve to stay in the business. Today, that's all changed.

EBay automatically issues end-of-auction notifications to high bidders and sellers, providing details of the item sold, the final bid, and contact information for the two parties. Better still, during the listing phase of offering an item, the seller is able to post details of payment method and shipping charges so, essentially, the end-of-auction notification can conceivably contain all the information the buyer needs to pay right away without further details from the seller. (Refer to the listing process described in Chapter 13, "Immediate Success with Your First Listing," and the discussion of online payment in Chapter 16.)

NOTE This is a real efficiency gain for you as the seller: The more information you can include at the time of listing, the less time you'll need to spend interacting on a customer-by-customer basis to answer questions such as, "How much is shipping?" or "Can you ship to my P.O. box?" By taking full use of the item listing specifications at the time you post items for auction, you can conceivably answer all these sorts of questions up front and, when the auction ends, the eBay notification to your buyer should be enough to allow him to pay immediately without further informational intervention required of you.

Besides the eBay end-of-auction notification, you might also elect to utilize the seller tools made available from PayPal. If you've established a PayPal account (and I hope you will), you can find a special feature called *Winning Buyer Notification* when you click on the tab labeled Auction Tools at the PayPal site (see Figure 17-1).

figure 17-1

PayPal's Auction Tools tab leads you to some time-saving features.

Under the section titled Invoicing Your Buyer, select the Winning Buyer Notification text link. In the succeeding screen (see Figure 17-2), you'll be able to customize your end-of-auction e-mail to provide a more personal touch while offering additional instruction to your buyer, automating the entire process.

As for *my* customized e-mail message, it reads something like this:

Congratulations on your win. Please include the specified shipping charge (for domestic shipments; international customers should contact me via e-mail for an updated cost). The insurance amount listed is optional.

I prefer PayPal payments and will ship immediately upon confirmation of your payment. I also gladly accept money orders, cashier's checks, and personal checks (must clear my bank). You can mail such payments to.

Dennis Prince

1234 Any Street

Anytown, CA 12345

USA

I leave positive feedback upon your confirmation the item has arrived safely and you are satisfied with it. Most buyers confirm by posting positive feedback to my eBay ID; I'll reciprocate immediately thereafter.

Thanks for bidding!

Best,

Dennis Prince

eBay ID: dennis_prince

As you can see, this message will provide the necessary payment information to help the buyer pay me quickly and easily. Here, I've also included a restatement of some of my sales policies—those most pertinent to the

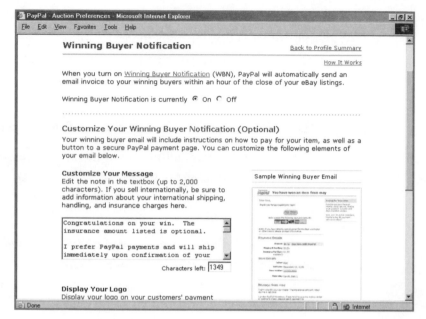

figure 17-2

Customize the Winning Buyer
Notification e-mail message
to further instruct your
buyers without having
to put forth extra effort.

payment process. Also notice that I've encouraged the posting of positive feedback, a topic I'll discuss in depth in Chapter 20, "Building a Stellar Online Reputation."

Payment Receipt

With the buyer duly notified, either via eBay's own end-of-auction e-mail, via PayPal's Winning Buyer Notification tool, or any other third-party tool you might use, it's now time to monitor receipt of payment. Recall your sales policy and the time limit you've put on receiving payment after the auction has ended. Now it's time to keep tabs on the buyer's honoring of their payment commitment.

Beyond the Winning Buyer Notification at PayPal, I've also made good use of another PayPal feature—the *Invoice Manager*—which is a feature of the overall *Post-Sale Manager* functionality. Here, I can track who has paid me and monitor when I need to ship an item, follow up with a buyer, and post feedback (see Figure 17-3).

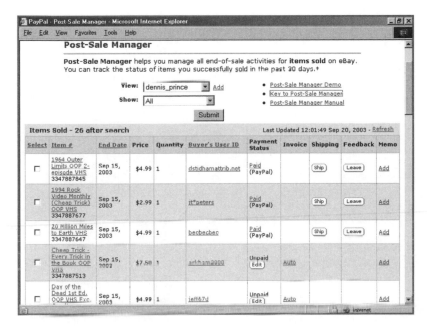

figure 17-3

PayPal's Post-Sale Manager tool allows me to easily keep track of the status of my outstanding closed auctions.

You might also want to utilize the variety of similar tracking and post-auction processing features found on the My eBay page within eBay. Here, you can track the items you've sold, send invoices, monitor payment (with active links to PayPal payment confirmation), and quickly send payment reminders if need be (see Figure 17-4). The My eBay page is highly customizable and provides additional tabs of information to allow you to track buying, watching, and account details.

Shipment Notification

Simply enough, when you ship an item that's been paid for, it's a good idea to let the buyer know. Some sellers state within the body of their sales policy something to the effect of "items will be shipped within 5–7 days of payment receipt." Other sellers elect to send individual e-mail notifications to their buyers upon item shipment. (Use a premade template and simply fill in the item specifics to save time.) Whichever route you choose, it's a good idea to let your anxious buyer know when the goods are in transit.

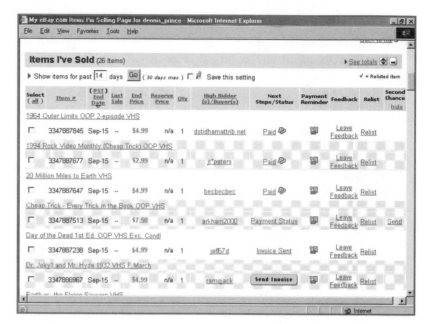

figure 17-4

The My eBay page is another terrific one-stop source of auction tracking to help you manage your sales.

Receipt Confirmation and Feedback

Finally, solicit receipt confirmation from your buyer to ensure that the item shipped has arrived safe and sound. I've utilized my Winning Buyer Notification message to solicit this confirmation and then go on to request the feedback exchange. Remember: It's that eBay feedback number that will represent your reputation at the auction place, and it's an invaluable asset to have on your side as you seek to attract more and more bidders and buyers. Again, you'll find a full discussion of eBay feedback and your seller's reputation in Chapter 20.

Controlling Costs to Pump Up Profits

Similar to the venerable "penny saved, penny earned" vernacular, a large factor in truly securing better auction income is your ability to retain more of your earnings for yourself. By controlling selling fees and other expenses, you'll be in better control of your overall business performance and bottom line profit than if you rack up costs indiscriminately and unmonitored. No, you don't need to become an absolute "tightwad" and you needn't relegate your auction listings to the bare-bones minimums. (That would be poor selling strategy, remember?) This section helps ensure that you remain aware of the fees and costs associated with online selling and how you can apply effective strategy to keeping those costs down while fortifying your fortune.

Controlling EBay Fees

Upon your first listings, you might have been surprised or perhaps concerned over the number of various fees eBay can levy. Although it's true that almost every little enhancement seems to have some sort of associated cost, it should be comforting to you that many of the listing-related fees you'll encounter can be significantly reduced or flat out avoided with a bit of foresight and careful planning. No, you can't escape every fee out there, but you can reduce and avoid many that really don't add much to your ultimate sales success and profit potential.

The Fees You Can't Avoid

Be realistic; you *will* pay some sort of listing fee when you sell at eBay. The days of free online auctioning are long gone. (Those sites dried up in the late 1990s due to low traffic and sparse listing volume.) Still, some cantankerously contend that eBay is getting rich because of their tariffs, yet it's important to understand that the fees you pay provide the needed capital to fund useful new features, costly infrastructure (hardware and software maintenance), and user services and tools. Much like your own business, as eBay continues to grow, it needs to reinvest to ensure it can satisfy the needs and wants of the more sophisticated online seller. The listing and usage fees wind up being a small price to pay for the ability to list, sell, and collect at a site so large, and the advanced methods and tools (such as Turbo Lister) become worth the cost when you consider the time, effort, and, yes, money *you'll* save in the long run. Internet and online auction history has already proven free sites simply cannot compete and perform to these levels.

The Little Things That Can Cost Big

So while it's reasonable and affordable to manage basic eBay insertion fees, there *is* a lot of fluff in there and you *can* cut costs by carefully selecting which features and services you'll use in your listings. In fact, after doing some research and investigating, you might find that although some adornments and extras add plenty of eye-candy, they also might offer little true return on the investment.

Cast a frugal eye on these questionable, and often costly, eBay listing enhancements:

- **Title enhancements.** Be it bold, highlighted, or whatever, few bidders really pay much attention to the visual style of your item's title. Save a buck and make conservative use of capital lettering (not exclusively, though) to highlight the key element of your title. Make sure you use plenty of good "hit words" because most items are found via keyword searches.

- **Special icons.** Whether it's a birthday cake, a Christmas tree, or a firecracker, when it comes to added title icons . . . who cares? When did you last leap at an item because of the cutesy little picture that accompanied it? Again, save the buck.

- **Home page featured placement.** This is one of the most expensive listing options at eBay and, unless you have an item that will gain you thousands of dollars in high bids or if you're continually selling a product in tremendously high-profit volume, it's best to bypass this one if you're trying to cut costs. Again, it's typically the keywords that get noticed, not the site real estate where your item is listed.

- **Cross-category listing.** This ability to have a single listing appear in two categories simultaneously will almost double the fee you'll pay yet might not truly pay off in the end. Revisit your research methods to determine the *best* category to list under and be willing to use a different category if your research indicates a better home for your goods. Besides, if you double-categorize, how will you know which category was ultimately responsible for your success?

■ **Gallery listings.** For an extra cost, eBay allows you to have your item featured in a picture gallery for those shoppers who prefer to view images rather than titles. The jury's still out whether the Gallery is bringing in more bidders and higher bids, though. Without definitive proof of greater success, save the extra cost of the Gallery listing.

Learning to Choose Fees Wisely

Of course, this isn't to say that *all* fees are inherently evil and detrimental to your eventual profit. Just as it makes perfect sense to pay reasonable fees for site and service usage, it's just as prudent to occasionally make use of features and enhancements when the situation calls for it. For example:

■ **Opening bids.** Of course, if current demand for your item easily will gain you your target price without the use of a reserve, then list in the lowest fee bracket and let the bidders work their magic. For example, notice how specifying an opening bid of $24.99 will incur an insertion fee of $0.55 whereas an opening bid of $25.00 (just one penny more) will cost $1.10 in insertion fees. Refer to the listing fees chart in Chapter 13 or review the fee information within eBay's help section; then use your noggin and study the various fee scales at eBay to get the most for the least.

■ **Reserve prices.** You might hate to pay the reserve surcharge, but do the math between putting a $200 reserve price on your item versus listing it with an opening bid of $200. At eBay, you'll find that listing an item with a $9.99 opening bid and a reserve of $200 costs $1.30. If you opt for the opening bid of $200, sans reserve, the same listing will cost you $3.30. But don't be penny-wise and pound-foolish: If you need the reserve to protect you from losing on your investment, then by all means use it.

■ **Relisting.** If your item fails to sell the first time around, relisting is the easy and inexpensive way to reposition the goods for sell again. It's free to relist (well, at eBay, you'll pay insertion fees a second time, but you'll be refunded if the item sells), and the benefit is that you can make changes to the item title, description, category, pricing, and so on to find your buyer on the site's dime. Take advantage of that.

■ **Online payment.** Some sellers might not be happy that fees are levied by online payment sites, but remember that buyers who can pay with credit cards (via services like PayPal and Billpoint) will invariably spend more than if they must surrender their cash on hand. If your items sell at good prices, make it easier for your buyers to pay by offering the online payment opportunity; then collect their higher bids at the relatively low cost to you.

These are the key areas where you can cut your auction costs to save a dime, a buck, or more. There are even more opportunities to shave your expenses, but these are points you'll want to focus on at the outset. As you refine your selling process and continue to explore new ways of managing your business, you'll be poised to recognize cost savers and cost wasters.

Add More and Save More Using HTML

If you want to get more into your auction listings without increasing your costs, it's often effective to incorporate the language of the Internet. Hypertext Markup Language (HTML) is the resident coding language used across the World Wide Web. HTML can also be incorporated into your eBay listings to provide more content at less cost.

Recall in Chapter 13 where I explained that eBay supports use of HTML coding within the description section of your listings. Using this code is easy—if you let it be—and requires that you merely insert some predefined markers or "tags" to enhance the appearance of your item description while enabling you to embed more images and add special links for your customers' convenience.

HTML tags are simple notations that are inserted into a regular text listing or document. These tags are alphabetic characters embedded between the < > signs. Appearing before and after portions of text, tags enhance the look or positioning of that text beyond the simple typeset you would otherwise see. A tag (such as) precedes the text to be enhanced. Then a closing tag that contains the forward slash (such as) ensures that the effect is not continued to the rest of the text that follows. Here are the most common tags you can use to achieve professional-looking results:

Font Tags

- bold results in **bold**.

- <i>italics</i> results in *italics*.

- <u>underline</u> results in underline.

- <font size=12 color=black face= "comic sans"> results in text that looks like this. This font will remain in use until you insert the </font> tag or specify a similar font equation with different settings.

Paragraphs, Line Breaks, and Lists

- <p> brings about a paragraph break

-
 results in a line break (similar to a carriage return)

- <li> generates a bullet mark before the text, as in a bulleted list

Inserting Image URLs and Other Web Links

- <img src= "http://my.starstream.net/dlprince/aromadisc.jpg"> inserts the specified image into the text. (You can add as many images as you like now, free of charge.)

- <img src= "http://my.starstream.net/dlprince/sales_policy.jpg"> inserts a graphic representation of my sales policy text. (You can also use a reference to a text document if you like, as seen in the "href" example that follows.)

- <a href= "http://cgi2.ebay.com/aw-cgi/eBayISAPI.dll?ViewFeed-back&userid=dennis_prince">My Feedback</a> provides an active (clickable) link labeled My Feedback to direct bidders to your eBay feedback page.

■ <a href= "mailto:dlprince@bigfoot.com">eMail Me</a> provides
an active link labeled eMail Me to immediately create an e-mail
message to your address.

Many more tags are available for use in HTML. If you want to gain a better understanding of the language, grab just about any book that discusses
introductory or intermediate HTML coding. For the purposes of your eBay
listings, though, these are the essential tags that will make your listing more
robust without emptying your wallet in potentially added fees.

Listing More by Doing Less

As promised, there is an easier way to list tens or hundreds of items in a single effort. To save time and achieve greater results for your listing efforts, use
eBay's bulk listing tool, *Turbo Lister*. This application allows you to create
bundles of item listings in a single screen, avoiding the need to navigate the
numerous screen steps you saw when listing a single item. If you want to
make more items available in a fraction of the time, Turbo Lister is the tool
for you.

Beyond the mere time savings, here are some additional reasons why bulk
listing makes sense:

■ Bulk listings can be created offline as eBay's Turbo Lister application runs directly on your PC without an active Internet connection required. You can create bulk listings on the go, too, using a
laptop if you like.

■ Bulk listings can be assembled whenever you choose at a pace to
best suit your needs.

■ Bulk listings can be uploaded in a single effort to start immediately
or to be delayed for a later date or time.

■ Bulk listings allow you to combine similar items to simultaneously
list and effectively cross-sell your goods.

The best news about bulk listing at eBay is that Turbo Lister is completely free to download and use. Here's how to do it.

Go to eBay's site map and seek out the link to Turbo Lister (see Figure 17-5) and follow the simple download instructions.

Upon successful download, you'll see a new icon on your computer's desktop from which you can easily launch Turbo Lister (see Figure 17-6).

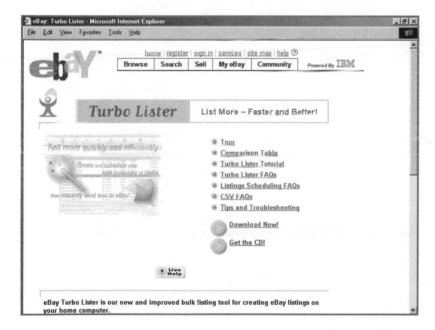

figure 17-5

The eBay Turbo Lister page can help you download this indispensable tool.

figure 17-6

The Turbo Lister "shortcut" is ready on your desktop; just double-click and launch.

Upon first use, you'll need to provide your eBay user ID and password and then verify your registered contact information. On subsequent uses, it's only necessary to provide your eBay password.

To begin creating a listing, click on the Create New button at the top of the initial Turbo Lister screen, navigating you to the new listing screen as shown in Figure 17-7.

Creating Turbo Lister listings is a simple three-step process. Much like listing single items within eBay, begin by selecting the auction format in the first screen. In the next screen, enter an item title, description, and images (see Figures 17-8 and 17-9).

 NOTE Turbo Lister defaults to eBay's IPIX image-hosting service (as does the single-item listing form), uploading images from your computer. If you'll be hosting images from a Web page elsewhere on an ongoing basis, you can change the default by clicking the appropriate check box when you select the Change Photo Hosting link.

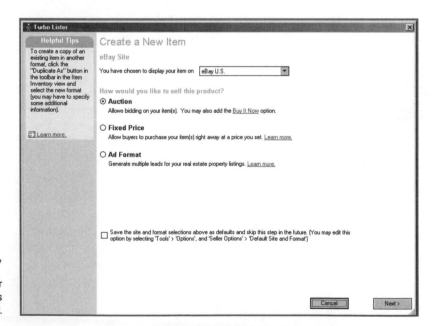

figure 17-7

Creating items in Turbo Lister follows the same screen layout as creating single items within eBay.

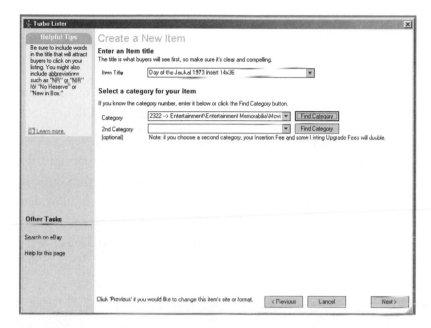

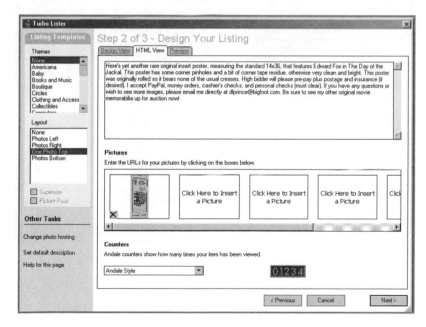

figure 17-8

Enter an item description in the appropriately designated text box and select a category.

figure 17-9

Specify item description, images, and counters for your listing.

In the final step of the listing creation, designate auction particulars including duration, pricing, shipping and payment instructions, and any listing upgrades (see Figure 17-10).

When you're finished with Step 3, simply click the Save button to complete the listing creation process within Turbo Lister (see Figure 17-11).

With listings now resident in your Turbo Lister Item Inventory, select those you want to upload to eBay (simply clicking on the item to highlight it), determine when you would want the auction to begin (the selection buttons at the bottom of the screen allow immediate start upon eBay upload or designating a later start date/time). Click the Add to Upload button to transfer the selected items to the Waiting to Upload queue (see Figure 17-12).

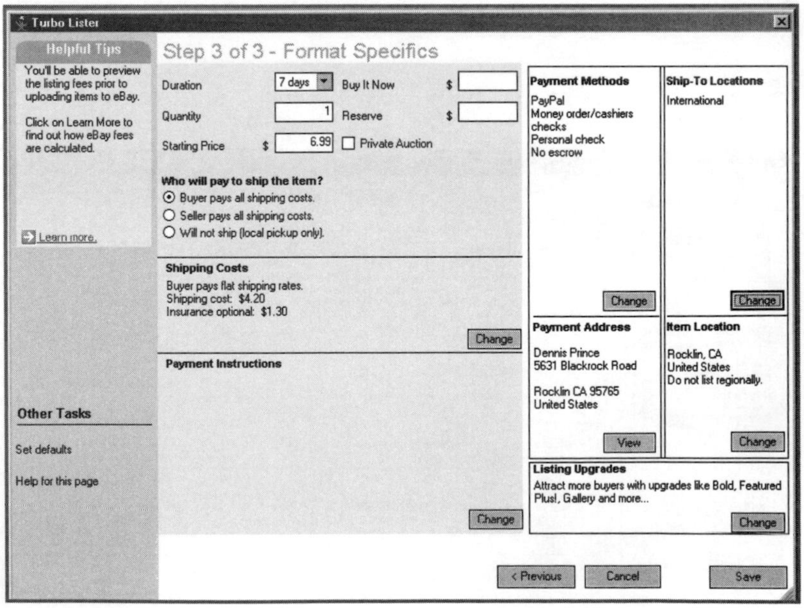

figure 17-10

Step 3 of the Turbo Lister process includes designating auction specifics.

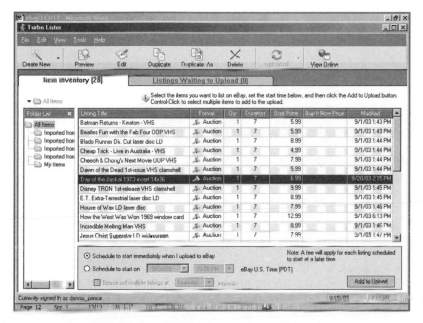

figure 17-11

When saved, Turbo Lister provides an overview of the items you have created that are ready to be uploaded to eBay.

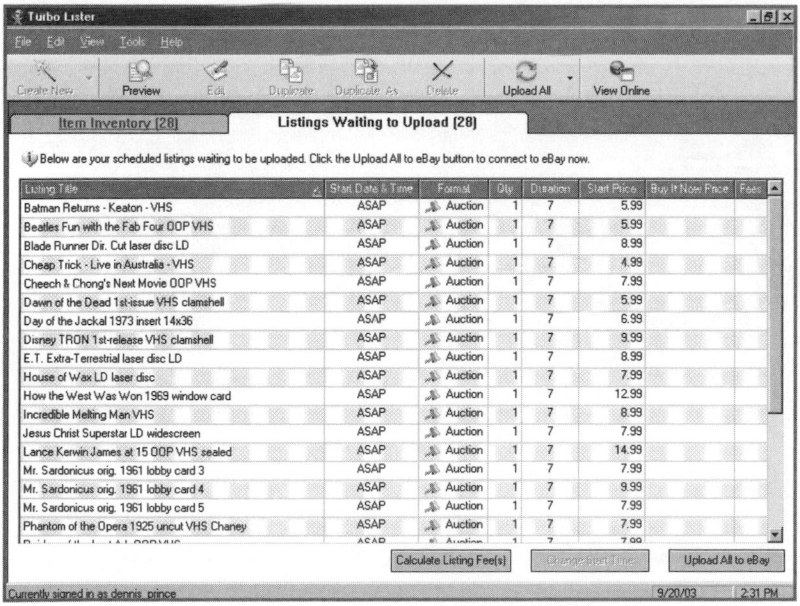

figure 17-12

With many items now ready to launch, it's time to upload to eBay.

NOTE Before actually uploading the items to eBay, make use of Turbo Lister's Calculate Listing Fees button to determine how much each item will cost in terms of insertion fees. If the fees are higher than you like, you can easily go back and modify some of your individual listing specifics and enhancements.

From the Waiting to Upload item collection display, click on the Upload All to eBay button to enact the item transfer (see Figure 17-13).

When the upload is complete, click either the Go to the Pending Listings text link (if you specified a later date/time) or Go to My eBay link (if you selected immediate auction launch) to view the results of your upload. (The results are shown in Figure 17-14.)

DID YOU KNOW? Did you know that, using Turbo Lister, you can schedule and upload up to 3,000 items at a time? Now that's bulk listing!

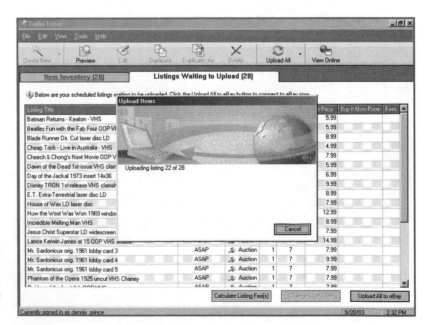

figure 17-13

Upon choosing to upload items, Turbo Lister connects directly to eBay to begin the data transfer process.

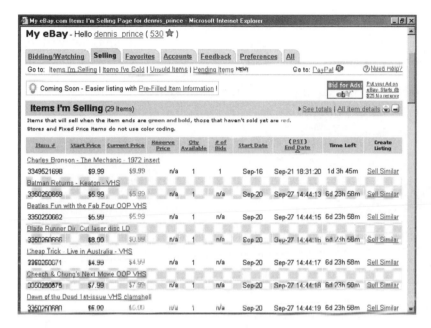

figure 17-14

Immediately, you can visit eBay to verify the launch status of your bulk-listed auctions.

Clearly, bulk listing makes it easy to manage a large volume of items and allows you to schedule and otherwise stagger when your auctions will begin. So while you're creating your listing collections, keep these important listing considerations in mind:

- List similar items so that multiple-item bidders can find related goods to maximize cross-selling potential or list a wide variety of goods to provide a range of items to attract more single-item bidders.

- Upload listings to coincide with peak bidding days and times.

- Always calculate listing fees before uploading to ensure you're aware of the costs.

- Try to stagger the end day of listing collections so that you'll be able to tend to end-of-auction activities one collection at a time.

■ Be certain you're fully prepared with all shipping materials and other supplies to quickly package and queue sold items that will be awaiting payment.

Now that you're a listing champion, it's time to move on to the next chapter to sharpen your shipping skills.

chapter 18

Pack It In:
Shipping Like a Pro

When the auction ended, you leapt into action to make contact with the high bidder and collect your earnings. But your job isn't finished yet. After that payment arrives, you have to do a little more work. The excitement of selling at eBay often overshadows what's really going on: A seller is offering to sell and ship an item to a buyer. After the auction ends and the buyer pays, the onus is on the seller to bring the deal to a successful close by getting the item there quickly and safely.

Packing and shipping is something of an art and nothing to be underestimated or taken lightly. This is the point of the transaction where you, the seller, establish your reputation in the buyer's mind. Take this step seriously, and you'll be recognized as a stellar seller. If you're new to packing and shipping, don't fret over the how's and why's of the process; this chapter can help you determine the best supplies to have on hand, the best way to use them, and the best methods to use to ensure that the item gets from Point A to Point B safely, to your buyer's delight.

Setting Up Your Ship Shop

Believe it or not, many sellers overlook a key element in their packing process—*where* they will pack up their items. You might think you can grab a box, bubble wrap, and packing peanuts and do your packing anywhere at any time. Certainly, you can take that approach, but it's not the most efficient way to work; besides, a transient "ship shop" can result in loss or damage to the items you'll pack.

Free yourself from rummaging for the last roll of tape or endlessly searching for the right box for an item. If you're going to manage a volume of sales, you need a supply room that will be well stocked with all the goods necessary to make the easy transition from listing an item to packing an item.

Establishing a Supply Room

A supply room is where you'll neatly and efficiently store and work with your packaging goods. This is also an area where you'll pack your items, preferably, rather than lug boxes and bubble pack from one room to another, leaving a trail of shipping debris in your wake. For the best sort of supply room, do your best to incorporate the following qualities:

- **It's a dedicated area.** No, you don't need a 10-bedroom home or condo to be an organized auctioneer. A single auction office located in a spare room can serve multiple auction uses (office, staging area, supply room). In fact, if you can find a large enough living space, the best auction environment is one where *all* your auction activity can be contained within a single space. If not, find another corner where you can set up a supply shop.

- **It's a clean and well-lit area.** Cleanliness and good lighting will work in your favor as you pack up those items that customers have already paid for and are anxiously awaiting.

- **It's large enough to allow organization.** Again, a mansion isn't necessary, but you'll do better if all your supplies aren't stacked in a cramped corner or dumped into a carton that requires upending to get to what you need.

■ **There's adequate work space to pack items.** It's where you'll keep your supplies and where you should expect to use them, too. Make sure you have enough room to work.

Stocking a Supply Room

Now you need supplies. What supplies? Here's the laundry list of things every well-stocked supply room should have:

■ **Boxes.** You can get them in all shapes and sizes these days, many designed to hold specific kinds of items (videotapes, for example) and keep them safe. Store them flat so they'll take up less space, preferably under your work surface to keep them handy yet out of the way.

■ **Mailing tubes.** If you'll be shipping rolled items, you'll want tubes or special tube-like mailing boxes. They're also free from many shippers. If they're the box type (triangular), you can store them flat. If they're actual tubes, store them in a half-box to keep them contained but easy to use.

■ **Box fill.** You know it as packing peanuts and environment-friendly Eco-Foam; it's some of the best lightweight material to fill a box and provide necessary interior cushioning. Wadded or shredded paper also works fine, but it tends to weigh in costly if a large amount is required. Box fill can take a bit more space to store; consider a large box or a clean garbage bag to store it in. Some people hang it from the ceiling and dispense it from a reclosable "spout." Neat, huh?

■ **Bubble pack.** Excellent for wrapping items and adding an extra layer of protection (both for cushioning and cleanliness) to items. Sheets of varying size can be stored in a box; bigger quantities can be rolled on a spindle.

- **Tape.** And lots of it. Store your tape in a drawer or on peg hooks for easy view and easy access. You'll want different types of tape for different needs:

  - Wide shipping tape (clear or otherwise, used for sealing and reinforcing boxes)

  - Brown paper tape, pregummed and often with filament reinforcement—also used for sealing or reinforcing boxes

  - Masking tape or cellophane tape for securing interior packing such as bubble wrap around an item

- **Backing board and stiffener.** Smaller sheets and sections of cardboard (either corrugated or chipboard) are useful for providing interior stiffening to prevent bends and creases for flat items. This can be stored in a suitable-sized box or a drawer.

- **Envelopes.** Have a good assortment of these, ranging from standard letter-sized envelopes up to (and beyond?) heavy-duty 9" × 12" manila envelopes. Padded envelopes are also good but are comparatively costly, and the protection they provide can be gained by using a combination of cheaper materials (such as stiffener or bubble pack in a manila envelope). Store envelopes in a box or drawer.

- **Mailing labels.** Again, these are now free from most carriers, and most of them—even USPS Priority Mail—will arrange to have your return address preprinted on them for even easier use. Store labels in a drawer or on a shelf.

- **Supply shop tools.** These are the other things you'll need (although not necessarily in bulk) in your supply shop:

  - Bold waterproof marking pens

  - A utility knife

  - Scissors

  - Blank white paper (for notes or correspondence)

Organizing a Supply Room

The key to organization is to have what you need, when you need it, and within easy reach. As you establish your supply room, envision the actual flow of work: picture an assembly line process (moving from left to right) or a single-item packing station where all packing materials are within reach (boxes underneath, box fill up above, tape to the left, labels to the right). Think *ergonomics* (working within the natural range and makeup of the human condition), and work to have items within easy reach without too much stooping, stretching, or otherwise contorting to get to the supplies you'll need. Keep it all within easy and painless reach, and you'll make your work much easier. Although it might sound a bit silly, the organization of your supply room is what will allow you to develop a repeatable and time-efficient packing process.

Source of Shipping Supplies

Although you would be right to consider the cost required to stock up a ship shop as I've described here, you'll be happy to learn that the bulk of the materials and supplies can be had for free. For starters, begin with the United States Postal Service (still my preferred carrier) to stock up on all manner of boxes, envelopes, tubes, labels, and more, to handle the majority of your shipping needs. Besides these supplies being free, they're easy to order right from your computer. Simply go to http://www.usps.com in your favorite Web browser and select the All Products & Services option from the top menu. In the ensuing menu, find and click Supplies (Shipping) and then select Shipping Supplies, Business Use in the left menu of choices (see Figure 18-1). Although it's a bit difficult to find, the effort will be well worth it because you'll soon arrive at a page that offers a wealth of free shipping goods. Order the items and amounts you need to stock up your ship shop and then use the simple *checkout* screen to have the items sent to you. Just like the regular mail you receive every day, the USPS will deliver these supplies right to your doorstep.

figure 18-1

Visit shop.usps.com on the World Wide Web for free Priority, Express, and Global Mail supplies.

If you'll be using United Parcel Service (UPS), Federal Express, DHL, or another carrier, look them up on the Internet; they, too, offer free shipping supplies for packages you ship using their services. (Look out, though, because some of their supplies are *not* free.) Of course, you can also get these same supplies at your local carrier's offices or designated partner stations.

Some packing supplies, though, are not free whichever carrier you choose. When it comes to box fill, specialized cartons, and the like, you might actually need to purchase these items. Visit your nearest wholesale or "club" warehouse for better prices on packing tape or specialized envelopes that are not readily available from the carriers. Visit your local office supply store or shipping office for large bags of Styrofoam peanuts and rolls of bubble pack.

DID YOU KNOW? Don't be bashful about picking up such supplies free from time to time. Workplaces, liquor stores, and even grocery stores routinely throw out reusable packing supplies. Ask around if you see those materials ready for the dumpster and, if they're clean and seem suitable for your packing task, ask if you can take those supplies for yourself.

Don't forget eBay itself: It's full of merchants selling these sorts of packing supplies, and usually at better prices than you would expect. If you're actively buying while selling, be sure to recycle the packing materials that protected the items you received. Most interior packing material can be used over and over again without significant degradation.

DID YOU KNOW? If packing supplies are costing you money on a regular basis, you can consider recovering that cost in your shipping and handling fees. If you're maintaining a high volume of sales, those costs can likely be recovered by adding as little as 25 cents to your shipping fee. Be careful, though, because any cost much higher than that can be construed as a form of final price manipulation.

Packing Protocol

Although packing is something of a profession, it's a skill easily acquired if you have the right supplies and know how to use them properly. Here are some things to consider as you approach your packing job:

- Think "lightweight" to save on shipping costs, but not at the expense of safe delivery.

- Pack items snugly in boxes, but don't overdo it lest you damage the item before it ever leaves your site.

- For fragile items, use the "box within a box" method to ensure extra cushion and protection (still mindful of total package weight).

- Use rigid mailers, padded envelopes, or insert cardboard stiffeners to protect flat items.

- Be considerate of the recipient, and don't over-tape or otherwise excessively seal a package; the item could be damaged as the buyer tries to wrest it free.

With the item ready to ship, send it on its way at the nearest carrier's office or authorized forwarding station. Be sure to retain your receipts, insurance forms, delivery confirmation numbers, and so on; not only will you want to have these important documents when verifying shipment and ultimate delivery, but many such expenses are also suitable as a business tax deduction. (See Chapter 21, "On Becoming a Business," for more details.) After the package is en route, send another message to the buyer to indicate that the item is on its way and provide tracking numbers (if available) so that the buyer can monitor the package's journey (see Figure 18-2). In your message to the buyer, request a confirmation response to indicate when the item has arrived and whether all is satisfactory.

NOTE Recall the discussion in Chapter 8, "E-Motions and Auction Affronts," of anxious buyers—those who can barely wait to receive their item. Remember that providing a tracking number for their coveted package can provide them the self-sufficient ability to pore over the step-by-step progress of their delivery, freeing you from repeated e-mail updates.

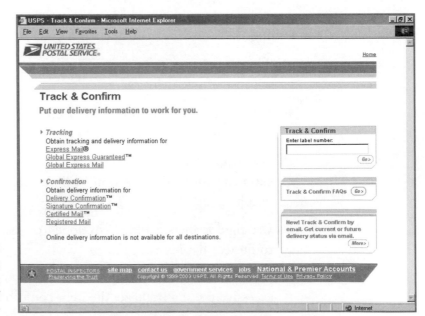

figure 18-2

Here's an example of the USPS online package tracking service, helping you and your buyer monitor a package's journey.

Getting Specific: What Are You Shipping?

When it comes to shipping and packing prowess, you'll need to develop a reasonable expertise in how to best prepare different sorts of items for transport. Not all items can be slipped into an envelope or dropped into a box. So, for added guidance into how to approach different shipping situations, here are a few rules of thumb that the experts use when they approach a particular packing job:

- **Photos or other nonbreakable flat items.** Use a suitably sized envelope with a same-size piece of cardboard for stiffening. For particularly old or delicate flat merchandise, consider putting the item in a plastic sleeve and then sandwiching it between two pieces of cardboard. Don't just lick that envelope flap; use a strip of packing tape to seal it shut. If it's a particularly large item, consider rolling it (if it won't cause damage) and send it in a sturdy (repeat, *sturdy*) mailing tube with both end-caps taped down.

- **Glassware, pottery, and other fragile items.** Wrap the item in light tissue paper first and then wrap it again with bubble wrap. Put it in an appropriate-sized box with a cushion of packing peanuts around the item. Next, place this box inside another box, again using a cushion of packing peanuts around the box within a box. Styrofoam sheets also work great as outer box siding material.

- **Framed items.** Size matters here, and you'll need to carefully assess the task to see whether it's within your potential to do a good job and whether you'll be able to work with the supplies you have. For starters, if the item is behind glass, it's best to disassemble the piece and pack the elements separately (see the preceding tips on flat items). Bubble pack and foam sheets are a must here, and you should wrap frame corners with sheet foam to prevent them from puncturing the packing box or causing damage to the piece (be it a litho, photograph, or whatever). Although you can find special packing boxes just for framed items, if the piece is too valuable or too unwieldy for your comfort, take it to a professional.

- **Big tickets.** If it's too big to handle, if you feel you'll have to improvise a patchwork of packaging, or if you just don't think you'll be able to get it in and out of your car when you're all done, then by all means, hand the job over to a pro.

- **The little things.** Whether a small piece of jewelry, a stamp, or any other "little" collectible or item that could have big value, be sure it doesn't get lost in the mail. First, protect it: Put the item in an appropriate-sized box with the right amount of packing peanuts or foam sheets to cushion it. Next, make it visible: Put that little box into a medium-sized box with appropriate interior cushioning. The second box might add more protection than required, but the goal is to be sure that little darling doesn't fall into some crevice, crack, or piece of mail-sorting machinery after which it might never be seen again.

Additional Packing Considerations

You might never have thought there could be so much to simply packing an item. This discussion isn't intended to over-complicate the process but does recognize how important it is to you and your customers that the items are shipped and received in satisfactory, undamaged condition. To that end, here are a few more considerations to take into account.

Shake and Break?

One USPS employee imparted this bit of wisdom: "If you can shake it, we can break it."

With that in mind, all items you ship should be given the *shake and rattle* test: Before sealing an outer box, hold the flaps closed and give the item a few shakes. Do you hear movement inside? If so, you might want to add a bit more interior padding until it's whisper-quiet in there. Movement could be the opportunity for items to shift and become damaged during their journey to their new home.

Help Fight Wetness

Other postal and shipping employees tell of water hazards. Somehow, even if there's not a cloud in the sky, items can get wet during transit. Expect that most water damage is irreversible, so take a simple step to ward it off: Put the item in a plastic bag whenever possible. It typically doesn't have to be hermetically sealed, but a simple Ziploc bag or a larger poly bag sealed with packing tape is usually enough to keep out the wet weather. Also, experienced handlers recommend that clear tape be used to seal the address label on the package's outside. If that gets wet and smeared, your package might end up in the Dead Mail vault for all eternity.

Don't Overpack It

If a little cushion is good, a lot should be dynamite, right? Not really. Too much interior packing can literally cause an explosion. Remember that boxes will get bumped, stacked, kicked, and tossed about on their sometimes perilous journeys. Use enough interior packaging to keep the item safe and secure, but if the box bulges like an overpacked suitcase, the item that's inside will probably get damaged the moment you seal it shut.

Seal the Deal

Not only will too much interior packing lead to potential damage, but an overzealous packer might likewise present buyers with something of a challenge as they try to extract their treasure from a practically impenetrable tape-and-cardboard sarcophagus. Seal the item enough to ensure it won't accidentally open in transit, but don't feel you have to extinguish an entire supply of tape, staples, and whatever else to guarantee the item's safety. Many buyers tell of accidentally damaging an item as they struggle to free it from its packaging. And don't forget: Excessive packaging adds excessive weight—which results in added shipping costs.

Small Touches with Big Impacts

If the item is particularly fragile or will fare best if unpacked by a certain method, put special unpacking instructions inside that can be found the moment the recipient opens the package. Also, be sure to include an extra shipping label *inside* the package; often labels come loose or become unreadable during the journey, or they might get wet. In some instances, packages are opened by the carrier in the hope that he or she will find an extra label to get the item on its way again.

Now that you're a packing and shipping genius, it's time to go back and consider exactly what it is that you'll be sealing up and sending off. That's right—*what* will you be selling at eBay and elsewhere? If you've wondered just what it is you might offer and where you might find the good stuff to offer, turn to the next chapter.

chapter 19

Building and Maintaining Your Inventory

By now, you've probably found several items to sell—things around the house, in the closets, under the beds, and in the back of the garage. EBay is a terrific venue for cleaning up the house and yard and bringing home a few extra dollars. However, serious sellers are in this for the longer term and must take a more focused approach to developing and growing their auction business. After you get into that league, *inventory* becomes your concern and budgeting and maintaining that inventory are what keep you (hopefully) operating in the black. Just as it is important to have a steady flow of merchandise to auction at a profit, it's equally important to control that inventory to be sure you can track it, value it, and even find it when the time is ripe to sell.

Reality Check: Know Your Margins

As you approach the concepts of acquiring, maintaining, and replenishing an inventory of merchandise, your first considerations should center around costs and profits. Ask yourself:

- What will it cost to establish an inventory of the items I want to sell?
- What will it cost to store and maintain my inventory?

■ What will it cost to list or advertise my inventory?

■ What prices can I expect to get for my items? (Be realistic!)

■ What percentage of return must I realize to make a profit?

As most sellers quickly find out, without a proper plan of how their incoming cash covers and surpasses their outgoing expenses, an online auction endeavor can quickly dry up before it's had a chance to flourish. For this reason, you need an *inventory plan* before you begin to invest in goods to sell.

When you begin to establish your inventory plan, keep these things in mind:

■ Am I doing this for the long haul or just a limited-time stint?

■ How much inventory do I already have, what return might it bring, and how long will it sustain my selling activity?

■ How much capital (expendable cash or access to it) will I need to establish my inventory of goods?

■ What sorts of goods do I want to sell? Will I need to spend significant time researching certain goods? Should I generalize or specialize? (Hint: It's best to specialize; too many folks try to be "all things to all people" and get tangled up in the effort.)

■ At what prices can I purchase goods, and what profit percentage can I expect to pull down?

■ How popular are the items I want to sell, and what kind of inventory turnover can I reasonably expect?

■ How (and where) will I store my inventory, and does it require any special environmental conditions (temperature, humidity, or whatever)?

■ Can I work directly with a distributor or drop-shipper and pay them to manage the inventory for me?

■ How many auctions do I want to stage each week or month, and what levels of inventory will I need to support that?

■ What is the lead time to replenish my inventory?

- Will the items I sell be seasonal, selling best at certain times of the year, or can I look for sustained sales levels year round?

As you can see, much of this revolves around the supply of your items, the demand for them, and the costs involved in acquiring, maintaining, and selling them. Consider these aspects of inventory acquisition and management before you head off buying up truckloads of widgets and whatchamacallits that might or might not be profitable for you.

Establishing Sources of Inventory

Most sellers have a variety of sources from which to draw items for sale. The truly prolific sellers will usually tell of finding "inventory" anywhere and everywhere (literally). Where does their great stuff come from? First, consider these traditional troves that are being tapped on a regular basis:

- **Garage sales.** When you're looking to pay only pennies on the dollar, look no further than your neighbor's driveway. Garage sales are perfect for finding great items, odd items, and hopefully lightly used items that resell online at terrific profit. To truly maximize your effort when cruising the garage sales, plot a course the night before to hit as many sales as possible within an area—and be prepared to offer a price for an entire boxload or table full of items. (Bulk offers are worth a try at any time, but they work best near the end of the day when the seller is anxious to close down; think in terms of going back to sales that seem likely to have auctionable items left over.)

- **Flea markets and swap meets.** Think of these as garage sales on a grander scale, where the sellers come to you—sort of. Many sellers tell of finding great items (along with great gobs of garbage) at flea markets. The key is to arrive early (usually before the sun comes up). You'll be in the company of many other "pickers" and "treasure finders" who all swoop upon the various sellers looking to cherry-pick the best stuff before the sun comes up and the masses come out. Again, don't be bashful about haggling, especially if you've gone back for more shopping near the end of the day.

■ **Thrift stores.** Sometimes, folks don't have the time or patience to attempt a sale of their own and will settle for packing up their unwanted goods and carting them off to the local thrift store. They get a receipt to take a deduction at tax time and you have a new venue to find great bargain items that folks might be paying well for at the online auctions. Warning: Thrift stores are often somewhat cluttered and disorganized. Be prepared to do some serious digging.

■ **Tag sales and estate sales.** These are indoor events where a private individual is selling off possessions or has hired a professional to manage the sale of items owned by someone recently deceased. Regardless, the quality of items is often a step up from what you'll find at garage sales and flea markets. Competition is a bit stiffer here and incredible bargains are more difficult to come by. However, there's still good opportunity to find deals and make purchases that you can later resell to discerning buyers for a reasonable profit.

■ **Auctions.** Of course, there's the auction in its many forms and appearances. In the physical world, be sure to visit private auctions (possibly part of an estate or tag sale), phone auctions (often geared toward collectors), and public auctions (such as those held at flea markets as well as government and police auctions). Online, many sellers tell of purchasing items for resale at the very auctions where they list their wares. It's not uncommon to find a seller who is offering merchandise that was acquired right there at a great price just a few weeks earlier. With a bit of repositioning and attention to timing, many sellers turn quite a good profit from online auction purchases.

■ **Specialty shows and exhibits.** Collectors and dealers regularly congregate at special shows that cater to their interests. Often, you can find interesting items at these shows that could bring a profit upon resale, but remember that dealers at the shows are there for that exact purpose: to make a profit. Don't expect to find garage sale or flea market prices, but keep a keen eye open for unique items that, based on your knowledge of the online market, look underpriced at the dealer's table. And don't forget to ask what else the dealer might have that isn't currently displayed; that bargain might still be packed in a box behind the table.

Although the preceding sources offer a sea of goods from which to choose, many "home run" items cannot be uncovered easily in multiple quantities, and many others that look like they'll pull down big prices can sometimes fizzle out and be candidates for the seller's own garage sell or flea market junket.

If you're looking to play like the big sellers—the eBay PowerSellers—play, you'll need to investigate more of the breakthrough methods of sourcing inventory. To that end, consider these sources of endless items that can work to truly fuel a bona-fide eBay business for years to come:

- **Closeouts, liquidators, and outlet stores.** If you decide to sell recently manufactured items, always look for the no-frills venue where you can buy a manufacturer's overstock, either from a clearance-type store or direct from the manufacturer's distributor. (You'll typically require a valid resale license to purchase direct from the distributor; you'll hear more about that in Chapter 21, "On Becoming a Business.") Be wary of loading up and relying too much on the goods that every other PowerSeller is offering lest you become just another drop in the bucket. Before purchasing goods in bulk, go back to your eBay research and check to see if there's truly a market for such items. If the market is flooded, avoid joining the pool party; if, however, the market seems to be underserved, you might have found something that could have viable appeal. It's healthy, though, to cast a critical eye on many of the overstocked and liquated goods you might find. Keep in mind that the reason the merchandise is overrun and being closed out is likely because people weren't buying it. Get it?

- **Drop-shippers.** If you're looking for the next wave in online auctioning and selling, you've just found it. Although not without its snags, drop-shipping is the *stockless retailing* solution whereby you source items from a distributor and wholesaler, list those items for auction or sale (*without* having purchased them yet) and, upon successful sale, instruct the drop-shipper to send the item to the buyer *as if it were delivered from you or your business*. How cool is that?

Today, many manufacturers and distributors have begun to embrace drop-shipping as a new way to attract more retailers to sell goods. A drop-shipper requires you to have a valid state seller's permit (also known as a reseller's license or tax ID number) before you can open an account.

After your account is set up, the drop-shipper will usually provide you with images and full descriptions of the goods you might want to offer to your buyers. You'll pay the wholesale cost of the item after it has sold plus a nominal drop-shipping fee (about $2–4 per address shipped to cover warehousing and carrier charges); the balance of the selling price you received is your profit. Better yet, if the item doesn't sell, you never purchased it in the first place!

The logical next question, therefore, is *where* can you find such manufacturers and distributors who are ready and willing to drop-ship goods for you? Well, take caution here because if you merely surf the Web for "drop-shippers" and the like, you'll find a number of outfits ready to make you rich (or so they say). Many of these are fronts for middlemen, those "clever ones" who say they're drop-shippers and are really just standing between you and an *actual* drop-shipper, taking a piece of the action away from the potential profit you could make if you had direct contact with the real product source. In my travels, I've learned quite a bit about drop-shipping and reliable sources of supply. To date, the most reliable portal into drop-shippers is the Drop Shipping Source Directory from World Wide Brands, Inc. at http://www.mydssd.com (see Figure 19-1). Founder Chris Malta and business partner Robin Cowie have scoured the various sources and established the most comprehensive and reliable collection of bona-fide drop-shippers.

■ **Networking.** As it's often said, "It doesn't matter what you know; it's *who* you know." Many sellers find terrific buys and resale

figure 19-1

World Wide Brands, Inc. should be your first stopping place when you decide to enter the exciting world of drop-shipping.

opportunities as a result of their interactions and relationships with others. As you make your rounds to discover new veins of inventory, get to know the people you'll frequently rub elbows with. When people help people, the result can be most satisfying—and profitable.

A Closer Look at the Inventory You Already Own

If you're like most people these days, you're probably sitting on a ready-to-go inventory within your own living space. It takes practically no time at all to accumulate mounds of stuff that continually gets in your way but is also excellent auction fodder. Before you throw something out or donate it to a charity, look for the sorts of items listed here. These are all excellent sellers— and they could be common items you see around the house every day.

■ **Antiques.** Do you have stuff that's been passed down from generation to generation, like furniture, artwork, tools, simple appliances, statuary, or whatever? Many folks have quite a collection of odds and ends that might have surpassed the 100-year mark, earning them the rightful name of "antique." This is the stuff that bidders are actively seeking online right now, so (provided it's not a beloved family heirloom) why not cash in?

■ **Advertising, premium, and promotional items.** Remember all that mail-away stuff you and your kids clipped box tops to get? How 'bout those silly trinkets from cereal boxes that you've had stashed in your Cap'n Crunch treasure box since you were a kid? Gas station give-aways? Fast food toys? Take a close look around and see if you have any of this stuff that has aged 20 years or more. Chances are, there's a good market for it online.

■ **China and silverware.** You might be sitting on a gold mine disguised as a buffet or china cabinet. Check it closely: The awful stuff that sits there year after year because you don't want to look at it could be quite valuable.

■ **Old product packaging.** It's not just Prince Albert in a can that draws the attention of collectors. Today, folks are bidding handsomely for product paraphernalia such as old cans, spice tins, soda bottles, cereal boxes, and just about anything else that conjures up memories of years past.

■ **Anything in the kid's room.** If your kids are at least into their 30-somethings today, you can expect that anything that might have remained in your attic from their youth is commanding good prices online. Toys, games, comics, trading cards, posters, records (and 8-track tapes), and other relics from the 1970s and earlier have become quite desirable to others in their age bracket. Of course, your kids know this, too, and will probably be visiting any day now to reclaim their treasures.

Although I already mentioned it near the beginning of this chapter, look no further than your own living space for auctionable goods. If you've been meaning to get around to decluttering your living spaces, take a second look and determine if what you have lurking in the garage, attic, back bedroom, or even at the off-site storage facility is the kind of thing folks online would love to pay you for. Most often, that stuff is inventory, and you should retrieve, catalog, and list it as such.

Reinvestment: Budget and Buy for Resale

You already understand that one great buy or an attic full of stuff isn't going to be enough to support your auction business for an extended period. Although you can do well in online sales while your great stuff lasts, it is of finite supply and, when your intention is to sell for the long haul, you're going to need to develop a profit-friendly method of replenishing your stocks. That means buying (or selecting drop-ship goods) with an eye on resale goals. Therefore, be sure to consider the following *before* you make your inventory investments:

- Can you purchase an item or items at a price that affords you reasonable profit?

- How quickly can you resell your prospective purchase? You don't want your money tied up in inventory for too long.

- Is there demand for the item that has been proven in the online auction arena?

- If you're dealing in collectibles, do you know which items are more elusive and which are more common? You'll want to hunt down the elusive items to make larger profits. (Hint: Talk with other sellers and dealers to learn what their customers are most eager to purchase; then explore the availability of those items for yourself.)

- Is there an upcoming event (news development, movie release, and so on) that could repopularize a particular item or group of items you have a chance to purchase cheaply?

Your key to sound inventory investment is to either have a good mix of items that appeals to many customers or a focused set of items that are sought after by serious buyers. Whichever route you take, be sure that you can gain a profit of at least 40 to 50 percent (and higher is always better), including allowances for business expenditures, which you'll read more about in Chapter 21.

Tools and Techniques to Keep Track of It All

So here you are with your terrific, cost-effective, and profit-bearing inventory of great items. But what a mess! How will you ever get it all in order, easily identifiable, and properly documented in a way that will streamline your efforts while helping you track the details of your business health? Organization of your inventory will be a key asset to you and will make your business run more cost effectively.

First, you'll need a system to help you keep records of your inventoried items.

Database Application

Many database or spreadsheet computer applications are up to the creation, maintenance, and storage of inventory records. Look to such products as Microsoft Excel, Microsoft Access, FileMaker, or something similar. Be sure that the application makes it easy to add, delete, update, and calculate your inventory. Make sure you have adequate PC storage to keep not only your growing inventory list but also a disaster recovery backup copy in case your work file is ever corrupted.

DID YOU KNOW? Before you run to the local software retailer to purchase a database or spreadsheet tool, look to the Internet for some excellent free database tools. When you're starting up, consider the spreadsheet package that comes with OpenOffice.org (http://www.openOffice.org), which has almost all the features of MS Excel and is *free*. When you're ready for a more serious database tool and don't mind writing a bit of SQL code, take a look at MySQL (http://www.mysql.com) as a solution that can help you manage full-fledged relational databases. If you want the SQL power but aren't a coder by nature, look at SQLYOG (http://www.webyog.com/sqlyog), which provides a user-friendly interface that is similar to Microsoft Access.

Inventory Ledger Book

Many people still think hard copy is best. Inventory ledger books work as well now as they have for decades. A good hard-copy ledger is expandable (perhaps a three-ring binder sort of format) and has adequate room for all details of the item to be entered. (Consider using a single page for each item.)

Now, consider the kind of information you'll want for each item in your inventory:

- **Item number.** Develop a simple numbering scheme to make item identification easier—and make sure you always assign a number to incoming items.

- **Item name.** What is it?

- **Item description.** This should be a detailed enough description to highlight unique attributes of the item.

- **Item image.** Although this takes a bit more effort up front, an image makes identification easier. An image is also useful when it comes time to list your item. That way, the image is ready to use whether it's a hard-copy photo you'll scan or a link to a digital image that you'll upload later.

- **Item cost.** How much did you pay for the item? (Don't forget to keep all your receipts.)

- **When purchased.** This helps you keep track of how long the item has been in your inventory.

- **Where purchased.** You might have stumbled on a great source of inventory and will most likely want to visit it again.

- **Estimated value.** This can be subjective, but try to refer to generally accepted market values by reviewing price guides, talking with other sellers and collectors, and researching previous auction prices.

- **Storage area.** *Where* is it now? If you keep inventory in several places (as many sellers do), you'll want to minimize time spent hunting down an item.

Of course, you should tailor this list of information to best meet your needs, but be sure you can accurately identify, retrieve, and list any item in your inventory.

Let EBay Keep Track of It All

Don't forget that eBay's Turbo Lister and My eBay tools can track and store much of this information for you as well. Although neither is tantamount in providing a total solution to your inventory management needs, you can rely on either of these tools (or both) to help you sort, collate, and categorize your inventory activity.

In addition, although the thought of assembling all this information can give rise to moans and groans about the amount of work required to properly catalog everything you have to sell, after you've established your initial inventory log, adding items and deleting them from the log is much easier if you merely keep up with it as your inventory turns.

Storage Concerns

Many sellers have tales of woe about the time when they didn't have a good storage system. Whether an item got lost or damaged, inadequate attention to storage has cost them in the long run. Although you might begin with a small table full of items to sell, be aware that your inventory can quickly swell to fill up desk drawers, closet spaces, and whole rooms. Here's what you should consider as you decide where you'll store your physical inventory:

- **How big (or small) will the items be?** If you're selling furniture or other large items, you'll be faced with the need for a larger storage area than if you're selling knickknacks.

- **Does the inventory require climate control?** All items are best stored in clean, dry environments, but some items need special care in regard to humidity and exposure to sunlight.

- **Can the inventory be secured?** Although you needn't distrust friends or family, you will want to be able to "close up" your inventory area to ensure nothing is inadvertently moved or mis-placed. And, of course, truly valuable items such as jewelry and the like should be locked up for safety's sake.

- **How large will the inventory grow?** Although you might start off with low expectations, many sellers who find their rhythm tell of storage facilities that are quickly outgrown. Keep expansion in mind and be prepared to deal with overflow from your initial stor-age solution.

- **Will storage cost?** Some sellers have so much inventory that they have to move much of it to offsite storage facilities. Keep those costs in mind as you figure the rest of your selling expenses and profit expectations.

- **How accessible will the inventory be?** If your items are stored off-site or up in the attic, always work to keep items relatively within reach. Clambering over boxes or trying to access an off-site facility with limited business hours can become inconvenient and time consuming.

 ALERT Although it might seem a slam-dunk solution to simply go that drop-ship route, letting the actual source of the goods manage all storage headaches for you, refrain from putting all your eggs into one basket. Drop-shipping can solve many of your inventory issues, but you'll likely still need to invest in and store physical goods to keep your business running at full tilt. For that reason, always consider the storage concerns brought up in this discussion.

Rotate Your Stock; Follow the Trends

Remember that Britney Spears won't be hot (or young) forever, nor will there be consistent demand for beach balls or fast-aging PC goods. Give your inventory a "shelf life," and try to keep it moving in line with public demand. You'll want to avoid these common traps that lie in wait for sellers:

- **If it's hot today, it's gotta be hot tomorrow.** Wrong. It's much bet-ter to figure an item will be cold tomorrow. Trends and fads are fleeting. Think of Cabbage Patch dolls, Furbies, Y2K paraphernalia, and Pokémon. Buy before or just at the onset of the newest craze, and sell as it peaks. Your goal is to have your inventory depleted before everyone else catches on and floods the market with similar goods.

- **It's bound to be popular one of these days.** Avoid investing heavily in trendy merchandise that could take years to "mature" (that is, to develop a significant rise in value long after the demise of the original burst of popularity) unless you can truly afford to tie up your cash assets. Some items can be an instant gold mine, whereas others simply languish without much demand at all. To you, that's either cash that's forever tied up or a loss if you decide to dump the goods for whatever they'll bring.

- **Nobody shares the really good information.** Actually, trade papers and collector's reports are full of useful news about buyers' changing attitudes. Never before have buyers been so bombarded with appeals to their money, and you'll need to read widely to be at precisely the right place with the right stuff at the right time.

- **The older it gets, the more it'll be worth.** Avoid holding inventory too long in anticipation of potentially higher profits. Find your profit goal and, if the market will meet it, sell. If you wait too long to sell, hoping for even higher profits, demand might fall off quickly and steeply, and you're apt to find that the opportunity has ended as quickly as it first appeared.

So, with your inventory matters addressed, it's time to move on and address the next big aspect of your business, the aspect that will make or break your ability to turn a profit regardless of what you're selling: your reputation. Turn to Chapter 20, "Building a Stellar Online Reputation," and learn how you can excel in your efforts if your good reputation precedes you at every turn and every click of your buyer's mouse.

part 5

Beyond EBay

chapter 20

Building a Stellar Online Reputation

In today's competitive eBay market, sellers are scrambling to bolster their business and beef up their bottom line. At the online auction place, you know you're contending with literally millions of sellers who are vying for the attention and patronage of the assemblage of bidders. Although there was a time when a good variety of merchandise was the only hook needed to attract eager bidders, now the attitude has shifted, and bidders are just as interested in *how* they will be served as they are in *what* they will be served. Part 4 of this book offered advice, approach, and insight into how to stay atop your auction matters, how to best engage your bidders and buyers, and how to keep the transaction on track for a successful close. If you've maintained a good focus on providing excellent service along the way, you have presented yourself as a committed seller who is intent on providing good products and a great experience to those with whom you've dealt. Through it all, you've begun to establish a name for yourself within the eBay community. Your good name, then, is among your greatest assets at eBay. Keep your name polished, keep it prominent, and promote it with pride.

This chapter illuminates the importance of your eBay reputation (buoyed by actual user comments shared with me), helps you get off to a good start in building an excellent eBay feedback rating, and brings to light the additional elements that can affirm you as a stellar seller, helping you attract and retain loyal customers in the virtual marketplace.

Building an EBay Feedback Rating

Have you seen what people are saying in the eBay Feedback Forum?

> "The best of the best! A true pro! Highly recommended!"

> "Okay to deal with, but kind of slow to ship."

> "Looking for a great deal? Keep looking. This #$+@!% just robbed me."

Yes, people are definitely talking, and when it comes to eBay feedback, what will they say when it comes time to rate *your* performance? By this point, you already know that feedback is the barometer by which buyers grade and critique the sellers they've dealt with (and vice versa). When you were a newcomer to the auction space, I cautioned you to investigate a seller's feedback rating and encouraged you to avoid sellers who have a spotty record. Now *you're* the seller and it becomes your task to build a respectable feedback rating as quickly and cleanly as possible. There are ways to bolster your auction reputation, starting with these tactics that will help you build a feedback rating that lets buyers know you're a seller they can trust. Feedback, you see, works a dual role for you: It's your calling card *and* your report card.

The Origin of the Feedback Forum

Simply enough, the Feedback Forum is a virtual public notice board where buyers and sellers can share their comments, good and bad, about their transactions with one another. Those who are serious about advancing their auction opportunities have been conscientious in their dealings to better ensure they will receive good marks from others. Those who are less than sincere in their auction exploits are quickly exposed to the rest of the community. That's what it's become—a community. Thanks to the Feedback Forum and the community's eagerness to utilize it, eBay for the most part has developed as a safe venue for online trading.

Getting Past the Goose Egg

First things first. Sellers who are new might face the quandary of "How can I get buyers to trust me if I don't yet have a feedback rating?" Yes, it can become something of a paradox: For bidders to have trust in you, you need a decent feedback rating yet, to gain a feedback rating, you have to be able to create and complete transactions. Thankfully, this predicament is not quite the "chicken and the egg" dilemma that it might appear.

To effectively get past the under-10 rating stigma (the inherent eBay initiation period), sellers should consider some active buying first. Remembering that feedback applies to both buyers and sellers, it's wise to do some buying, to be a stellar customer when working with the seller, and subsequently earn those prized initial feedback points before you begin selling. After you've received 10 positive feedback points from at least 10 unique users, eBay awards you with your first visible feedback star; you're on your way. Even though the feedback you receive will be identified as buyer-related feedback (see Figure 20-1), it will nonetheless convey that you're

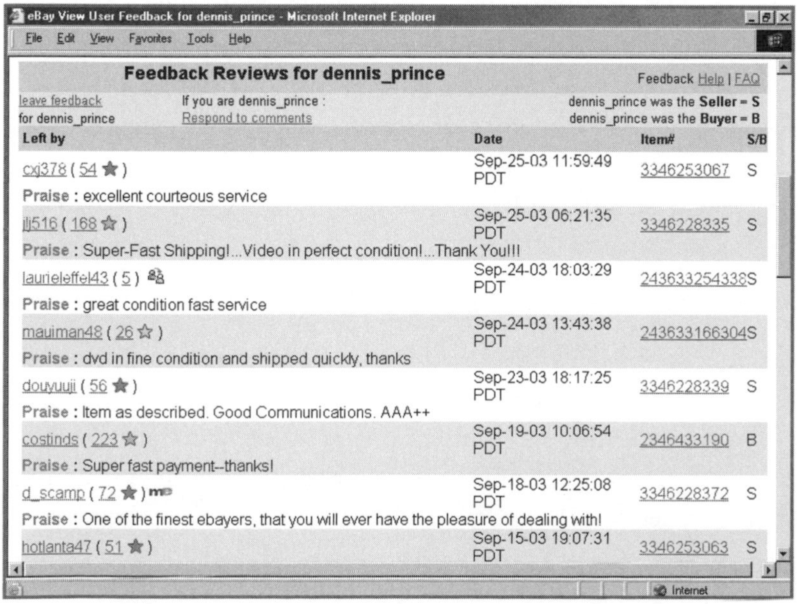

figure 20-1

To the right of each individual feedback comment, notice the S or B indicator that denotes whether the feedback was posted in relation to a sell or buy transaction.

reliable and accountable in completing deals. Just like that, your initiation period is over and you're ready to sell.

You Can't Win If You Don't Play

Of course, the key to building an impressive feedback rating is participation. If you're a seller who is eager to gain a respectable rating for yourself, you'll have to post feedback for others. Regular auction-goers tend to work under the mode of "You leave positive feedback for me, and I'll reciprocate." Essentially, it's a mentality that promotes a better trading environment because users (especially sellers) reap the rewards of their good business style and active online community involvement. When you become a serious seller who covets a stellar reputation, you'll be more than motivated to perform well in every deal, hoping to build a chart-topping feedback rating.

Yet, many folks I've talked to have complained about the time required to manage feedback at eBay. No doubt about it, feedback *does* take time, but it's time well spent in enabling you to reap the reward of comments to be left for you. EBay has made feedback management much easier. The My eBay area provides buyers and sellers with a way to easily review those transactions where feedback is yet to be posted. All you need to do is click on the tab labeled Feedback and then click on the button labeled Leave Feedback. From there, you'll see a comprehensive listing of those transactions in which you need to complete the feedback phase of the transaction (see Figure 20-2). Rather than sift through your backlog of completed listings or purchases, let My eBay lead the way to fast and fruitful feedback management. Neat, huh?

Don't Be Afraid to Get Suggestive

But what if that buyer or seller with whom you've dealt seems a bit delinquent in posting feedback? Well, the next way to grow your feedback rating is to, well, *suggest* it be posted. Although some buyers are touchy about sellers asking for positive feedback (some denounce this as begging for brownie points), it's generally safe and reasonable for sellers to communicate the following:

> "Your item is on the way. Please let me know when it arrives and we'll exchange positive feedback."

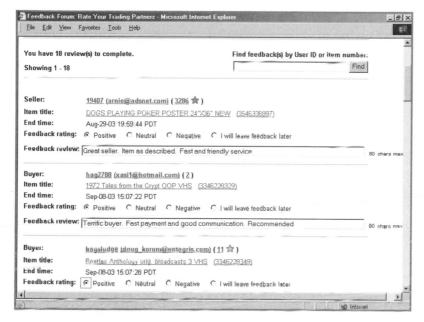

figure 20-2

From the My eBay area, you can post feedback quickly and easily.

(Recall that I suggested as much in my Winning Buyer Notification from PayPal.)

Who should post feedback first? There's no right or wrong answer here because it becomes a matter of personal preference. Although you should expect to post feedback for the buyer first (remember that as seller, you're in the business of reaching out as much as possible), if that buyer is satisfied with his purchase and your service, he'll likely respond in kind.

ALERT Some sellers swear they'll not post positive feedback *until* the buyer has done so first. Why? Some sellers impart horror stories of dutifully posting feedback for their buyer when the item is shipped, only to be slapped down with a negative feedback posting from a disgruntled (sometimes unmanageable) buyer. To that effect, sellers often await the buyer's e-mail confirmation that all is well and positive feedback will be posted. Then, all is safe in the seller posting feedback as well. You decide which approach you'll take.

Of course, don't be hurt if some buyers never post feedback for you; some simply don't do it and become angered if they're pestered for it. Leave that one alone. But, assuming you're listing plenty of items for sale and are behaving in a polite and professional manner through every transaction, you should find that your feedback rating will blossom in no time.

So Much Ado 'Bout Feedback?

But *why* does feedback matter? If it's just the opinions of average people on eBay, what noticeable impact can it really have?

The answer springs from the need to feel safe and confident in a virtual trading environment. Return to the initial discussion of how safe you feel sending money to an absolute stranger. Wouldn't you feel better if you could learn a bit more about the people you'll be dealing with? Feedback serves both buyers and sellers and, although it's not foolproof, it helps you gain a better feel about who's who in the online auction space. Although I have not doggedly chased down every buyer or seller with whom I've dealt over the years, wringing out a positive comment at every possible opportunity, I remain eternally vigilant in dealing quickly, fairly, and respectfully at all times lest I would bring about bad news of my business. Feedback *is* important and, best of all, it's easy to manage.

Mind Your Business

Although feedback—that precious customer testimony—is integral to your ability to draw and delight customers, you'll need to offer many of the "intangibles" of excellent customer service and product quality. Your feedback rating will serve you well in helping to gain the trust of buyers, but here are some other key aspects to successfully attracting buyers and further enhancing your online reputation.

Get Noticed

It's tough to be seen among the millions of other sellers online, and you'll need to employ every method available to rise above the crowd. A critical step in building a stellar online reputation is to ensure that your presence will be acknowledged. Forget the bold type and fancy icons for your listings. (Those just add to your selling costs.) Instead, take advantage of these more effective attention-getting moves.

- **Practice peak timing.** Remember to stage your auctions for 7 days, ending on a weekend, and closing between 6:00 and 8:00 PM PT for maximum bidder exposure. Adjust the auction durations and timings to coincide with special events such as holidays and such.

- **High hitting.** Carefully choose keywords that are most likely to be searched by bidders, ensuring that your listings appear in the maximum number of result lists.

- **Category savvy.** There's a sea of categories to choose from, so continue to research which categories are host to items like yours and where the most active bidding seems to take place.

- **Detail oriented.** Give ample information about the items you sell so that bidders won't feel like they're gambling on a long shot.

- **Image conscious.** Provide clear photos of your items or thumbnail links to a gallery of images in your listings. Don't overdo it, or your page will take too long to load, causing bidders to lose interest and leave.

- **Cross listed.** Cross reference your concurrent auctions in the descriptions of your listings. Use HTML links to make it easier for bidders to jump from item to item.

Although this might seem like repetition of what was stated in previous chapters, the importance of these listing and visibility strategies becomes clearer as you recognize how these tactics work to boost exposure of *you* as well as your items. Taking deliberate and well-thought-out steps in how and when you'll list your items will gain you and your growing business greater exposure to the millions of bidders who are searching for goods.

"I look for sellers who have the things I want and are presenting them well," asserted eBay regular Mark Munoz. "If they've got a lousy description or [inferior] photo, I'll bolt and go to another seller who does a better job and knows how to properly offer items for bid."

If you serve up high-quality listings utilizing well-founded methods, you'll be more likely to be remembered by customers who like what you sell. "Those are the sellers I'll be looking for the next time I search for stuff," confirms Munoz. That's about all the convincing I need.

Get Knowledgeable

To truly carve a presence in the auction world today, you need to convince bidders that you're an *expert* who can be trusted and is worth seeking out again and again. If you merely dabble in the goods you sell and have a limited knowledge to match, some might perceive you as risky.

"It's scary to see how some people totally misrepresent things," complains memorabilia collector Joe Medeiros. "They're either ignorant or dishonest. [I] don't know if they're trying to pull a fast one, but I'm not sticking around to find out."

To gain bidders' confidence as well as capture their bids, sellers need to establish themselves as being reliable sources of goods *and* information. If you don't know the facts, find out. Read collector's books, trade journals, historical references, and anything else that will give you the inside information that bidders are looking for. By offering up accurate descriptions, key details, appropriate pricing, and answers to specific questions, sellers provide proof of their knowledge and become recognized for being a trustworthy source that bidders learn they can count on. With the ever-present spectra of fraud and tomfoolery lurking online, bidders are taking greater precautions to be choosy about whom they'll buy from.

Get Committed

You know that your sales are your bread and butter; you must realize that it's your customers who are feeding your fortune. Strive to exceed customer expectations with every sale, and you'll do some of your greatest work in boosting your online reputation. Be prompt, professional, and pleasant in all communications. Don't make customers wait, and never leave them wondering about you, your products, or your commitment to ensure a stellar exchange.

How? Offer clarification about your products and your sales policies whenever asked. Give clear and concise answers to a bidder's questions. Then provide additional information that you think will help potential bidders feel more confident about bidding on your auctions, be it product related or policy related.

And go the extra mile if a transaction gets a bit muddled and requires special handling. Keep that customer satisfied. Show the customer your commitment to better business by actively working to clear confusion and resolve potential problems. You're not only working for that customer's satisfaction; you're also protecting your reputation from the sort of disgruntled retribution that could mar your otherwise blemish-free reputation.

Get Personal?

By all means, don't pry into your bidders' private lives, but do allow them to peer in a bit on yours. Given that this is the "faceless world" of the Internet in which you're dealing, be sensitive that bidders aren't able to make that face-to-face contact as they would at a shop or show. Remember, if your customers can't see you, they might have trouble trusting you. Remedy the situation by sharing something of yourself. At eBay, there's a quick and easy solution to this dilemma: *About Me*. Actually, it's about *you* and your business, and it's the area of eBay where you can post a photo of yourself while sharing some personal details about your interests, hobbies, pets, or whatever.

Although it might sound silly on the surface, many bidders are eager to see and know just whom it is they might be dealing with. Consider it an icebreaker, if you will, as well as another way to gain recognition and rapport with the bidding public. You needn't invest days or even hours when setting up your About Me page. The style can be as simple as following along eBay's pre-prepared templates. Let me show you how easy this can be.

To begin creating your About Me page, visit the eBay site map and locate the About Me link under the Buying and Selling heading. Click the link to access the starting page that explains the feature. On that page, find and click the Create and Edit Your Page button and choose a format for your page (readily available as a two-column layout, newspaper layout, or centered layout, as shown in Figure 20-3).

Select a format and begin filling in the content for your About Me page (see Figure 20-4).

After you've entered the information you would like to share, click on the Preview Your Page button to review your work (or you can select the Choose New Layout button if you would like to start again). Figure 20-5 shows the humble beginnings of my new About Me page.

If you are satisfied, click the Save My Page button at the bottom of the screen. Of course, you also have the option of utilizing the Edit Some More, Edit Using HTML (for you serious Web programmers), or Start Over buttons.

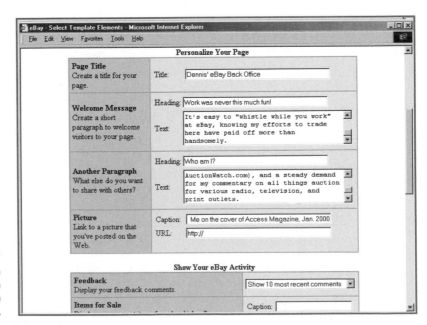

figure 20-3

EBay makes it easy to create your own About Me page by offering three easy-to-use layout templates.

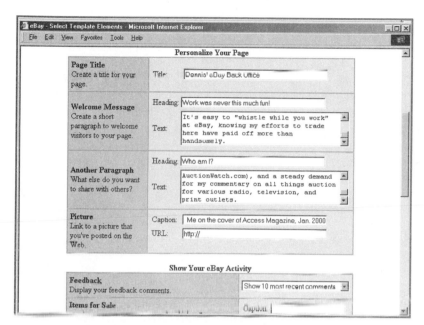

20-4

Fill in information to be displayed on your About Me page.

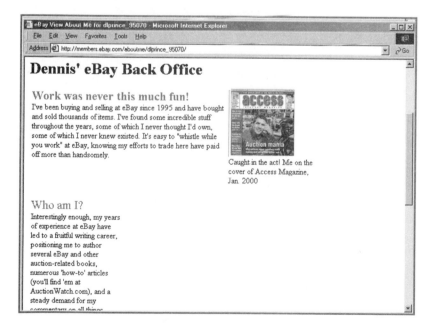

figure 20-5

In mere minutes, a simple About Me page is ready to display.

NOTE Although I've kept the text in this example About Me page light, think about what you can tell visitors that will help them feel more comfortable and confident about dealing with you. In my example, I clearly state I've been *eBaying* since 1995 (I have extensive experience, you see) and I have fun doing it (I'm suggesting a pleasurable experience to those who will deal with me). I also indicate that I've written many books about eBay (I could be a useful source of information to visitors) and I've written about the auction industry as a whole (I have a breadth of experience). It's not my intention to toot my own horn here, but I hope you'll see how you can instill calm and trust in visitors based on what you choose to share about yourself in your About Me page.

Serving the Auction Newbie

Recall in Chapter 8, "E-Motions and Auction Affronts," where I discussed the various auctiongoer personalities and introduced the newcomers—the *newbies*—who are fresh on the scene. Most sellers agree that working a sale with a first-timer can require extra effort, extra explanation, and occasionally extra patience. Those sellers who welcome this interaction, however, and stand prepared to assist and encourage the wide-eyed wanderers through their initial encounters will find themselves in prime position to adopt a long-term customer in the process and significantly enhance their eBay reputation.

Now, certainly, no seller wants to be in the business of baby-sitting newbies, yet it is the wise eBay merchant who will recognize that these new bidders will benefit—and likely appreciate—a bit of extra help. When newbies set their sights on your offerings, it's in the seller's best interest to ease the potential apprehension and improve the ensuing transaction for both of you. Here are three simple ways to do just that:

- **Set the tempo.** Remember that many new buyers aren't exactly savvy to the protocol of auctioning. They might be overanxious; they might be undercommitted. When the auction is over, promptly get the exchange in action. Exemplify your tried-and-true process of managing auctions, and newbies will know they're working with a real pro whom they can trust.

■ **Be their guide.** It's always good business to help new bidders (*your new customers*) better understand how eBay and online auctioning works, showing them the ins and outs of the bidding realm. Remember: If you're there to help them, chances are they'll be inclined to become a repeat customer.

■ **Build a better community.** As a seller, do your part to ensure that the auction venues stay active and positive by shouldering part of the burden of keeping the community growing. Help the newbies along, and you'll fuel their desire to bid and buy more often.

Beware the New Bidder?

Of course, a seller must look after his own business interests as he courts new customers. Although new bidders don't have a lengthy bidding history that can be reviewed, sellers can nonetheless ascertain whether the new bidder is taking one of two common shopping styles: risk-averse or reckless.

Some newbies bid cautiously at first, utilizing conservative high-bid amounts or limiting their bidding to just an item or two. After they gain some confidence and experience, they'll likely loosen up. Until then, your auction might truly be the only item in their sight, and they might interact with you as if they're your only customer. Anticipate that and be ready to serve them to the best of your ability.

Conversely, watch for the newbies who run amuck in a bidding frenzy. Caught up in the fun of shopping and the ease of bidding (often overlooking the potential sum total of all their bids), these are the newbies you need to tend to quickly. Before the euphoria of the win wears off—and before the ultimate sticker shock sets in—be sure to engage these apprentice auction-goers fast to collect your payment. Although it's not always the case, this sort of newbie is prime to become a deadbeat after he realizes he has overcommitted his finite funds to a sea of online sellers.

It's not just newbies who sometimes require additional attention, but the opportunity to lend a hand to a novice bidder is the foundation upon which a lasting customer base is formed. Take the time to understand and assist the auction newbies, and you're likely to become a seller they'll visit again and again.

Then, of course, they'll tell their friends, and they'll tell their friends, and so on, and so on . . .

Making the Grade

Next, let's look at you again and how you're presenting the items you'll sell. Experienced sellers know how important accurate item representation can be, not only for the sake of an immediate sale but also for their long-term reputation. *Item grading*, however, remains a gray area in online selling. It's a subjective assessment that, if not properly understood and communicated, can lead to a contentious matter between buyer and seller.

Understand that there are no universally accepted grading definitions for all sorts of merchandise; different terms are used to describe the condition of different items (such as furniture, stamps, glassware, or trading cards). If this multitude of terms isn't enough cause for concern (and it is), similar terms are used across a variety of items yet don't represent the same "state of being" within each commodity. Therefore, accurate and responsible use of grading terms becomes something of a *learned* discipline with application of a stated grade often depending on the experience of the seller.

The bottom line, though, is that bidders are looking for high-quality items (especially true for collectibles and vintage goods). Because they're willing to pay high dollars for top-quality merchandise, bidders are looking for sellers who are accurate and dependable in their grading techniques. So, when it comes time to advertise your goods as well as further establish your good reputation, consider these guidelines when communicating the condition:

- Use the recognized grading terms for the item you'll offer. (There's no universal grading system or terminology because different commodities use different grading criteria; educate yourself on the proper terms and appropriate application thereof.) Steer clear of off-the-cuff terms like "super condition," "really nice," and "great specimen." Avoidance of accepted terms makes you appear inexperienced or potentially dishonest.

- Accompany the grade with a full disclosure of the item's details. Help the customer decide if your assessment of the item seems reasonable.

- Consider using "half-grades" (Very Fine +, Near Mint -) if you're on the fence about where the item truly grades out.

- Consider carefully undergrading your item. Without taking too much away from the item, let buyers know you're using a strict grading system, and then grade down a half step. This usually results in feedback from buyers proclaiming your items arrive "better than described," exactly the sort of good PR you want.

- Be sure to apply a suitable offering price (if using a reserve or stating a Buy-It-Now price) to the grade you select. A noticeable mismatch in price compared to condition does not sit well with bidders.

Bidders are seeking out sellers of desirable goods and will make note of those sellers who seem to be most dependable and trustworthy in terms of item grading. By properly representing your items, you'll develop a reputation for being honest and reliable in all sales.

One Last Look at the Distinctive Differentiators

To close this discussion about your eBay reputation, turn your attention once again (and always as you do business) toward your customers. They are the ones you are seeking to entertain and satisfy, and they are the ones who will keep you happily in business or woefully on the sidelines. Your reputation begins and ends with your ability to recognize your customers' needs and to balance those with your duties as a seller. It sounds preachy, I know, but customer satisfaction simply cannot be stressed enough.

Recognize that bidders are looking for a seller to be interactive and responsive. Bidders at eBay are usually engaging in business with complete strangers, often across the continent and sometimes across the globe. The successful seller understands the potential anxiety this can cause and remains ever ready to respond to any and all bidder inquiries. When a bidder (or especially a *potential* bidder) contacts you, be sure to respond quickly, completely, and professionally. Answer the bidder's questions directly, and then provide extra information you think could help them better understand your item or your way of doing business. Remember: You're courting a potential customer here, so be friendly and forthcoming. Your goal and duty is to help bidders feel at ease when dealing with you.

Next, bidders are looking for your sales policy—one that they hope will not be difficult to find or interpret. Bidders want to be clear about how you intend to do business with them. Develop and publish your sales terms and conditions up front so that your customers can quickly understand how you will manage an eventual transaction. Therefore, make your policy easy to find by including the terms directly in your auction descriptions. The key here is to make your policy readily available and conspicuously visible. Customers don't appreciate guessing games or having to hunt down your sales conditions. If you don't think this is a key to customer service and your online reputation, keep in mind that most bidders don't feel well served if they have to hunt *you* down to determine what kind of business you're running. They'll run to another seller instead.

And what kind of business *are* you running? Bidders will determine if your sales terms are sensible. That's a subjective matter, but many terms are generally accepted among auction goers. Bidders (your customers) need information regarding what payment methods you'll accept, what sort of shipping charges you'll apply, and how quickly you'll deliver an item won. Be reasonable here. Don't mandate "money orders only" or "payment by credit card—no exceptions." The same goes for shipping charges: Don't charge a flat rate of $6.50 if what you typically sell only incurs $3.85 in postage costs. Customers don't appreciate being trapped by unfounded terms that make it look as if the seller is more interested in his convenience at the expense of the customer's. That bidder will most likely bolt from your auction and find another seller who is operating in a more customer-friendly manner.

Don't overlook the fact that customers are looking for a bit of appreciation. Although some might argue that dealing with customers can be a grueling exercise in patience (which it sometimes can be), the fact is that most bidders you'll deal with at eBay are honest folk who are intent on doing good business. Simple things like including a thank you note with their item or suggesting an alternative shipping method that can save them a buck or two will go a long way along the road of satisfaction. If you treat your customers like you would like to be treated, they'll be more inclined to work with you to improve the transaction. Then, upon completing a successful transaction, be fast to post that positive feedback, letting them know how important and appreciated their business has been to you.

Lastly, it's been said that to truly excel in customer satisfaction, a seller needs to have a passion to serve those he sells to. "Real customer service comes from the heart," offered a fellow seller. "If you don't truly and deeply value what the customer means to your business' health, you might as well not bother." That's so true, although it's not easy to maintain such a credo. Your key, though, to ensuring that you remain completely customer focused is to let the customer—not you—determine what's satisfactory. Only the customer can tell you if he has been satisfied, and it's the wise seller who keeps a pulse on his customers' satisfaction as a means to understand which direction the business is going.

By applying these key principles to your business, your approval ratings and online reputation will have nowhere to go but up.

chapter 21

On Becoming a Business

For many of the driven eBaysians, this is the goal: to become a full-fledged auction business. In the days prior to the dot-com bust, many sellers glee-fully announced that they had proudly quit their day jobs, electing to sustain their income on eBay alone. Many tried, few succeeded. You see, after the dot-com crash and after the fevered novelty of eBay wore off (not to mention that the marketplace was more plentiful with once-costly items that had suddenly become quite plentiful), those sellers who were high on aspiration but low on planning simply couldn't maintain a consistent level of sales. Yet, some *did* make it and continue to do so thanks to careful planning, a well-thought out "migration," and a full understanding of what it means to go into business for oneself. It's not a get-rich-quick scheme—no way—but it is a bona-fide business possibility.

Establishing your own eBay or other such online business can provide you the freedom and flexibility that you might never have dreamed possible. Although it's a lot of work, running your own show puts you in control and gives you the opportunity to explore new ways to make a living. But don't forget there is still much of the real world to contend with and, to small business owners, that means licensing, registration, tax liabilities, and more.

This chapter highlights the major business requirements and liabilities if you're truly committed to going into business, staying in business, and keeping out of trouble with your local and federal government agencies. Despite the many regulations you'll encounter, government interest isn't all burdensome. There are also small business assistance programs and exclusions that can help your business grow and prosper.

ALERT   *But first* . . . the disclaimer (you knew it was coming): The information provided here is intended to guide you toward a better understanding of some of the elements of legally establishing your business and reporting your business activity to government agencies (such as the IRS). The rules differ from state to state and even from town to town, so please consult the proper agencies as well as a CPA to be sure you fully understand the limitations and liabilities as they pertain to your own business. (There, that wasn't so bad.)

Licensed for Business

Although people often conduct their auction activities without one, in many states, the act of buying items wholesale for the purpose of reselling them online or elsewhere requires a valid *Resale License* (also known as a *Seller's Permit* or *Tax ID*). Licenses might be required at the city level, county level, or with other states. Because the requirements can vary significantly from state to state, it's wise to visit your local state's business administration home page. Resale licenses are usually free, although you might need to pony up a small deposit. When you're buying wholesale, you need to have this license so that you can purchase goods—tax free—from wholesalers and distributors. Because the requirements differ from state to state, start by visiting the Small Business Administration (SBA) site at http://www.sba.gov. There, you can find links to your state-specific Web site to get more information on the local business license regulations you must comply with.

But is registering your business simply an exercise in wading through red tape? Actually, no. Although you might not see the need when your business first starts up, there are a number of SBA-provided services and protections to be gained as your business grows. Consider these, for example:

- Business structure assistance
- Business tax liabilities and advantages

- Business insurance
- Trademark registration and protection
- Patent protection and assistance
- Copyright protection and assistance

Those are just a few considerations that will help you or haunt you depending whether you properly register your business. According to the SBA, failure to comply with business licensing and adherence to regulations could leave you legally unprotected, expose you to penalties, and generally put your business at risk of dissolution.

Charging Sales Tax

One of the most active discussions of online auction sales centers around the levying of sales tax. In general, businesses are required to charge state sales tax for all retail sales made within their state of residence (or the state of business residence). Your resale license indicates to wholesalers, manufacturers, or distributors from which you purchase goods that you will charge sales tax to your in-state customers and will remit those taxes collected to the Federal government; that's why your suppliers don't charge you tax. However, with online auctions easily and regularly spanning multiple states and even countries, there has been some confusion regarding when and where to collect sales tax from buyers.

The Internet Freedom Act of 1998 was passed to waive the need for out-of-state sales taxes for Internet sales. That effectively solved the interstate tax collection problem (at least for now), but there is still the in-state tax requirement to contend with. Technically, sellers with valid business licenses are responsible for collecting and remitting taxes on retail sales made within their state of business; out-of-state sales do not require collection and remittance of taxes for such transactions.

So why else has the collecting of sales tax become a much-discussed topic within the eBay community? Many buyers complain that some sellers are falsely collecting sales tax; they're either charging taxes for in-state sales without holding a valid resale license, or they're attempting to collect taxes for out-of-state purchases. *This is illegal.* Therefore, before you think you might be able to glean an extra buck or two on an online sale (not that you would really be so tempted), be prepared that a buyer could ask you to provide your resale license number for verification. If you don't have one, you could be accused of tax fraud. (And if you have one and aren't using it to report taxes, you're in even more trouble if the state finds out.)

Tax Liability for Online Sales

Now, let's move from one tax discussion—collecting sales tax—to another tax discussion: paying income tax. Wherever you make a profit, income taxes are to be paid. Although you might well consider skirting the issue of paying taxes related to your garage sale, your baby-sitting gig, and your appearance at collector's shows, understand that your state and federal governments aren't as likely to be so permissive when it comes to eBay activity. Given the billions of dollars in e-revenues generated by online auctions, the tax collectors have duly taken notice of who's making how much and how much of that the government can tap into.

For Fun or Profit?

Although it's probably clear that, in reading this chapter, you're in this for the profit, it still bears discussing the tax liability of your eBay endeavors, whether you deem them for business or pleasure. The majority of online business owners regularly identify and declare their sales to the tax man, but others believe they are exempt because their online efforts constitute a mere hobby: selling trinkets they've picked up during their travels and outings.

"All income is taxable, even hobby income," counsels Tax Consultant Jill Dutcher. "The difference between hobby income and business income is *intent* and if you *make money.* If you buy from garage sales, for example, and resell [online] at a profit, you are operating a business."

Okay, but how is this income to be declared? Dutcher continues: "Hobby income is reported as other income (under $400.00) . . . [but] as a matter of practicality, I put most hobby income on a Schedule C [income tax statement] and deduct any expenses directly to it."

The rules are simple: Wherever you make a profit, taxes are to be paid. Even if you decide to infrequently sell off prior investment pieces such as fine art, vintage automobiles, antiques, or what have you, if any sale earns you a profit over and above your original purchase price, the IRS deems the profit as taxable income. Conversely, if such a sale fails to recoup the original investment, you'll be faced with a loss, which could be deemed a "declarable loss." (Again, consult a tax professional in these matters.)

Naturally, you would prefer to see your gains exceed your losses (and the government would like that, too). When you're successful in your money-making enterprise, you must share the wealth with the IRS.

Further, if your approach is to regularly buy and sell items at online auctions, you're essentially operating a *sole proprietorship*—a business that is in the business of making a profit. If you're this sort of happily self-employed business person, recognize that you're responsible for making *quarterly estimated tax payments* based on the income realized for the tax period. Required payment dates are April 15, June 15, September 15, and January 15 of the following year. These payments are filed using Form 1040-ES (OCR). There's a catch to paying these taxes on your business: Besides paying a regular tax on any profit, you're also responsible for paying an additional 15.3 percent to cover Social Security and Medicare contributions.

So, when it comes time to file your annual tax return in April, you should consider reporting your business' activity using Schedule C, Profit (or Loss) from a Business or Profession, with your Form 1040 income tax filing.

On a final note, Dutcher strongly encourages keeping your personal and business transactions clearly separated. "I always recommend a separate bank account for your business expenses. Keeping your personal and business expenses separate makes the accounting easier."

How Big Is Your Business?

The type of business you desire, your individual situation, your business goals, and other personal and financial factors all play a part in choosing an appropriate *business structure*. Before choosing one over the others, be sure to discuss your business plans with your accountant or attorney; they can guide you on the pros and cons of each structure option and help you understand the requirements and liabilities of each.

Staying on the discussion of taxation, one of the many complicating factors about how your business income is taxed depends on how large your business is and how you have formally established it. Not all businesses are taxed the same because not all businesses are structured to operate the same. Familiarize yourself with the different types of business organizations to best suit your business goals as well as to make the best of the tax laws.

- **Sole proprietorship.** If yours is a one-person show without special corporation designation, you fall into this business type. Taxes on sole proprietorships are identical to individual income taxes; you and your business are considered one and the same. But that doesn't mean business income is just like salary; you're responsible for paying self-employment taxes, which include roughly an additional 15 percent liability for Social Security and Medicare. Here, you'll use the Form 1040 Schedule C (Business Income and Expenses) as well as Schedule SE (Self-Employment).

ALERT An eBay "home business" is the most common type of sole proprietorship and is easy to establish and maintain, legally. However, be certain not to overlook or ignore the fact that, just because you're operating your business from your home, you're not exempt from certain legal or other business-related liabilities. Be sure to review the section "Business Insurance and Other Protections" later in this chapter. Also, be certain your local municipality doesn't prohibit operating a business from your home; some towns and cities forbid this.

- **Partnership.** Work with another person and claim it as such without claiming corporate status, and you'll be deemed to fall into this business type. This is more complex than it sounds, however, and you should seek out professional advice if you intend to create a partnership or *limited liability partnership*. Interestingly, taxes on this sort of business model are treated similarly to those on a sole proprietorship: Two self-employed individuals who are working for a business but are not *employees* of the business file individual tax returns based on their share of the partnership income. The business, not claimed as a separate entity, is not taxed. The partnership files its business activity information via Form 1065 Schedule K-1. The partners, then, report their personal income and tax liability using Form 1040 Schedule E.

- **C corporation.** After you officially name your corporation and go through the registration process that lets you include *Inc.*, *Corp.*, or *Ltd.* along with it, you qualify as a C corporation. A corporation is taxed as a separate entity by way of the *corporate income tax*. For corporations, taxable income can be affected by how much the owners withdraw in the form of salary, benefits, or dividends. In addition, corporate income can be subject to *double taxation*; that is, any profit that a corporation claims is taxed; if the owners withdraw it for their own use, that profit is then considered *dividends* and will be taxed as personal income on the owners' individual tax returns. A corporation files an individual return using Form 1120 using tax brackets that are different from individual (personal) tax filings.

- **S corporation.** This acts more like a partnership in that the income is taxed as if it were all claimed by the owner—which might be just one person or a group of people. The corporation reports activity via Form 1120S Schedule K-1 and the owners file Schedule E to report their share of the business profits.

- **Limited liability company.** The LLC structure is available to businesses that have two or more owners, who have the liberty to choose if they will be taxed as a partnership (using Form 1065 Schedule K-1 and Schedule E) or as a corporation.

Clearly, the government hasn't made determining which business model is best easy to do. Be sure to consult a tax professional for an accurate assessment of your business, its potential, and the best choice for business declaration. Then check with your state to determine any limitations or special fees that might be levied on different business structures. Also visit the IRS Web site at http://www.irs.gov/forms_pubs/index.html for a more than generous dose of documentation and explanation of the different tax forms and application to the different business structures.

A Couple More Taxing Matters

As a self-employed individual who is earning income, you are responsible for certain federal payments that most employers manage for you. The total is calculated as a fixed percentage of your business income as follows:

- **Social Security liability.** 12.4 percent of a base amount (a ceiling amount stated by the government). You should be so lucky as to get anywhere near the ceiling these days.

- **Medicare liability.** 2.9 percent of *all* profit your business realizes.

Self-employment tax often comes as a rude surprise to those who conduct auctions or a separate business as a sideline activity. Remember: These are the deductions that your regular employer splits with you, paying half while you pay the other half. But when it's your own business, you're responsible for the whole amount.

The Expense Defense

Naturally, it takes money to make money. Whenever your business incurs expenses in its striving for a profit, those are probably deductible costs that can offset a portion of your net income (that is, your receipts less the cost of the goods you sold). Although some consider taking business deductions as sly and maybe even illegal (which occasionally it can be, if the deductions aren't legit), most who aren't already aware are surprised and pleased to learn the different expenditures that can be justifiably deducted from their business proceeds.

To begin, understand the normal business expenses that you should be deducting from your net income:

- Supplies
- Office furniture
- Office equipment (PC, fax, printer, phone, and so on)
- Business-related postage costs
- Training and other business-related educational expenses

- Business counseling fees
- Tax preparation fees
- Rent or mortgage interest
- Phone and Internet connection fees
- Legal fees
- Bad debts (unpaid sales)
- Business travel costs (transportation, meals, lodging, entertainment)

These are just some of the common deductions you can legally claim as your operate your business. Be sure to consider other expenses that you incur as part of keeping your business alive and thriving, and consult your tax adviser to see what additional deductions you might be letting slip through your fingers (and into Uncle Sam's hands).

Taking Shelter from Taxes

Although the name has oft been maligned as a business's loophole to evade tax liability, tax shelters or breaks are legitimate, and each business owner should make the most of them.

The goal of a tax shelter is to reduce your business's net income by deflecting some monies to recognized state and federal investment programs. As you operate your business, consider these prime tax reduction opportunities:

- **Retirement plans.** Many financial advisers encourage small business owners to take advantage of income deferment programs such as IRAs, Roth-IRAs, and Keogh Plans. The money you filter to these investment accounts can be deducted from your business income prior to taxation.

- **Family employment.** If you have your under-18 kids lending you a hand in your business, consider employing them and paying them for their efforts. The money you pay them is nontaxable up to an established ceiling amount. Those wages can help reduce your business income and the tax liability that accompanies it.

Business Insurance and Other Protections

Your business is a profit-making machine, and it deserves to be protected properly. Business insurance, therefore, should be considered to ensure that you don't lose the farm—literally—in the case of an unforeseen incident.

Depending on the size and scope of your business, you should investigate these forms of business insurance:

- **Property insurance.** Many home business operators don't realize their homeowner's insurance fails to cover any potential business losses as a result of fire, natural disaster, theft, or vandalism. Some homeowner's policies only cover personal property to a maximum value (regardless of actual value), and many have exclusions that render your property uninsured if it's not at your principal place of residence (such as portable electronics or offsite storage).

- **Liability insurance.** Although your home is usually covered if personal visitors hurt themselves on your property, business visitors might not be covered.

- **Employee insurance.** If your business has grown and you have a staff helping you run the shop, be sure to look into these employee-related protections:
  - Unemployment coverage
  - Workers' compensation
  - Disability insurance

- **Miscellaneous insurance.** Don't forget the other types of coverage that can help protect your business:
  - Auto insurance (business vehicles)
  - Business interruption coverage
  - Health insurance
  - Product liability insurance
  - Employer practices liability

Again, take the time to consult the SBA site to learn more about business insurance options and how you can determine which coverage is best for your business.

chapter 22

Venturing Outside of EBay

So you're ready for the big time, are you? Good. Many sellers have found a level of ongoing success that has them itching to take the next step beyond routine listing and selling of merchandise at eBay, electing to establish and advance an actual business portal of their own. Thanks to the Internet, practically anyone can set up a viable business entity provided they have a product to sell and a motivation to succeed. For many folks, eBay has become the equivalent to dipping a toe in the water to see if buying, selling, and interacting with others is a business venture worth embarking upon.

If you've been following along up to this point and have found enough success to whet your appetite, then it's time to stop testing the waters and consider jumping in with both feet. Ready?

A Self-Assessment to Determine If You're Ready for the Next Step

It's really quite straightforward: Look at the following statements, make an honest assessment, and see if you're ready to step up your business potential.

You know you're ready to move ahead when the following are true:

- EBay seems to be more limiting than enhancing to your overall business potential.

- You've established a customer base; that is, you have a rapport with many different individuals who are eager to know what merchandise you'll offer next.

- You've established a routine with your eBay sales that allows you to work a reasonable amount of hours while pulling down a decent and consistent income for the effort expended.

- You've seen other opportunities to serve your customers that go beyond what can and is being done at eBay.

- You're eager to learn and apply new skills, be they computer oriented, sales oriented, or research oriented.

- You're financially able to extend yourself into additional sales venues that might require additional commitment of time and money. (Remember: Time *is* money in the sales world.)

- You've already begun to draw a consistent income from activity outside of eBay (perhaps direct sales to your established customers) and are ready to shift more effort to it.

Then again, you might want to delay starting up a commercial endeavor if what follows applies to you:

- You enjoy auctioning but are rather sporadic with your listing efforts.

- You are easily distracted by temptations to surf off and shop instead of focusing on selling.

- You dread having to manage the end-of-auction routine.

- You avoid competition.

- You aren't quite comfortable with online business and interactions with strangers.

■ You can't afford to invest any more time in online sales.

■ You're generally too reserved to ever consider promoting yourself.

If you're considering taking the leap and becoming a bona-fide "Web merchant," you need to honestly assess your skills, desires, drive, and aptitudes. Many folks plunk along at eBay and are successful in bringing in some extra cash here and there. That's success. Others, though, are driven to build the better mousetrap and are eager to give the public what it really wants, earning an increased cash flow in the process. That's success, too. For you, it's a situation of defining what success is for your situation and how hard you're willing to work to grab the brass ring away from others in your arena. It's not necessarily easy to break into these merchant ranks, but bear in mind that more and more regular folks are doing it—successfully—every day.

The Do-It-Yourself Marketing Campaign

As defined by Webster's, a campaign is "a series of activities designed to bring about a particular result." If you seek to further enrich your sell-through rates and sales prices at eBay and elsewhere, you can do several things to propel your results upward and increase your business' visibility to as many potential customers as possible. If you're ready to hit the campaign trail, here are several paths you should consider traveling.

Creating an EBay Store

Your commercial Web experience begins within eBay itself when you create an eBay Store. From eBay's home page, click on the eBay Stores link under the Specialty Sites header; then, on the eBay Stores main page, click on the Open Your Store Now text link to begin the Store-building process. The first step in building a Store is to establish who you are and what your Store will be from the Store Content page (see Figure 22-1).

Enter the basic content for your Store by typing information into the various screen fields, much like when you created your About Me page. When you're finished, click the Continue button at the bottom of the page. The next step is to choose your Store colors and graphics (see Figure 22-2).

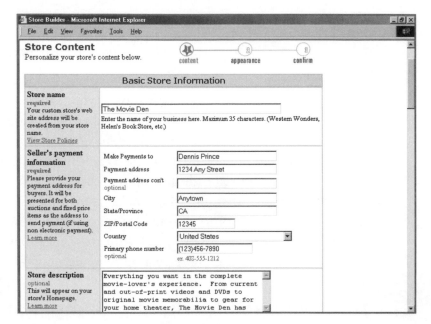

figure 22-1

Begin building your eBay
Store by specifying your
Store Content information.

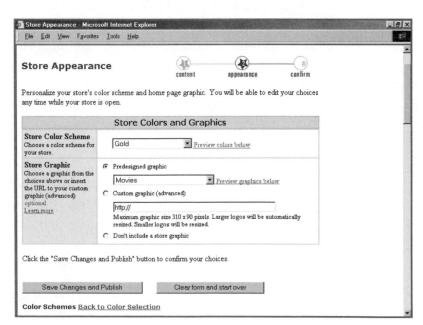

figure 22-2

Choose the color and graphic
scheme for your Store.

NOTE When you're choosing your color scheme, think about matters of readability and ease on the eye. A green color scheme with bright red text (or something similar) can be garish to behold.

When you're done, click the Save Changes and Publish button at the bottom of the screen. Immediately, your eBay Store will be open and ready for business. The screen you see reflects your initial Store design (see Figure 22-3).

If you're not satisfied with your Store and want to make changes, click on the Seller Manage Store text link from within your Store page and make any changes you would like, whenever you like (see Figure 22-4).

With your Store now created, you can easily stock your virtual shelves in identical fashion as when you list auction items. Now that you're a Store manager, eBay's item listing form (both in the single item listing as well as in the Turbo Lister forms) will display the additional selling format of Sell

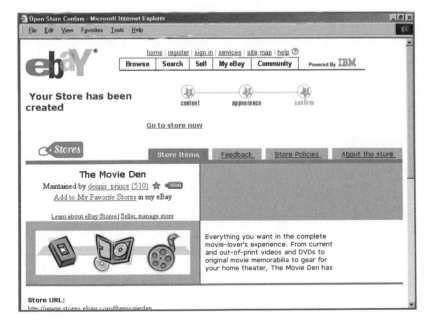

figure 22-3

This image shows how quick and easy it is to establish an eBay Store.

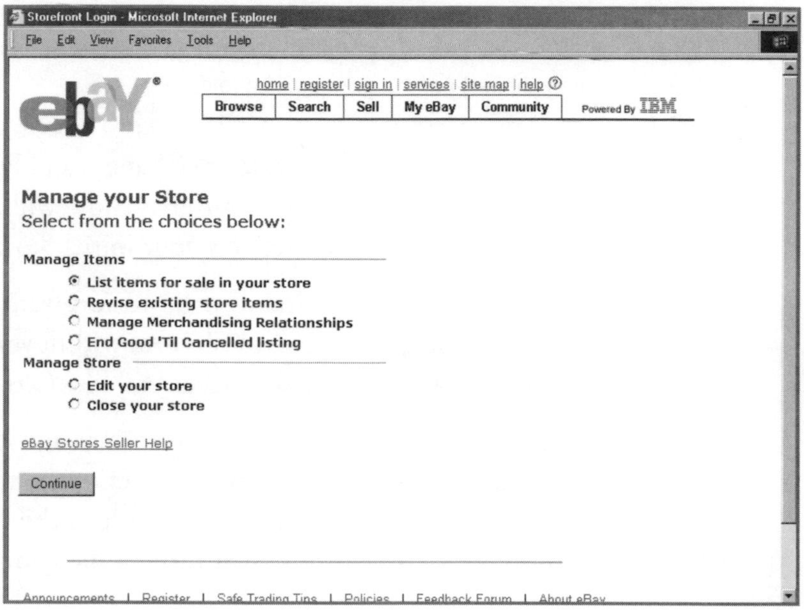

figure 22-4

Use the simple selections
from this screen to
manage your eBay Store.

in Your eBay Store. In addition to being able to easily host auction items and
fixed-price (store) items, here are more benefits you'll find when you operate your eBay Store:

- The ability to showcase auction and fixed-price items in one place

- Your own eBay Store Web site address (for example,
  www.stores.ebay.com/themovieden)

- Your Store's name and link highlighted in all your eBay listings

- Your Store's name featured in eBay's Store directory, where buyers
  can browse or search for your Store

- A built-in Store search engine for your customers' use

- A Store icon next to your eBay User ID so that buyers can easily
  visit your Store

- The ability to create custom item categories within your own Store

Considering an Official Web Site?

If you're ready to truly move beyond eBay, join the millions of other online entrepreneurs who know that commercial Web sites are among the easiest and most effective ways to get noticed and conduct business. However, not all Web sites are created equal, and not all sites (or their proprietors) effectively achieve their commercial goals. As you consider your business Web site, first consider the following:

- What products or services will you sell?

- Who will your customers be, and what are their needs, likes, and desires?

- How often will you need to update your site?

- How will your site leverage from and tie back to your other selling activities (such as your auction sales)?

- Who (or what) is your competition? (Don't get overwhelmed by this, but be aware of who might be trying to carve a similar niche and what steps they've taken to do so.)

- What other similar sites have you seen? What about them did you like and what didn't you like?

As you embark on actually assembling your site, keep these thoughts in mind:

- Keep the site simple and easy to navigate.

- Be sure the site will load quickly. Visitors won't hang around long if it takes minutes for your pages to load.

- Be sure the site works! Test, test, test.

- Be sure the site is running on a stable server. (Watch out for free servers; they have a tendency to go down frequently. If you use a free server, keep checking to see what your customers will find.)

- Provide plenty of useful links, but keep annoying advertising and banners to a minimum.

- Provide easy contact links for your visitors to communicate with you.

- Establish your sales policies and ordering methods clearly.

■ Get to the point. Show the visitors the goods and not your skills at Web authoring.

■ Keep the site fresh by listing new merchandise to sell, removing sold merchandise, and listing new information or links that might be useful to your visitors.

After you have a well-designed and well-functioning site, you'll want to let the world know that you're open for business. Here are some of the easiest and most effective ways to do that:

■ **Register your site with search engines.** There's a whole gang of search sites out there on the Web, so begin by registering your site with some of the biggest engines first (such as Yahoo, Lycos, Alta Vista, and any others that leap to mind). Be sure to include all appropriate *metadata* to tell the indexers what can be found on your site; that will help your site show up on more searches.

■ **Link your site to your eBay auctions.** If you'll still be running auctions at eBay (and why shouldn't you?), make sure to include an active link from your site to your active auctions.

■ **Link your site to other sites.** When you find other sites that complement yours, check with the Webmasters to see if they will add a link to your site. Be sure to return the favor, and you'll be networking with others on the Web in no time.

■ **Develop a mailing list.** Provide a link on your site that allows visitors to be included in a regular mailing list and product update. Because it's an "opt-in," you needn't worry about being accused of spamming. In addition, many recipients will probably share the message with their friends, who soon might be telling their friends, and so on.

■ **Become a member of an online consumer advocacy organization.** Nothing speaks louder about your commitment to good business than when visitors see logos from BBBOnline (the Better Business Bureau) or other such groups. After you're a member, organizations allow you to display their logo on your site.

■ **Enhance your Web development skills or hire a professional developer.** As you seek to better serve customers who visit your Web Store, you'll need to provide high-powered search utilities, online catalogs, shopping cart functionality, and payment services. Some Store owners find this part of the business demands ongoing skill development or subcontracting to a Web developer. If your business warrants it (and hopefully it will), you'll need to ensure that your site will keep up with customers' wants and needs.

No one likes a stale site, least of all your customers. One of the biggest challenges to new online merchants is the need to keep their site current. What should you keep fresh on your pages?

■ Your inventory, of course.

■ News about your products (new releases, industry developments, and so on).

■ Special stories that relate to your products or that your customers will relate to.

■ News about upcoming merchandise, sales, contests, giveaways, or any other promotional efforts you'll undertake.

■ Your links. Many useful sites change their URLs or cease to exist. Keep your links to other sites current.

Calling In the Experts

If the home-grown approach isn't for you, if you've seen great return on your own efforts yet still feel there is an untapped potential for your business, or if you just want some additional advice on some of the fringe areas of your business, you might consider calling in some helpers. The nice thing about this sort of Web business approach is that several help sites won't cost you an arm, a leg, or your business's first-quarter profits to boost your knowledge and increase your results. Here are just a few of the helpful online resources you might like to make use of:

■ **The Small Business Advisor.** I mentioned this one in the previous chapter but will mention it again; I like this site as a source that focuses on assisting entrepreneurs who are either just starting out or are looking to advance their business.

- **Bizoffice.com.** This is another site that offers all sorts of tools, information, and advice to entrepreneurs. Check out the easy search engine submit tool to get your site indexed at more than 2,000 search engines and directories.

- **SquareTrade.com.** Here's a site that offers assistance in problem resolution. It's sort of a new cyber-twist on BBBOnline, but SquareTrade assists buyers and sellers in reaching a mutual understanding and agreement, even if an impartial mediator is required to help both parties sort out the situation. SquareTrade offers a logo that you can include on your Web site (upon registration) to show your customers another indication of your interest in doing good business.

Who's Visiting Your Store?

This is a sort of "before and after" exercise as well as one you'll want to conduct regularly throughout the life of your business. Customer profiling is the sort of thing big corporations spend millions of dollars on every year, seeking to better understand their industry, their customers, and what sells and why. For you, millions of dollars aren't required to get useful and telling information on who's visiting your site, what they're doing while visiting, and how they came to find you in the first place.

You probably did some up-front work back when you were deciding what product or service you intended to offer, either at eBay or at your budding Web store. Because keeping pace with ever-changing customer consciousness is your ongoing responsibility, here's a restatement of what initial (as well as ongoing) customer profiling should include:

- Who are your target customers? Are they male or female? Young or old? Do you know their average income? Do you know why they're buying what you're selling?

- How big is your customer pool? Is it growing or shrinking? Is it seasonal or year round? Do other economic events have a direct impact on customer purchasing decisions?

- Are there regional considerations to take into account? Do the bulk of your customers reside in a certain geographic region, either stateside or elsewhere in the world? If so, why and what can you do to tailor your sales to specific regional needs or desires?

- Who's competing for your customers' attention? Be aware of pricing, service level, and anything else the competition might be offering that will draw away your customers.

With a finger on the market pulse, look deeper into your customers' wants and desires and see if you're serving up what they're looking for in the following key areas:

- **Price.** This is perhaps one of the most immediate differentiators for sellers and buyers. To truly understand your customers, you need to understand their perception of what your product is worth. Understand when higher prices drive customers away (if they can get it cheaper elsewhere) or draw them in (if they perceive increased quality when they pay slightly more). Understand what the market will bear and which items will gain you different levels of profit.

- **Value.** Not the same as price, value involves how useful the customers will perceive what you provide to be, not only in inventory or price, but also in quality, service level, and reassurance. What "creature comforts" are your customers most wanting, and can you cater to those wants?

- **Availability.** Simply enough, are your customers willing to wait for a particular item, one you say you can get but don't have at the current moment, or do they want their goods *now?* Some customers are willing to wait for a precise item knowing that you're capable of providing it to them in a way that pleases them. Others might be looking for the first item they can find and don't have the luxury or inclination to delay the acquisition.

- **Guarantees.** Many items don't really require guarantees, but many more (especially in the online collecting realm) do. But you don't always have to promise the world to help your customers feel assured in their purchases. What simple guarantees are your customers looking for, how can you assure them (and yourself) about the quality or authenticity of an item *before* the sale, and what might the cost be to your business when you honor your guarantee?

- **Follow-up.** Some customers want to make a purchase and never be bothered again. Some want to feel you are a valuable connection that they can call upon again and again. And some want *you* to keep *them* posted about new items, offers, or other opportunities that would interest them. Determine whether your customers want to build a lasting relationship with you and your business or if they'd rather be left alone to browse at their discretion.

Assuming you've learned about your customers and their desire for your products, you need to understand how well your business is serving them. Here, though, concern yourself with how well your business presence—your Web site—is performing to make visits to your storefront a pleasant and sales-generating experience. Here are some of the things you'll need to monitor:

- Which areas of your Web site are visited most?

- What days of the week do the majority of visits occur?

- How long do visitors spend at your site (including at different areas within your site)?

- How do visitors branch to your site?

- How many visitors turn into customers?

- How effective are your advertisements (banner ads) in terms of click-through usage?

- How effective are partner sites' links to directing their visitors to your site?

- How many errors occur at your site?

It seems like a lot to keep track of (and it is), but the good news is that Web tools can help you get all this information and more in easy-to-retrieve and easy-to-analyze forms. A *Web traffic analyzer* is a tool that's designed to help Webmasters (and businesspersons like yourself) keep a good eye on how a site is performing. Where do you get a Web traffic analyzer? Check out the following products. They're available for free introductory download:

- **WebLogManager Pro.** This product is available for a 30-day trial at http://www.monocle-solutions.com.

- **Surfstats Log Analyzer.** A 14-day trial download is available at http://www.surfstats.com.

- **W3Perl.** This freeware offering is available at http://www.w3perl.com/softs/index.html.

Developing a Brand

From flying windows to a leather "swoosh" to a colorful upsy-downsy site moniker, brand names and brand logos can mean immediate customer recognition. If you want to be considered among the favorite places to do business, you'll want to establish *your* mark.

Although branding can be relatively simple, big businesses spend millions upon millions of dollars each year hoping to establish the next big name in consumer goods. Oftentimes, millions upon millions of dollars go down the drain on failed efforts. So keep your sights appropriate to the immediate size of your business, but don't be afraid to dream a bit about the potential for your piece of the pie.

To start, your business needs a name. According to some of the greatest minds in marketing, a good business (or product) name will do the following:

- It will define the benefit of your product or service.
- It will be easy to remember.
- It won't be too similar to established business names or brands.
- It won't be too generic or too specialized.
- It will differentiate you from other businesses or competitors.
- It will be multinational.

Those points might seem vague at first, but consider the other businesses you can rattle off the top of your head or products that have firmly entrenched themselves in your mind. Then avoid them. Don't overwork your business name, but don't give it merely cursory attention.

After you decide on a name, see if you can secure a Web domain name for it. This is tough because so many domain names have been snapped up, often for the mere purpose of selling ownership later. Visit any domain registry (such as Dotster.com, Register.com, or others) to determine if the domain name you have your heart set on is still available. If the exact name isn't available, experiment with different spellings or formations, but don't create such an esoteric URL that customers won't remember how to enter it to find your site.

 ALERT Be wary of some domain registry services. Some shady operators have been known to advertise Internet searches for the availability of a particular domain name only to buy it up upon your query (if it was still available) and then sell it back to you at a marked-up price. If in doubt, consider contacting your Internet Service Provider (ISP) directly for assistance.

Now you need a logo or a brand mark. This is strictly extra credit, but a well-designed emblem can help establish your business in the minds of your customers. Be it cute, clever, professional, or personable, your special design can be a great marketing tool.

And don't forget: Whatever name, logo, or brand mark you decide on, be sure to have it clearly visible on your Web site, your auction listings, and all correspondence with your customers.

Is Your Web Store Sticky?

No, this isn't an examination of your good housekeeping skills nor is it another "Helpful Hint from Heloise" for eliminating grubby fingerprints from computer monitors. *Stickiness* here refers to how well your Web Store attracts customers, whether it entices them to thoroughly explore your virtual booth, and if it will compel them to return again, soon. To prevent your site from becoming a bit dusty—that is, not getting the sort of traffic you would like or not keeping visitors around longer than a few seconds—here are some ways to better ensure drawing power and to encourage visitors to shop longer and return more often.

Keep Them Browsing

It's disheartening to learn that visitors to your Web Store have dropped by, taken a cursory look around, and then headed out as quickly as they came. Why did they leave? Well, like any of us, your customers are likely looking not only for quality merchandise but also for a quality shopping experience that caters to their needs and interests. Although you'll naturally begin with desirable merchandise that is (hopefully) enticingly priced, don't overlook these other "products" that will attract more customers, extend their time of stay, and establish your showcase as a favorite and frequent destination:

- Provide useful and interesting articles that further discuss the sorts of things you sell. Written by yourself or gleaned from other sources (with permission, of course), added information that helps educate your visitors about your wares and related items—be it historical data, industry trends, or even trivia—gives your show-case increased value in your customers' eyes.

- Customers love a forum where they can offer their opinion or ask a question. You can satisfy this urge by providing even the simplest of customer surveys, reader polls, or suggestion boxes. The information they share benefits you, too, because it helps you learn more about what your visitors want, like, and seek in an online dealer.

- Serve up plenty of useful links that can further benefit visitors. You can cooperatively exchange links with others online—you pro-mote their site and they yours—while your customers benefit from the "hub-like" quality that your Web Store now provides.

- Don't overlook the oldest form of promotion: a contest. Be cre-ative and challenge the astuteness of your visitors. Reward the win-ner with a discount or some sort of freebie.

Keep Your Web Store Current

This is the most enticing aspect of a well-maintained destination yet the most difficult to sustain. After you've succeeded in keeping your visitors browsing your store and purchasing your goods, you'll need to ensure there's something new for them upon each return visit.

Online studies have concluded that if you can offer new content (either information or merchandise) on a daily basis, visitors will return every few days. If you provide only weekly updates, visitors will likely return once every few weeks. And, if you're limited to updating just once a month, visitors will probably only visit once every few months. As these findings bear, the more often you can update your site, the more frequent your customers will return. And, the more they visit your store, the more likely you remain in the forefront of their mind when it comes to shopping for the sorts of goods (and information) you regularly offer.

Keep Your Web Store Simple

After you get in a rhythm of updating your Web Store, you might find it tempting to go all out and deliver so much content (especially images and cute decor) that you risk bogging down the display. Aside from large images that can take a while to display, overdecorating your site can become counterproductive, often hiding your great offerings amid excessive visual hoopla. Avoid clutter by keeping your store neat, well organized, and fast loading. If possible, adopt a design that customers can become familiar with, can navigate easily, and can feel at home in upon future visits. This, again, makes your Web Store a pleasure to visit, helping visitors easily find what they're looking for while quickly determining what's new for today.

Transforming Customers into Repeat Buyers

I've already discussed the importance of the "customer experience" in previous chapters, but recognize how important that experience becomes to your ability to encourage a customer to return again and again. Remember: It's no longer a matter of goods alone; serving your customers well and gaining their loyal and repeat patronage is critical to the long-term health of your business.

Again, online shoppers are interested not only in *what* they will be served but equally *how* they will be served. If you invest your efforts only in the particular merchandise you offer, ignoring your responsibility for the customer's shopping experience, you'll soon find you're lagging behind your competitors. Don't believe it? Here are some revealing statistics presented by Vicki Henry, CEO of Feedback Plus, Inc., on why customers *don't* return:

- 1 percent die.
- 3 percent move away.
- 5 percent buy from friends.
- 9 percent prefer competitors.
- 14 percent judge by first encounter.
- 68 percent leave because of rudeness or indifference.

Remember: With the millions of items online up for sale or bid on any given day, it's highly likely that another seller will be offering the same sort of thing that you have on the block. If another seller greets the customers with a bigger smile and a more attentive policy than you, he might well win the customers that you just ignored.

Little Things That Can Make a Difference

Delighting customers and gaining their loyalty doesn't require grandiose efforts that are difficult to sustain. In fact, your consistent attention to the simple elements of customer service is often all that is needed to build a devoted customer base. Here are a few things you can do to keep that customer satisfied:

- Always follow up after a transaction to ensure that the item your customer purchased was received intact and as expected.
- Ask for your customers' feedback (and really want it) regarding how they felt about their transaction with you.

- Listen to your customers; they're the ones telling you if you're doing well or not.

- Sweat the details; look for ways to continually improve your correspondence, packaging, product appearance, quality, and so on.

- Underpromise and overdeliver. Customers should be delighted at how well the product and service has *exceeded* their original expectations, not the other way around.

It doesn't take a Herculean effort to show your customers that you care. In fact, some small business owners are discovering that they're better equipped to establish and foster good interpersonal relations with their customers when compared to the often distant and prerecorded personalities of the larger firms.

Customer Satisfaction: Their Words, Not Yours

"Sure my customers are satisfied; just ask me and I'll tell ya."

Although that might sound funny, there's more truth in that seller-centric sentiment than many would want to admit. It's a trap that's easy to fall into: believing your *own* praises. Experts often remark that to truly excel in customer satisfaction, a seller needs to have a passion to serve customers, leaving it to them to decide when they've been satisfied.

"Real customer service comes from the heart," notes a veteran seller. "If you don't truly and deeply value what the customer means to your business' health, you might as well not bother." These comments underscore the need to let the customer—not you—determine what's satisfactory. It's one way to ensure that you remain totally customer focused. For better or worse, you don't give out the grades here; the customer does. The wise seller keeps a pulse on his customers' satisfaction as a way to understand which direction the business is going.

And at the end of the day, it's an undeniable truth that customer service should become and remain a seller's top priority in the effort to develop lasting customer relations, at eBay or anywhere else you might sell.

appendix A

Additional Resources

And then the protests rang out:

"But you didn't tell me *everything* about eBay and online auctions."

"I want to know more about selling."

"I want to know more about buying."

"I want to know more, more, MORE!"

Excellent. I was hoping you would. Clearly, I can't provide *every* detail for you in the confines of this book while keeping with my initial promise of getting you to the point as quickly and crisply as possible. If I've done my job well, you have a well-defined road map for striking off into eBay and perhaps beyond. But knowing that with every question I answer I potentially give rise to even more queries, this appendix of references will hopefully guide you to the founts of knowledge you so anxiously seek.

More About EBay and Auctions

Likely you've seen plenty of other eBay and auction-related information sources, both in print and online. I've sifted through most of them, and here's my list of the best of the best.

Books

I'm glad you've chosen this book to help you along in your eBay ventures. Still, you might want to read further on some of the topics I've covered. Among those texts I have found most useful, here's my recommendations for your further research:

- *Auctions: The Social Construction of Value* by Charles W. Smith; Berkeley: University of California Press, 1989. This is a detailed yet easy-to-read analysis of the business of auctioning. Smith provides excellent narrative and examples of auctioning at work in global economies. If you're looking for more insight on how auctions play out and how they shape and direct market values, this is the book for you.

- *Auctions and Auctioneering* by Ralph Cassady; Berkeley: University of California Press, 1967. This was my primer to auctions. Although I hadn't read this book until after I became well established in the online auction realm, the information that it provides filled in many of the gaps. Even though this book was published almost 40 years ago, the vast majority of information is still timely. Unfortunately, this book has been out of print for quite a while. That, of course, is a call to you treasure hunters and book finders to start the search for a copy. Don't forget to check your local public library, which was the first place I was able to find it.

- *The Perfect Store: Inside eBay* by Adam Cohen; New York: Little, Brown and Co., 2002. This makes for interesting reading if you're looking for more insight into the creation of eBay. Cohen, a writer for *Time Magazine*, was given unfettered access to eBay, its founders, and employees. Sometimes it reads like a "company reviewed and approved" text, but it's insightful and entertaining nonetheless.

Web Sites

If you're looking for auction information that's only a mouse click away from where you're currently buying and selling, try these sites:

- PlatinumPowerSeller (www.platinumpowerseller.com). Mike Enos has seen the eBay prize and grabbed it. He confides that he's successfully quit his day job, having been able to secure and maintain a lucrative income from his auction exploits alone. His Web site is chock full of helpful information, and his weekly newsletter is useful and engaging. If you want to learn from another of the premier auction "big dogs," visit Mike's site.

- AuctionBytes (www.auctionbytes.com). Ina and David Steiner have been at the auction business for a long time and have produced a user-friendly site that is brimming with useful tips and tactics plus up-to-the-minute news flashes that affect the eBay community. They also publish a free newsletter, so be sure to sign up.

Learn More About PCs, Web Browsers, and the Internet

I know I never went into the intrinsic details of the hardware and software aspects of surfing the wide-open cyberspace. Here are some useful resources that will help you power up and dive into the online waves.

Books

Here are a few books that I read and reviewed when I needed answers to pesky PC, software, and online questions:

- *Upgrade Your PC to the Ultimate Machine In a Weekend* by Faithe Wempen; Rocklin, CA: Prima, 2002. This is a great guide for weekend warriors who want to rev up their PCs in a hurry. Written in a way that follows the flow of an actual weekend, Wempen's book guides readers through various hardware and software upgrading techniques that help squeeze more oompf out of any PC.

- *Young@Heart: Computing for Seniors* by Mary Furlong; New York: McGraw-Hill, 1996. Sadly, this very good book has gone out of print but can still be found at Amazon and on eBay in used condition. I like to include this book in my list of recommended references just because it has appeal. Even if you're not a senior, you'll find some useful bits of information about computing. But for my senior auction-going friends (and I know there are a lot of you), get this book and get cozy with your PC—it's the best start for getting the most of those auction sites. The book is a bit outdated now, but it has so much relevant information, regardless.

- *Searching and Researching the Internet & WWW* by Ernest Ackermann and Karen Hartman; Rockland, MA: Franklin Beedle & Assoc, 2000. Data mining is what it's all about, and this book is all about that. This one's a bit more heady than your casual sort of Internet reference (having been adopted for use by many colleges and universities). Still, it does a fine job helping readers learn to tap the almost infinite amount of information to be found online.

Web Sites

- Finding Information on the Internet: A Tutorial (http://www.lib.berkeley.edu/TeachingLib/Guides/Internet/FindInfo.html). Here's a great Web-based tutorial presented by the University of California, Berkeley. Besides the wealth of knowledge about the Internet, this tutorial also covers Web browser comparisons, search tools, and even Lynx information. It's well worth the visit.

- Learn the Net (http://www.learnthenet.com). Here's another great self-paced learning site presented by About (Internet for Beginners). Features include Web browser tutorials, e-mail primers, and even Web site building instruction.

Internet Safety and Good Practices

Here are some resources if you're a bit Internet-anxious or otherwise want to fully prepare and protect yourself while surfing the Internet.

Books

I've given you quite a bit to consider within the pages of this book regarding your online safety, but it's a topic that can never be overstudied. Here are some additional texts that I have found intriguing and empowering:

- *Net Crimes & Misdemeanors: Outmaneuvering the Spammers, Swindlers, and Stalkers Who Are Targeting You Online* by J.A. Hitchcock; Cyberage Books, 2002. Written by an Internet crime and security expert, this book runs the gamut in exposing the various online offenses including spam, hoaxes, identity theft, encryption, and more. It's written in a surprisingly engaging style that's as interesting as it is informative.

- *Naked in Cyberspace* by Carole A. Lane; Cyberage Books, 2002. One of the best ways to protect yourself online is to gain a full understanding of how you might already be exposed. The fetching title of this thorough reference delivers on its promise: It reveals the information you can gather about others and yourself online, and then counsels how to best safeguard your personal information and protect yourself from intrusion.

- *Caught in the Net* by Dr. Kimberly S. Young; New York: John Wiley & Sons, Inc., 1998. Remembering all I said about the alluring draw of online bidding and buying, this excellent book takes a frank approach to helping online users identify whether their activities have gone too far. The good news is that Dr. Young also provides several methods to cure Internet addictions and methods to keep yourself fully in control.

Web Sites

There are a lot of home-grown and professional sites about matters surrounding Internet safety. New sites are always springing up, but here are two sites that I visit time and time again (and you should, too):

- Federal Trade Commission: E-Commerce & the Internet (http://www.ftc.gov/bcp/menu-internet.htm). Well, you know that the FTC means business and is interested in keeping your online business safe. This URL links to a specific section with the FTC's Consumer Education area. There are several great articles and analyses that you'll find enlightening in regards to online trading. If you're so inclined, visit http://www.ftc.gov/ftc/consumer.htm as well—it's not all Internet related, but it's good consumer information all the same.

- CERT Coordination Center (http://www.cert.org). This page is a clearinghouse for Web security information. It's one of the best places to get the real scoop on viruses (and hoaxes) as well as some very good articles on home security. It's also the place the professional security experts go to get the latest information.

Building Web Sites with HTML

If you want to explore your options with HTML, either within the description area of an eBay listing or to produce a full-fledged Web Store of your own, here are some tasty resources to feed your hunger to know more. Of course, these are online resources, which is the best place to learn about the Internet's design and programming style.

- HTMLhelp.com (http://www.htmlhelp.com). This terrific reference on HTML coding is presented by the Web Design Group. Learn about good HTML construction and find excellent information regarding Cascading Style Sheets (CSS) and design help. This resource is critical for adding top-notch HTML formatting to your online auction pages.

- HTML—An Interactive Tutorial for Beginners (http://www.dav-esite.com/webstation/html/). This offers a nice tutorial on HTML from Dave Kristula. You can practice writing the code directly in the tutorial to see immediately how it works. Kristula also has a good interactive guide on CSS.

- HTML Home Page (www.w3.org/MarkUp). This is the official home page of the W3 Consortium, which is an international standards body charged with standardizing Web formats. This resource includes information on the upcoming XHTML standard.

Index

Symbols